The Editor

FREDERIC L. BENDER is Emeritus Professor of Philosophy at the University of Colorado, Colorado Springs. He is the author of *The Betrayal of Marx* and editor of *Karl Marx: The Essential Writings*.

NORTON CRITICAL EDITIONS IN THE HISTORY OF IDEAS

Karl Marx

THE COMMUNIST MANIFESTO

PREFACES BY MARX AND ENGELS
ANNOTATED TEXT

SOURCES AND BACKGROUNDS

THE *COMMUNIST MANIFESTO* IN
THE HISTORY OF MARXISM

INTERPRETATION

SECOND EDITION

Edited by

FREDERIC L. BENDER
UNIVERSITY OF COLORADO AT COLORADO SPRINGS

W. W. NORTON & COMPANY
Independent Publishers Since 1923

W. W. Norton & Company has been independent since its founding in 1923, when William Warder Norton and Mary D. Herter Norton first published lectures delivered at the People's Institute, the adult education division of New York City's Cooper Union. The Nortons soon expanded their program beyond the Institute, publishing books by celebrated academics from America and abroad. By midcentury, the two major pillars of Norton's publishing program—trade books and college texts—were firmly established. In the 1950s, the Norton family transferred control of the company to its employees, and today—with a staff of four hundred and a comparable number of trade, college, and professional titles published each year—W. W. Norton & Company stands as the largest and oldest publishing house owned wholly by its employees.

Composition by Westchester Book Composition
Manufacturing by Maple Press
Production Manager: Sean Mintus

Library of Congress Cataloging-in-Publication Data

Marx, Karl, 1818–1883.
    [Manifest der Kommunistischen Partei. English]
    The Communist manifesto / Karl Marx ; prefaces by Marx and Engels ; annotated text, sources and backgrounds, the Communist manifesto in the history of Marxism, interpretation, edited by Frederic L. Bender. — 2nd ed.
        p. cm. — (A Norton critical edition)
    Includes bibliographical references and index.
    ISBN 978-0-393-93560-8 (pbk.)
    1. Communism.   I. Engels, Friedrich, 1820–1895.   II. Bender, Frederic L.
III. Title.
    HX39.5.A5213 2013
    335.4'22—dc23

                                                    2012019995

W. W. Norton & Company, Inc., 500 Fifth Avenue, New York, NY 10110
wwnorton.com

W. W. Norton & Company Ltd., Castle House, 75/76 Wells Street, London
W1T 3QT

    4 5 6 7 8 9 0

To Joe,
who was born on Marx's birthday.

Contents

Interpretation   143

Preface

The little pamphlet at the heart of this volume has been, ever since its initial publication, the object of extraordinarily intense controversy—and remains so in our own day.

A refugee German typesetter named Friedrich Lessner, who had helped with the printing of the *Manifesto*'s first edition, recaptured in a memoir the enthusiasm the onset of revolution and the publication of the *Manifesto* elicited from its first audience, the revolutionary activists of a small clandestine organization called the Communist League. Describing the twenty-nine-year-old Marx he had met in 1847, Lessner could have been describing as well the *Manifesto* on which Marx was then working:

> His speech was brief, convincing and compelling in its logic. He never said a superfluous word; every sentence was a thought and every thought was a necessary link in the chain of his demonstration. Marx had nothing of the dreamer about him. The more I realized the difference between the communism of Weitling's time and that of the *Communist Manifesto*, the more clearly I saw that Marx represented the manhood of socialist thought.[1]

The immediate purpose of Marx's little pamphlet had been to help Communist League members spread the league's principles, especially in Germany. As it turned out, the *Manifesto* was launched on a career that would take it into countless editions around the world, in hundreds of languages, long after the events of 1848 had become dim memories.

Lessner continued:

> We in the Workers' Educational Society were in a certain state of excitement at that time. We firmly believed that it [the revolution] must start soon and we still had no idea how much education and organization work had yet to be done to make the proletariat capable of shattering the bourgeois world.

1. Friedrich Lessner, "Reminiscences of an Old Communist," rpt. in *Marx and Engels through the Eyes of their Contemporaries* (Moscow: Progress Publishers, 1972), pp. 103–4. The Workers' Educational Society to which Lessner refers was organized by the leaders of the Communist League.

The *Communist Manifesto* left the press in February 1848. We received it at the same time as the news of the outbreak of the February Revolution in Paris.

I cannot render the powerful impression that this news produced upon us. We were intoxicated with enthusiasm. Only one feeling, one thought filled us: to stake our life and all we had for the liberation of mankind!

"Proletarians of all countries, unite," was the key to his program and through this program the old society will fall. Under the flag on which the glowing letters of the solidarity of all oppressed stand, the great revolution will begin. With this slogan, the new society will emerge and stand.[2]

Barely a month after the *Manifesto*'s publication, an editorial discussing communism appeared in *The Illustrated London News*, the first of infinitely many denunciations to follow. This editorial laid down the main lines of criticism on behalf of property and propriety that the *Manifesto* would continue to receive, as well as what were to become the most widely disseminated distortions of Marx's views. The editorial reads in part:

The recent political convulsions have called out a whole host of regenerators of the world, "friends of humanity" by profession, fierce from excess of loving-kindness to all—the very fanatics of philanthropy, ready to compel everyone to be their brothers on pain of death. . . . A few phrases are all that is necessary to establish the theory of Equality; and, going a little farther, it is very easy to call the wants of rogues the rights of man.

The next step is to require, as the first duty of a Government, that it shall do everything for everybody; even plunder and confiscate on an extensive scale if necessary. . . . This is really no exaggeration of the doctrines preached by some of the continental Communists. They think they are apostles of progress, while they are really going back towards old and exploded despotisms, which treated men not as free and independent beings, but as a property belonging to the strongest. . . .

But if any Government, of whatever form, that of an Autocrat or a Republic, takes on itself all the business of a nation, it needs little foresight to predict the result. Everything will be a failure: it is proverbial that Government work is always the worst done and the best paid, and under the universal share system the profits would be unscrupulously absorbed by the agents, accountable only to themselves, to everybody and nobody. . . . It

2. Lessner, p. 104.

is scarcely possible to conceive the misery that would be caused by such a system, supposing it could be established.[3]

What, we may ask, does this controversy signify today? Extolled in its day as truth incarnate and the inspiration for a life-and-death struggle for humankind's liberation; condemned simultaneously as the vilest of propaganda on behalf of despotism—the *Communist Manifesto* remains today the most potent literary symbol of a century's struggle concerning the form and content of freedom.

With this Norton Critical Edition, the student is provided the very best documentation and scholarship with which to appreciate the *Manifesto* in its complexity and context and with which to comprehend the legacy of controversy the *Manifesto* bequeathed to posterity. The Second Edition interprets the *Manifesto* in relation to the dominance of globalized finance capital, socialist feminist critique, postmodernism, and the fragmentation/transformation of the global working class in this, the second decade of the twenty-first century.

FREDERIC L. BENDER

3. *The Illustrated London News*, March 25, 1848.

Chronology of Events Leading to the *Communist Manifesto*

1816   Congress of Vienna. Holy Alliance (Russia, Prussia, Austria) inaugurates Restoration, dominates European politics until 1848.

1818   (May 5) Birth of Karl Marx at Trier, Germany.

1820   (November 28) Birth of Friedrich Engels at Barmen, Germany.

1833   Abortive workers' rising at Frankfurt, Germany; revolutionaries include Karl Schapper.

1834   Exiled German workers found League of the Banned in Paris.

1836   League of the Just founded by Schapper, Heinrich Bauer, and Joseph Moll after split in League of the Banned.

1838   (May 12) Auguste Blanqui's unsuccessful uprising in Paris; Schapper, Bauer, Moll expelled from Paris, move League of the Just to London.

1840   Schapper and Bauer found German Workers' Educational Society in London.
        Accession of Friedrich Wilhelm IV of Prussia.

1843   (September) Marx emigrates to Paris.
        (Autumn) Engels's initial acquaintance with Bauer, Schapper, Moll.

1844   (Spring–Summer) Marx writes *Economic and Philosophical Manuscripts*, his first studies of alienated labor and communism.
        (September) Start of collaboration of Marx and Engels.
        (Autumn) Uprising of Silesian weavers.

1845   (January 16) Marx expelled from France; moves to Brussels.
        (Summer) Engels introduces Marx to Schapper, Bauer, Moll.
        (August) Marx and Engels begin writing *German Ideology*, first formulation of historical materialism.

1846   (January) Marx and Engels found Communist Correspondence Committee in Brussels; similar committees soon set up in France and Germany.

(November) First "Credo" formulated by League of the Just, presumably by Schapper and Moll.

1847 (late January) Moll discusses with Marx and Engels the league's desire to merge with their Correspondence Committees to form Communist League.

(June 2–9) First congress of Communist League, in London; Engels attends, Marx does not.

(September–November) Engels works on "Principles of Communism" for league.

(November 23–24) Engels abandons "Principles" and writes Marx that they should persuade league to authorize Marx to write a manifesto.

(November 29–December 8) Second congress of Communist League, again in London. Marx and Engels both attend. League assigns Marx task of writing *Manifesto*.

1848 (January 26) Central Committee demands Marx complete *Manifesto* by February 1.

(c. February 1) Manuscript of *Manifesto* arrives in London.

(February 14–18) First edition of *Manifesto* printed in London.

(March 3–July 28) *Manifesto* published in installments in the weekly newspaper *Deutsche Londoner Zeitung*.

(March 4) Marx expelled from Belgium; moves to Paris at invitation of French government.

(early March) Move of Central Committee to Paris, with Marx now its head; Marx opposes formation of "German Legion."

(early March) Liberal uprisings in six German states.

(March 18) Revolution in Berlin.

(c. March 20) About one thousand copies of *Manifesto* arrive in Paris, destined for Germany; most are seized at the border.

(March 24) Working-class riots in Amsterdam, resulting from a large public discussion of the *Manifesto*, of which some one hundred copies had arrived; at subsequent trial, the *Manifesto* described as an "excitive pamphlet [which], with an unprecedented cynicism, unveils the most scandalous intentions" of the Communists; on April 17 the king agrees to grant a new constitution.

(March 27) Marx and Engels write "Demands of the Communist Party in Germany."

(end of March) Marx moves to Cologne, Germany.

French translation of *Manifesto* by league member Victor Tedesco seized by Belgian police.

(March or April) Italian and Spanish translations of *Manifesto* begun in Paris. These translations never appeared.

(April 1) Annihilation of "German Legion" by Prussian troops.

Engels, in Barmen, works on English translation of the *Manifesto*, which he never finished.

(April or May) Second edition of *Manifesto* printed in London.

(May 18) National Assembly convened in Frankfurt, Germany.

(June 1) Marx and Engels found *Neue Rheinische Zeitung*, "Organ of Democracy," at Cologne; newspaper expresses radical democratic viewpoint throughout 1848–49.

(June 11) Worker and student uprising in Berlin.

(July 21) Copies of second edition of the *Manifesto* distributed at Cologne.

(November 10) Friedrich Wilhelm IV moves thirteen thousand troops into Berlin, meeting no serious opposition; political clubs are closed, newspapers submitted to censorship, and citizens' militia dissolved; the revolution in Germany is almost over.

(December) Publication of a Polish translation of the *Manifesto* in Paris.

(end of December) Publication of a Swedish translation of the *Manifesto* in Stockholm; title changed to *The Voice of Communism, Declaration of the Communist Party* and epigraph, "Proletarians of all countries, unite!" changed to "The voice of the people is the voice of God."

1849 (May) Marx leaves Cologne for Paris.

(August) Start of Marx's permanent exile in London.

1850 (March 24) Marx writes "Address of the Central Committee to the Communist League," announcing program of "permanent revolution."

(September 15) Marx and Engels repudiate "Address," split (and thereby dissolve) Communist League.

(November 9–30) Chartist leader George Julian Harney publishes, in *The Red Republican*, the first English translation of the *Manifesto*. The translation was by Helen Macfarlane.

Historical and Theoretical Backgrounds of the *Communist Manifesto*

Karl Marx wrote the *Communist Manifesto*, more correctly the *Manifesto of the Communist Party*, between December 1847 and February 1848 at the request of the Central Committee of the Communist League.[1] Through June 1847, Marx and his close associate Friedrich Engels had avoided joining the league, which had been in existence for a decade. Instead they had set up their own organization, a network of "Communist Correspondence Committees," first in Brussels (where Marx was living) and then in Paris, London, and other places. The merger of their Correspondence Committees into the league that June prompted the league to request in November that Marx compose a statement of its principles and aims. Since Marx is known to have corresponded with Engels during the *Manifesto*'s composition (though no letters of this period survive), it can be presumed that Engels played a role, albeit behind the scenes, in the *Manifesto*'s composition. Indeed, its title was originally suggested by him.[2]

The *Manifesto* is not one of Marx's major theoretical works. Rather, it is a concise outline of his theory of historical materialism written at an easily accessible, simplified level. It includes as well a statement of the league's hopes and plans for the impending revolution, a critical overview of rival socialist groups, and an assessment of political developments in a number of countries. Its primary purpose was to unify the divergent factions within the league and to aid members in their agitational work. It was a publication of the league, not of Marx and Engels, and presumably was subject to approval and revision by the league's leadership.[3]

---

1. Marx changed the organization's name to Communist "Party" in the *Manifesto* itself.
2. Engels to Marx, November 23–24, 1847. Karl Marx and Frederick Engels, *Selected Correspondence*, rev. 2nd ed, ed. S. Ryazanskaya, trans. I. Lasker (Moscow: Progress Publishers, 1965).
3. On the question of the league's possible revision of the manuscript of the *Manifesto*, see Albert S. Lindemann, *A History of European Socialism* (New Haven: Yale University Press, 1983), p. 96.

Because the *Manifesto* is primarily a tactical document, because it is extremely compressed, and because it is often the reader's first introduction to Marxist thought, to present it properly to the modern reader calls for a fairly detailed discussion of its context. We will consider then its place within the development of early socialism, in the Communist League's history and organizational structure, and in connection with the central concepts that Marx presupposed (alienated labor, communism, historical materialism). Only then will it be possible to give a full and balanced assessment of the *Manifesto*'s significance.

The Setting for Revolution

The decade preceding the revolutionary outbreaks of 1848 witnessed the rapid growth of industry, widespread famine, and intense political ferment in many parts of Europe.[4] The poor suffered terribly during this time and became increasingly attracted to socialist and communist ideas. These views acknowledged and explained the contrast between the misery of the masses and the wealth of the masters of the new industrial mode of production (the "bourgeoisie" or "capitalists"). They corresponded to what the poor saw around them: the great promise of industrial society, that free men and women might finally satisfy their material and spiritual needs, remained unfulfilled. Promise and reality diverged ever more sharply as the Industrial Revolution destroyed traditional social institutions and beliefs, while leaving the nature of the emerging society temporarily in doubt.

By rapidly altering the technology and scale of production, the Industrial Revolution held out the prospect of unlimited material progress. But at the same time many workers, those "proletarians" who could find work only under abysmal conditions in the new factories and mines, slipped into a new type of poverty, characterized by the noise, stench, and squalor of factory or mining towns. Small farmers, artisans, and shopkeepers (the "petit bourgeoisie") lost their livelihoods as modernized agriculture and industry undermined their traditional economic roles. These people fell to the bottom of society, joining there the desperate masses already seeking employment. As the owners of the means of industrial production grew wealthier and more powerful, the idea spread among the workers that the new economic system, capitalism, was responsible for this polarity of enormous wealth for the few and misery for the many.

Of course, this destruction of small independent producers was an uneven process affecting some trades more than others. Where

4. See Oscar Hamen, *The Red '48ers* (New York: Scribner's, 1969), pp. 89–92.

the small-scale, independent producers were threatened but not annihilated, their protest could be more volatile than that of the sometimes more docile factory proletariat.

A second source of revolutionary unrest in the 1840s was nationalism, which was especially strong in central and eastern Europe. Many different peoples sought to regain their cultural identity and political independence from the empires of Russia and Austria. German and Italian nationalists sought the unification of their countries and the modernization of their respective political institutions. Everywhere spread the impulse to recover national languages, the memory of past glories, and dreams of future independence. In particular, the cause of Poland aroused great sympathy in western Europe, where it was felt that an independent Poland might serve as a buffer to the westward expansion of "barbaric" Russia.

It was the bourgeoisie, by advocating liberal ideas of economic freedom (laissez-faire) and the limitation of monarchical power, who posed the most direct threat to the reactionary status quo established after the Napoleonic wars. In contrast, except as they might be manipulated by the bourgeoisie against the monarchies, the working classes were no menace to the existing regimes, despite their occasional outbursts against oppressive economic conditions. Many members of the landed aristocracy in the more rapidly industrializing nations embraced romantic, anti-industrial ideas in an effort to oppose the "crass materialism" of the bourgeoisie and the ruthlessness of the market.

For the working masses, the food shortages that began in 1844 and the business crisis of 1847 made starvation an everyday reality. Throughout western Europe, governments were unable to prevent the spread of famine caused by a blight that rotted potatoes in the ground. For the Irish this meant the death or emigration of nearly one half the population in 1844. The following year the blight had serious effects in France, Belgium, and Germany, where the potato crop virtually disappeared through 1848. With the failure of the wheat and rye crops in 1846 and 1847, the cost of food skyrocketed, just as wages tumbled during the depression of 1847. Food riots and demonstrations became common. The political upheaval that everyone expected was finally touched off early in 1848 in France.

Early Socialism

The main tributaries coming together into the stream of early socialism rose primarily in Britain and France. France is especially important, for in that country, between 1830 and 1848, socialism was transformed from a utopian ideal into a political movement. Nineteenth-century French socialism's origins can be traced back to the French Revolution and its grand ideals of liberty, equality, and fraternity—and to the growing realization that these ideals were being undermined by every advance of industrialism and of the bourgeoisie, the very class that had proclaimed these ideals in 1789.[5]

The incompatibility between private property and political equality was already a theme during the French Revolution. The Abbé Mably (1709–1785) wrote that "equality cannot exist in conjunction with private property, which is the source of all our social evils,"[6] and the utopian moralist Morelly wrote that private property must be abolished if the family and a rational social and political system, capable of realizing the moral regeneration of humankind, was to be established. But it was François Noël ("Gracchus") Babeuf's (1760–1797) Conspiracy for Equality that first attempted to put these ideas into practice. Babeuf's abortive coup d'état in 1795–96 gains added historical importance because the long dormant memory of this first attempt at a communist revolution was reawakened in 1828 with the publication of an eyewitness account by one of its participants, Filippo Buonarroti.[7] In his book *Babeuf's Conspiracy for Equality*, Buonarroti showed that Babeuf had grasped the tension between political equality on the one hand and the existence of private capital and the free market on the other. According to Buonarroti, since private property inevitably gives rise to material inequality (if all property were equalized on one day, inequality would reappear on the next), the only way to establish economic, hence political, equality would be to do away with private property altogether, oblige everyone to place the fruits of his or her labor into a common store, and establish an administration that would divide up social wealth according to the most scrupulous equality.

Babeuf's conspiracy illustrated as well some of the basic tactical tendencies of communism: the resort to conspiracy, the manipulation of the masses, and the intended establishment of a temporary dictatorship. During the winter of 1795–96 bread and wood were scarce. Speculators drove the prices of goods to record levels and wage-earners were unable to make ends meet. In this environment, Babeuf brought together some two thousand followers under the name of Society of the Panthéon, which had, however, a secret nucleus calling itself The Society of Equals. The Society of the Panthéon (so-called because it met in the vicinity of the Panthéon, a

5. See George Lichtheim, *Marxism: An Historical and Critical Study* (New York: Praeger, 1965) 21–30.
6. Lorenz von Stein, *History of the Social Movement in France* (1850; Totowa: Bedminster, 1964) 156.
7. On the linkage from Babeuf through Buonarroti to Blanqui and later anarchist and communist revolutionaries, see Arthur Lehning. *From Buonarroti to Bakunin: Studies in International Socialism* (Leiden: Brill, 1970).

former church in Paris housing the graves of Mirabeau, Voltaire, and Rousseau) sought to arouse a revolutionary fervor in the masses, whose participation was deemed necessary for the success of the anticipated coup d'état. After the seizure of power, according to the plan, a revolutionary dictatorship would be established, since the masses were judged incapable of ruling themselves. This revolutionary dictatorship would set about transforming society and the values, goals, and beliefs of its members, turning power over to the masses at some unspecified future date. The Conspiracy for Equality was eventually revealed to the police, and Babeuf, Buonarroti, and its other leaders were arrested.

In the period leading up to 1848, the most important French socialist movements were associated with Henri de Saint-Simon (1760–1825), Charles Fourier (1772–1837), Auguste Blanqui (1805–1881), Louis Blanc (1811–1882), and Pierre-Joseph Proudhon (1809–1865). Fourier was a utopian social critic who denounced the exploitation and hypocrisy concealed within the bourgeois family, society, state, and the church. He excoriated bourgeois "civilization" for its wastefulness, disorganization, and irrationality and denounced the force, caprice, and fraud by which it functioned. Fourier believed that bourgeois civilization could be replaced by a social order he termed "Harmony," in which the chronic misery of the masses would give way to their universal happiness. Fourier's idea was to divide society into a network of independent, primarily agricultural, communes of about eighteen hundred persons, each containing a carefully selected diversity of personality types. Land and property would be held in common, and each individual would have the opportunity to perform the work he or she most desired. In acting on his or her own desires, Fourier argued, each individual would also contribute to the common good. Under such circumstances, according to Fourier, work would be experienced as voluntary, joyful, and a constant source of personal fulfillment.

Saint-Simon was the first theorist of class conflict as the driving force of historical change. He believed that class conflict could be eliminated only when human affairs were regulated by an elite group of benevolent industrialists, scientists, and engineers who possessed the knowledge and skills necessary to ensure progress and universal happiness. In the society he envisioned, equal access to education would provide everyone with the opportunity to be selected for the elite. Saint-Simon believed that in such a society the need for government, laws, police, and a military establishment would be minimal and eventually would disappear altogether. But he deplored the possibility that the working classes might come to power, and he thought he could convince the bourgeoisie that it was in their interest to adopt his ideas so as to forestall this possibility. Although

Saint-Simon's highly centralized, technologically sophisticated utopia contrasts markedly with Fourier's decentralized, agrarian communes, both conceptions are socialist or communist (the terms were interchangeable until Marx distinguished them in the *Manifesto*). They both look forward to a postcapitalist society without private ownership of the means of production, in which an individual's social position and welfare would not depend on her or his wealth.

Blanqui was prominent in every French revolutionary uprising from 1830 until his death in 1881. Although he never wrote a systematic work, his writings indicate the influence of Babeuf and Buonarroti, and he was thus the main link between the Baboeuvists and the communists of 1848. He believed a communist society could be achieved only by abolishing "ignorance," which he held responsible for the evils of existing society. This required the destruction of those institutions, especially the church and state, which kept the masses ignorant. Like Babeuf, Blanqui advocated revolution by coups d'état led by small, secret revolutionary groups. Such groups, composed chiefly of educated *declassés*, would have to lead the proletariat, because under prevailing conditions the masses were too ignorant to know their true interests. Only when the revolution had educated the masses sufficiently would it become possible to replace the minority dictatorship with democratic self-government.

Blanqui had no use for Marx's view, as expressed in the *Manifesto*, that a lengthy period of capitalist development would be necessary before the proletariat could seize power. For Blanqui, the will and the deed were everything. The established order could, in principle, be overthrown at any time. He saw the proletarian dictatorship commencing with the confiscation of large landholdings, the state control of factories, and the introduction of a progressive income tax—ideas on postrevolutionary strategy that found their way into the *Communist Manifesto*. Despite a brief alliance with some Blanquists within the Communist League while in the depths of despair following the defeats of 1848, Marx showed little interest in Blanqui's tactics, although he always acknowledged Blanqui to be an authentic and important revolutionary.

Blanc was a journalist and politician who transformed French socialism from a sectarian ideal into a mass working-class movement. In 1839, under the influence of Buonarroti's book and Saint-Simon's idea of the organization of labor by the state, Blanc wrote *The Organization of Labor*, in which he advocated that the state guarantee regular work for every citizen. The railways, canals, mines, large industries, banks, and insurance companies would be nationalized, national workshops established, and loans guaranteed by the state to groups of workers who sought to start cooperative workshops. The central goal of Blanc's socialism was the replacement of capitalist enterprises with cooperative ones, under state control. He rejected the view that cooperative associations should be formed on only the workers' initiative, for if they were voluntary, he held, they would never come into being over bourgeois opposition. Following the February 1848 revolution, Blanc and two supporters were admitted to the new bourgeois government, but they were constantly outvoted and their attempted reforms undermined.

Finally, the "mutualist" Proudhon, who subsequently had a profound influence on anarchist and libertarian thought, was, like the socialists and communists, a mainstay of the "left" opposition to capitalism in the 1840's. In his first book, *What Is Property?* (1840), which Marx at the time hailed as a milestone, Proudhon defined the property of capitalists and absentee landlords as theft because such property was built on the exploitation of labor. Proudhon's sympathy for peasants and artisans led him to advocate a society of small holdings, each worked by the proprietor alone. He condemned communism because it denied each worker the right to property in his land and tools, and he rejected both communism and capitalism as authoritarian. Instead, Proudhon believed that once people understood the laws by which society functions, there would be no need for authority. Mutual aid or anarchy—administration without government—would then become the norm. Unlike Marx, Proudhon opposed any organization of workers for the sake of seizing the state. For a time (1844–46) he befriended Marx and made possible the latter's first access to workers' organizations, but their friendship ended as the differences between Proudhon's mutualism and Marx's socialism became apparent.[8]

Meanwhile in England, where there was no living memory of a great revolution, socialist ideas developed chiefly within the field of political economy (especially in the work of David Ricardo [1772–1823] and his socialist followers), and in social reform movements, chiefly the Owenites and Chartism. Although not himself a socialist, Ricardo was the first political economist to construct a systematic analysis of capitalism in terms of the mutual antagonisms among landowning, capitalist, and laboring classes. These antagonisms, Ricardo showed, were reflected in the fluctuating shares of the national income taken by rent, profits, and wages, respectively. Ricardo's analysis of economic classes and their interests departed significantly from the approach of his predecessors, notably Adam

---

8. The break between Marx and Proudhon became apparent when the latter turned down Marx's invitation to join the Communist Correspondence Committees unless that organization rejected theoretical exclusiveness, something Marx was not prepared to accept. Marx to Proudhon, May 5, 1846, and Proudhon to Marx, May 17, 1846. Robert Payne, *Marx* (London: W. H. Allen, 1968), pp. 141–43.

Smith, who had conceived a capitalist society as harmonizing the interests of all its members. Although Ricardo believed that the pursuit of individual advantage is connected to the good of the whole, he recognized that the fate of any individual is determined largely by that of his or her class.

Ricardo focused on the opposition between landlord and capitalist, which was the main social issue of his day. He claimed that landlords were parasites who contributed nothing to production, and that rent was simply wealth withdrawn from profits for consumption by the aristocracy. Marx, in the *Manifesto*, argued analogously that the interest of the proletarian was opposed to that of the capitalist, because profits represented that share of social wealth withdrawn from wages.

Robert Owen's (1771–1858) early achievements as a mechanic and later as a factory manager led to his becoming the director of the cotton mills at New Lanark, Scotland. These he reorganized into a model community so as to demonstrate that high wages and good working conditions could increase an enterprise's profitability. By 1819 Owen was advocating factory reform legislation, including a shorter workday and the appointment of government factory inspectors to enforce the legislation. He also proposed that society be reorganized into a network of cooperative villages, each engaged in both agriculture and manufacture. By 1830 Owen was the head of a movement that sought to eliminate the employing class and to reorganize industry on a self-governing, cooperative basis. Emphasizing the link between social reform and ethical potential, Owen regarded competition as the root of all evil. He denounced religion because it blamed social misery on innate sinfulness rather than on pernicious social conditions. He wanted religion replaced by a moral doctrine that would teach children from infancy the virtues of social cooperation and service and the vices of selfishness and competition.

Chartism was a widely influential working-class movement based on the "People's Charter" of 1836, which called for electoral reform and political power for the advancement of labor's interests. Many Chartists stood for social and economic reforms in such areas as factory legislation, protection of child and female labor, and the ten-hour day. By the late 1840s radical Chartist leaders were in close contact with Marx and Engels and the German exiles of the Communist League. But a massive Chartist demonstration in London in April 1848, stimulated by the revolutionary successes on the Continent, failed miserably, exposing Chartism's inner divisions and lack of widespread support, after which the movement disintegrated.

The upshot of all these developments in France and England was that the socialist critique of bourgeois society developed along three lines. First, it developed an analysis of the capitalist economic system that demonstrated the system's responsibility for the misery of the working masses. Second, early socialists developed a critique of liberal political theory, especially of its assumptions that society is composed of individuals with no interests in common and that man is essentially egoistic and acquisitive. Third, it argued the likelihood, if not the certainty, that a just society would emerge from capitalism through the very conditions created by capitalism itself. What set Marx apart from most other early critics of capitalism was his rejection of their faith that bourgeoisie and proletariat would eventually cooperate and find a way to transform capitalism into a more just social system. Although much had still to happen intellectually in the 1840s, a socialist program developing all three lines of argument was not fully formulated until Marx wrote the *Communist Manifesto*.

Above all, the socialist critique of bourgeois society depended on an economic doctrine that could counter classical political economy's apparently scientific claim that capitalism was inherently just. Early socialist writers had already established the basic theme of this doctrine: the exploitation of labor. This theme was based on a simplified version of the classical labor theory of value (which held that labor is the sole creator of economic value) and the notion that justice demands that those who perform labor receive its full value.[9] Socialists argued that exploitation could (and should) be eliminated and production be carried on voluntarily, cooperatively, and according to rational plan. They argued, further, that any such rational plan would make meeting the *basic* needs of all its first priority and would aim beyond that to satisfy the *human* needs pronounced in the French Revolution for liberty (a genuine role in the social decision-making process), equality (the elimination of privilege, especially as it pertains to questions of power), and fraternity (sympathy and solidarity, not egoism, as the underlying ethos of the community).

Socialists insisted that society, insofar as it molds individuals, has the moral responsibility for the welfare and development of all its members and, in some cases, that the state must actively promote these. On the other hand, the liberal view was that individuals are not molded socially and that society need offer them only the opportunity to rise or fall to the level appropriate to their abilities and efforts. Thus the sole legitimate function of the state, for liberalism, was to preserve life, property, and (economic) liberty—and otherwise

9. Marx's version of the theory of exploitation, as expressed in *Capital*, holds that workers are exploited under capitalism *even if*, perchance, their wages equal or even exceed the full value of their labor power, so long as they add more value to their products than they receive in wages.

to allow the market mechanism to determine individuals' relative social positions. Spokesmen for this viewpoint justified the poverty of individuals by implying that they lacked the personality traits, such as intelligence, industriousness, or thrift, necessary for economic success. Likewise, liberal spokesmen failed to take into account the fact that everyone does not start out equally: some people possess talents, wealth, and other advantages that others lack.

The bourgeois conception of liberty as the right to keep the profits earned by free exchange in the market was brought under attack by socialists in the interests of those who owned no property. Socialists considered labor, not property, to be the basis of social life. They sought to distribute work equally among all society's members, to have production undertaken for utility rather than for profit, and to have work allocated—as nearly as possible—corresponding to the talents, abilities, and interests of those who performed it.

Regarding the transition to postcapitalist society, no socialist before Marx had perfected an analysis that showed the forces underlying capitalism leading to socialism of their own accord. Thus, before Marx, socialism seemed to be a system that could be created only by persuading the capitalists themselves, or by establishing communist enclaves or colonies. Borrowing the idea of class conflict as the motor of history from Saint-Simon and the French restoration historians, Marx argued that capitalism's very success produces a constantly growing proletariat, which is forced by its dependent position to destroy capitalism and create socialism in its place. By withholding its labor, seizing the factories, and gaining control of the state, the proletariat would wrest power from the bourgeoisie, expel it from its position of political and economic privilege, and establish for the first time a genuine democracy: the rule of the vast majority.

The Communist League

It was within the context of these developments in France and England that the Communist League was formed. The league's origins can be traced back to the very beginning of the German workers' movement. In the early 1830s there occurred a number of uprisings among artisans whose livelihoods and social positions were suddenly threatened by the spread of British manufactures and the introduction of industrial production. The first German workers' organization, the League of the Banned, was formed in 1834 from among German artisans who had fled to Paris following an abortive rising in Frankfurt the previous year. Very little is known of this group, which, according to Engels, had ceased functioning by

1840.[1] But from this first organization a new group, called the League of the Just, split off by 1836. This group was prominent in the conspiratorial atmosphere of late 1830s Paris. Although it sought originally merely to introduce into Germany the ideals of the French Revolution and the *Declaration of the Rights of Man*, like the Baboeu-vists it came eventually to demand economic and political equality for all citizens, seeing its practical role as that of "enlightening the people and making propaganda for the collective society."[2] Among its members were three men who would later play central roles in the Communist League: the compositor Karl Schapper, the shoemaker Heinrich Bauer, and the itinerant tailor Wilhelm Weitling. The French authorities suppressed the League of the Just for participating in the Blanquist uprising of May 12, 1839, and its leaders were expelled from France.

Schapper and Bauer went to London, where they were joined by the watchmaker Joseph Moll, and together they founded the German Workers' Educational Society, a legal organization in which workers and their families met socially for their educational and cultural advancement. One of the Educational Society's posters proclaimed:

> The main principle of the Society is that men can only come to liberty and self-consciousness by cultivating their intellectual faculties. Consequently, all the evening meetings are devoted to instruction. On one evening English is taught, on another, geography, on a third, history, on the fourth, drawing and physics, on a fifth, singing, on a sixth, dancing and on the seventh communist politics.[3]

But these educational societies also served as conduits for the recruitment of revolutionaries for the League of the Just. Branches of the Educational Society were established throughout England, attracting large numbers of German refugees.

In 1843 Weitling was imprisoned in Switzerland for publishing a book called *The Gospel of a Poor Sinner*, in which he portrayed Jesus Christ as preaching communism and the abolition of the state. Upon his release in August 1844, Weitling went to London, where he received a tumultuous reception from Schapper and his friends and was hailed as the prophet of the impending workers' revolution. This demonstration on Weitling's behalf was in fact the first important

1. Friedrich Engels, "On the History of the Communist League," Karl Marx and Friedrich Engels. *Selected Works in Two Volumes* (Moscow: Foreign Languages Publishing House, n.d.), p. 4.
2. Karl Schapper to Marx, June 1846, quoted in *Karl Marx: A Biography* by Heinrich Gemkow et al. (Dresden: Verlag Zeit im Bild, 1968), p. 95.
3. Cf. Carl Grünberg. "Bruno Hildebrand über den kommunistischen Arbeiterbildungsverein in London," *Archiv für die Geschichte des Sozialismus und der Arbeiterbewegung* 10 (1925), pp. 455 ff.

occasion of international socialist solidarity. It was followed, that
October, by the founding of the International Society of the Democratic Friends of all Nations (or Fraternal Democrats), whose goal
was to coordinate the political activities of revolutionaries all over
the world. Meanwhile, the Educational Societies in England had
gradually attracted workers of other nations, notably Scandinavians,
Dutch, Hungarians, Czechs, Yugoslavs, and Russians, while also
maintaining contact with revolutionary organizations of Frenchmen
and Poles.[4] It was thus no surprise that the Educational Society soon
adopted as its motto the slogan "All Men are Brothers." Marx and
Engels, however, declined to join the Educational Society, even
though Engels, who lived in Manchester, had known Schapper,
Bauer, and Moll since 1843 and had introduced Marx to them in the
summer of 1845.

The theoretical program of the League of the Just was notoriously
weak. It relied first on Étienne Cabet's scheme for founding a communist colony in America and then to a great extent on Weitling's
religio-communist ideas.[5] Engels claimed that this weakness in
matters of theory stemmed from the league's class composition, the
German artisans standing predominantly in blind opposition to the
advance of industrialization:

> The members, in so far as they were workers at all, were almost
> exclusively artisans. Even in the big metropolises, the man who
> exploited them was usually only a small master. . . . [T]hey all
> hoped ultimately to become small masters themselves. . . . The
> greatest honor is due to them, in that they, who were them-
> selves not yet full proletarians but only an appendage of the
> petit bourgeoisie . . . which was passing into the modern prole-
> tariat and which did not yet stand in direct opposition to
> the bourgeoisie, that is to big capital . . . were capable of instinc-
> tively anticipating their future development and of constituting
> themselves, even if not yet with full consciousness, the party of
> the proletariat. But it was also inevitable that their old handi-
> craft prejudices should be a stumbling block to them . . . when-
> ever it was a question of criticizing existing society in detail, that
> is, of investigating economic facts. And I do not believe there was
> a single man in the whole League at that time who had ever
> read a book on political economy. But that mattered little; for

4. The German Workers' Educational Society had almost one thousand members by the
   end of 1847. See David McLellan, *Marx* (New York: Harper & Row, 1973), p. 168.
5. McLellan says that Cabet persuaded the London German communists to abandon
   their goal of seizing power (170). For this reason, they were skeptical of Weitling's call
   for immediate revolution. Schapper described their goal as that of calmly sowing seeds
   that humanity would later reap. The London Communists broke off relations with
   Weitling by March 1846. See Max Nettlau. "Londoner deutsche kommunistische Diskussionen, 1845," *Archiv für die Geschichte des Sozialismus und der Arbeiterbewegung*
   10 (1925), p. 371.

the time being "equality," "brotherhood" and "justice" helped them to surmount every theoretical obstacle.[6]

In contrast to the anti-industrial sentiments of the revolutionary artisans, Marx was developing his critique of capitalism from a different viewpoint. For him, it was the proletarian, not the artisan, whose class position made him the natural enemy of the bourgeoisie. For this reason Marx quarreled in 1846–47 with Weitling and Proudhon—both, far more than he, authentic leaders of the workers' movement—for their failure to abandon the artisan's standpoint.

Spurning all other groups because of their unique theoretical position, Marx and Engels established their network of Correspondence Committees in 1846. Precisely because the proletariat was a product of industrialization, its growth depended on the expansion of industrial production. This placed the proletarian in a different position vis à vis capitalist development from that of the artisan, whom it simply displaced. Marx's communism was the first to welcome the advance of capitalism as necessary for the formation of that new class that would in turn overthrow capitalism and reorganize society in the interest of humanity as a whole. In identifying his theory with the class position of the proletariat, Marx stood diametrically opposed to Weitling and other socialists or communists who identified their theories with either an abstract "humanity" or the struggle of artisans against industrialization. Marx and Engels believed their theory to be the only properly "scientific" socialism because they alone perceived the necessity of such a two-stage transformation from feudalism to socialism (communism) *through* capitalism. Therefore, throughout the 1848 revolutions and beyond, except for seven months in 1850, they *supported* the bourgeoisie in its struggles against feudalism and absolute monarchy.

Meanwhile, as the leaders of the League of the Just were growing increasingly aware of their own lack of a viable program, the time became ripe for a formal merger of the League and its Educational Societies with Marx and Engels's Correspondence Committees. By mid-1846, the London communists agreed to correspond regularly with Marx's committee in Brussels, despite their earlier suspicion of Marx's theoretical views. They were also wary of his tendencies toward intellectual arrogance, which had gotten him into bitter quarrels with Proudhon, Weitling, and others. On January 20, 1847, the London Correspondence Committee and the League of the Just decided to send Moll to visit Marx and formally invite him to join the League of the Just. For Marx and Engels the prospect represented an opportunity to gain influence in a large workers' organization. Marx

6. Engels, "Communist League," pp. 10–11.

set the conditions that at the forthcoming league congress his theoretical outlook be accepted as league doctrine and that it be published in a manifesto. Moll replied that this would be acceptable, but that there would be some opposition from within the league that would have to be overcome.

The congress to inaugurate the new Communist League took place in London from June 2 to 9, 1847. Marx did not attend, but sent Wilhelm Wolff (to whom he later would dedicate the first volume of *Capital*) to represent the Brussels group. The league was reorganized and statutes proposed to be circulated, modified, and accepted at the next congress. The old motto of the League of the Just, "All men are brothers," was replaced by Marx's "Proletarians of all Lands, Unite!" The first article drawn up at the congress declared the aim of the Communist League to be "the overthrow of the bourgeoisie, the establishment of the rule of the proletariat, the abolition of the bourgeois social order founded upon class antagonism, and the inauguration of a new social order wherein there shall be neither classes nor private property."[7]

The league's structure consisted of a number of "communes" of three to twenty members, who elected their own chairmen. From two to ten of these communes in turn formed "circles" within a city or town. The circles were made up of the chairmen of the communes, who in turn were to elect their own presidents. These circles were in turn coordinated by the "leading circle" of an entire province, which was to be nominated by the league's "central committee." The members of the leading circles and of the central committee were to be elected annually, subject to recall at any time by those who had elected them. Significantly, the central committee was allowed to make no changes in the rules except at a congress, when such proposals would be laid before the delegates, who represented every circle. The central committee participated in the congress in only a deliberative capacity; it did not run the congress. One can see from this that the league had a hierarchical but nonetheless democratic structure with power resting ultimately in the hands of the delegates elected from the circles.[8]

At the league's second congress, held in London from November 29 to December 10, 1847 (this time with Marx in attendance), the delegates discussed the problem of drawing up a general statement of principles. An attempt at a "confession of faith" had been made by

7. See Nettlau, "Londoner deutsche kommunistische Diskussionen."
8. Although the central committee handled the league's day-to-day business, power rested ultimately with the circles, which elected delegates to the central committee who were recallable at any time. Unlike Lenin's subsequent "democratic centralist" Party model, the Communist League's central committee did not control the organization dictatorially.

Schapper, Bauer, and Moll for the old League of the Just in the winter of 1846–47, and a second attempt had been made by Schapper and Wolff shortly after the first congress, but both were deemed inadequate. In November 1847 Engels also made an attempt at writing a catechism, titled "Principles of Communism," which, however, he abandoned and sent to Marx with the following suggestion:

> Think over the Confession of Faith a bit. I believe we had better drop the catechism form and call the thing: Communist *Manifesto*. As more or less history has got to be related in it, the form it has been in hitherto is quite unsuitable.[9]

After a debate on general principles that lasted ten days, during which Marx defended his theories in detail, the league followed Engels's motion and commissioned Marx (not "Marx and Engels") to prepare the draft of a manifesto. Marx then returned to Brussels to write.

While Marx divided his time in Brussels between writing the *Manifesto* and writing and lecturing on economics,[1] in London the league was growing impatient at his delay. Events were accelerating rapidly. Insurrections had already broken out in 1846 in Poland, and a conflict was brewing between Prussia and Denmark over the border provinces of Schleswig and Holstein. In Switzerland, liberals with support from England had defeated a coalition supported by the reactionary Holy Alliance of Austria, Russia, and Prussia, electrifying liberals everywhere. On January 3, 1848, there was a massacre of Italians by Austrian soldiers in Milan, creating a state of tension that would soon burst into open revolt. Shortly thereafter, insurrections broke out in Sicily and Naples. The league's central committee sensed the impending spread of such outbreaks to northern Europe and impatiently awaited Marx's manuscript.

Marx, who always had difficulty completing a manuscript, was trying to craft the *Manifesto* with an almost poetic care. Although no letters between Marx and Engels survive from this period, presumably Engels was consulted throughout. The central committee had expected to receive the *Manifesto* by the beginning of January 1848. At a meeting on the twenty-fourth of that month, they wrote Marx tersely that

> The central committee charges its leading circle in Brussels to communicate with Citizen Marx, and to tell him that if the Manifesto of the C. Party, the writing of which he undertook to do at the recent congress, does not reach London by February

9. Engels to Marx, November 23–24, 1847, *Selected Correspondence*, p. 45. See pp. 101–2, n. 5 in this volume.
1. "Wages" (written late December 1847), "Speech on the Question of Free Trade," delivered in Brussels, January 9, 1848.

1st of the current year, further measures will have to be taken against him. In the event of Citizen Marx not fulfilling his task, the central committee requests the immediate return of the documents placed at Citizen Marx's disposal.[2]

It is not known exactly when Marx completed the *Manifesto*, but the brevity of the last two chapters suggests that he hurried in order to meet the central committee's ultimatum. The printing of the first edition was completed sometime between February 14 and 28.[3] The first edition was run off the press for internal distribution among the circles and communes on the Continent, where events were indeed developing rapidly.

On February 24, Paris rose, toppling the bourgeois monarchy of Louis Philippe. In Germany, demonstrations demanding liberal reforms, including freedom of the press, trial by jury, the introduction of constitutions in all the German states, and the convening of a national parliament, began as soon as news came of the events in Paris. By early March, Hesse-Kassel, Hannover, and Saxony had liberal regimes. By mid-March, street demonstrations in Vienna brought about the downfall of Metternich, who had governed Austria for nearly forty years. His rigidity in the face of new social forces made him an embarrassment to the empire, in spite of his exemplary services on behalf of the Reaction. Despite the empire's attempt to keep the revolt under control, it soon found itself isolated against the combined forces of the big and petit bourgeoisies, students, workers, and peasants. At the same time, Austria was shaken by nationalist risings in Hungary, Bohemia, Croatia, Venetia, and Lombardy.

These events weakened Austria so decisively that Prussia remained the only reactionary bastion besides Russia. Very soon thereafter, demonstrations against the monarchy occurred at both ends of Prussia, in Cologne and Königsberg. Refusing all advice to compromise, Friedrich Wilhelm IV ordered his troops to crush all signs of popular unrest, which they did brutally in the Berlin uprising of March 13. On March 16, news of the events in Vienna reached Berlin, heightening tensions even further. On the eighteenth, Friedrich Wilhelm issued a proclamation that partly met the insurgents' demands. The proclamation lifted censorship, called an assembly of the United Diet, a parliamentary body created in 1847 by Friedrich Wilhelm to raise funds for railway construction, and acknowledged the need for new constitutions in the German states. But the language of the proclamation only incensed the Berliners further, because the king made it appear that these concessions were gifts to his subjects.

2. David Riazénov, *The Communist Manifesto* (New York Russell and Russell, 1963), p. 220.
3. Bert Andréas, *Le Manifeste communiste de Marx et Engels: Histoire et Bibliographie, 1848–1918* (Milan: Feltrinelli, 1963), p. 9.

Demonstrators demanded a real commitment to liberal reform and the withdrawal of troops. Royal forces responded by attacking the demonstrators. Barricades were quickly erected, and the people, including many artisans led by Stephan Born, a member of the Communist League, fought the army through the night.

Finally, Friedrich Wilhelm withdrew his troops, accepted the inevitability of constitutional government, and, in a major shift in policy, announced that Prussia would take the lead in creating a unified Germany.[4] At this point political freedoms were recognized in Prussia, setting the stage for the open activity of the Communist League.

The league had already moved its central committee to Paris in March, with Marx now its head. By the end of that month, the Paris central committee received from London about a thousand copies of the *Manifesto*, for distribution in Germany. Around March 27, the central committee drew up its "Demands of the Communist Party in Germany," which adapted the *Manifesto's* ten-point program to the altered German conditions.

The "Demands," which read as follows, circulated widely in the following months:

1. All of Germany shall be declared to be a single and indivisible republic.
2. Every German, having attained the age of 21, and provided he has not been a condemned criminal, shall be eligible both for election and as elector.
3. Representatives of the people shall be salaried so that manual workers, too, shall be able to become members of the German parliament.
4. Universal arming of the people. In future the army shall be simultaneously a worker-army, so that the military arm shall not, as in the past, merely consume, but shall produce more than is actually necessary for its upkeep. This will likewise be an aid to the organization of labor.
5. Gratuitous legal services.
6. All feudal dues, exactions, corvees, tithes, etc., which have hitherto pressed upon the rural population, shall be abolished without compensation.
7. Royal and other feudal domains, together with mines, pits, and so forth, shall become the property of the State. The domains shall be cultivated on the large scale and with the most up-to-date scientific devices in the interests of the whole of society.

---

4. By the following year, however, once he had regained control of the situation, Friedrich Wilhelm withdrew these concessions. Only the policy of unifying Germany remained.

8. Mortgages on peasant lands shall be declared the property of the State. Interest on such mortgages shall be paid by the peasant to the State.

9. In localities where farming methods are well developed, the landrent or the earnest money shall be paid to the State as a tax.

    The measures advocated in Nos. 6, 7, 8 and 9 have been put forward with a view to decreasing the burdens hitherto imposed upon the peasantry and the small farmers, without cutting down the means available for defraying State expenses and without imperilling production.

    The landed proprietor who is neither a peasant nor a farmer, has no share in production. Consumption on his part is, therefore, unwarrantable.

10. A State bank, whose paper issues are legal tender, shall replace the many private banking concerns now in existence.

    By this method credit can be regulated in the interest of the people as a whole, and thereby the dominion of the magnates of the monetary world will be undermined. Further, by gradually substituting paper money for gold and silver coin, the means of exchange (that indispensable prerequisite of bourgeois trade and commerce) will be cheapened, and gold and silver will be set free for use in foreign commerce. This measure in the long run is necessary in order to bind the interests of the conservative bourgeoisie to the cause of the revolution.

11. All the means of transport, railways, waterways, steamships, roads, etc., shall be taken over by the State. They shall become the property of the State and shall be placed at the disposal of the non-possessing classes gratuitously, for their own use.

12. Salaries of all civil servants shall be identical, except in the case where a civil servant has a family to support. His requirements being greater, his salary shall be higher.

13. Complete separation of Church and State. The clergy of every domination shall be paid by the voluntary contributions of their congregations.

14. The right of inheritance to be curtailed.

15. The introduction of a steeply graduated income tax, and the abolition of taxes on articles of consumption.

16. Inauguration of national workshops. The State guarantees a livelihood to all workers and provides for those who are incapacitated for work.

17. Universal and gratuitous education.

    It is to the interest of the German proletariat, the petit bourgeoisie, and the small peasantry to support these demands with all possible energy. Only by the realization of these demands will the millions in Germany who have hitherto been exploited by a handful of persons, and whom the exploiters would fain still keep in subjection, win their rights and attain to the power which they, as the producers of all wealth, are entitled to expect.

The Committee:

KARL MARX	KARL SCHAPPER
H. BAUER	F. ENGELS
J. MOLL	W. WOLFF

In Paris, the league tried to block the attempt organized by revolutionary petit bourgeois democrats to send a military force into Germany. Several thousand recruits were organized into this "German Legion," with the support of the revolutionary French government, which wished to be rid of these troublemakers. Marx organized a Workers' Educational Society to keep the workers in Paris, arguing that the German revolution must begin in Germany. Nonetheless, about April 1, the legion crossed the border and was annihilated by Prussian troops. A National Assembly was convened in Frankfurt on May 18, beginning a new stage of political struggle.

Meanwhile, most of the league's members had returned to their homes throughout Germany, leaving the league's organization in tatters. As a result its subsequent influence during 1848 was minimal despite the efforts of many individual members in leading strikes and organizing trade unions or producers' cooperatives. On June 1, Marx founded a newspaper, the *Neue Rheinische Zeitung*, in Cologne, in which he and Engels carried out a continued radical democratic (*not* socialist) critique of the affairs of the Frankfurt Assembly, until he was forced to shut it down on May 1, 1849. By September 1848, the democrats and liberals, who by then no longer cooperated with one another in the Frankfurt Assembly, were in full retreat before the reactionaries, as Friedrich Wilhelm IV regained control over political developments. Uprisings in May 1849 were crushed easily. On August 6, 1849, Marx arrived in London, where he was to live until his death in 1883.

Let us turn now to Marx's conception of the proletariat and of the factors that were to distinguish its revolution. This will take us directly into his analysis of alienated labor and its disappearance under communism—the heart of the Marxian outlook.

Alienated Labor and Its Elimination under Communism

On the basis of his studies of the class struggles in the French revolution, Marx decided toward the end of 1843 that a social revolution could succeed only if it were led by a class that, in seeking its own emancipation, could at the same time arouse a large segment of society to join it in opposing the prevailing social system.[5] To have its leadership accepted, such a class, like the bourgeoisie of the French Revolution, would have to inspire in other classes the feeling that they, too, were represented in its struggles against the established order. Thus the revolutionary class must act in the name of general human interests as well as in its own particular interest. In this light Marx asked, which class, acting in its own interest, could also emancipate humanity generally? His answer was that such a class would have to be one that is so thoroughly dehumanized that it would have nothing to lose and everything to gain from the destruction of bourgeois society, for only such a class could carry along with it those other classes that experience their alienation under capitalism to a lesser extent. As Marx conceived it, such a radical "human" revolution would entail the overthrow of "all [social] relations in which man is an abased, enslaved, abandoned, contemptible being."[6] In Germany, which was then in only the initial stages of industrialization, Marx believed such a revolution would not only replace feudal institutions with capitalist ones, as had the bourgeois revolutions of Britain and France, but would also project itself beyond the level attained by these earlier revolutions "to the human level which will be the immediate future of these nations."[7]

Thus the practical question for Marx was: which class is it that, in its own interest, could propel feudal Germany beyond bourgeois society to a level that would constitute a "human emancipation" from bourgeois society itself? In fact, no such class existed in Germany at the time. There was yet to be formed

> a class in civil society which is not a class of civil society, a class which has radical chains, which is the dissolution of all classes, . . . [whose] sufferings are universal, and which does not claim a *particular redress* because . . . wrong *in general* [has been perpetrated on it] . . . which is, in short, the *total loss* of humanity and which can only redeem itself by a *total redemption of humanity.* This dissolution of society, as a particular class, is the *proletariat.*[8]

Note that Marx defines the proletariat here in terms of its being the product of the disintegration of feudal society and not in terms of its place within capitalist production (as wage labor), as he would

5. Marx., "Towards a Critique of Hegel's *Philosophy of Right:* Introduction," *Karl Marx: The Essential Writings,* ed. F. L. Bender (Boulder: Westview Press, 1986), p. 49.
6. Ibid., pp. 47–48.
7. Ibid., p. 47.
8. Ibid., pp. 50–51 (some of Marx's italics deleted).

do by 1844. In 1843 he was still quite ignorant of capitalism as an economic system. Rather, Marx then had in mind the proletariat as it was comprised of artisans, serfs, agricultural laborers, and other groups displaced from their traditional ways of life by technological advances in agriculture and manufacturing. These people were forced, under threat of starvation, to migrate to the cities, where they had little alternative but to accept wage labor in the factories, under truly abysmal conditions. In 1844 Marx shifted his emphasis from this idealist conception of the proletariat as the redeemer of humanity to an economic sociology of the proletarian as urban, industrial worker. He argued that it is the *alienation* of proletarians' labor under specifically capitalist conditions that entitles them to claim that their revolution against capitalism represents the "total redemption" of humankind. That is, it is not their poverty or displacement per se, but the peculiar qualities of alienated labor, which gives the proletarians' struggle its all-or-nothing character.

The most fundamental condition embodied in the social relations of capitalism is that the worker is reduced to the status of any other commodity.[9] A commodity is an economically useful object that can be exchanged for another commodity on the market. In capitalism workers, as commodities, lose their human worth as free, responsible agents and become interchangeable with machines, energy supplies, or buildings. Workers become one among many factors of production, commodities to be purchased by capitalists for their utility and perhaps tomorrow to be discarded and replaced by machines. Likewise, the price of labor (wages), like that of any other commodity, fluctuates according to changes in supply and demand. If there is insufficient "demand" for their labor power, workers cannot find jobs and must go without wages. Some starve.

The discovery of this dehumanization of the worker under capitalism is the basic concept underlying Marx's analysis of alienated labor. Marx does not consider alienated labor primarily a matter of subjective feelings of estrangement or of difficult, tedious, unsatisfying work—although these are frequently characteristic of work under capitalism. Rather, "alienated labor" denotes the fact that the capitalist system reduces free, self-creative subjects to objects, that in their economic life people become mere commodities. This "dehumanization" of the worker in turn establishes his or her "radical, human need" to become a person, that is, to become a free, self-creative individual and social being. For Marx the needs of the worker go deeper than the necessities of physical life or the socially

9. Marx, "Wages of Labor," *Karl Marx: Early Writings*, ed. and trans. T. B. Bottomore (New York: McGraw-Hill, 1964), p. 69.

recognized amenities: the worker has the radical (human) need to revolt against the capitalist mode of production as such and establish a humane society in its place.

People typically acquiesce in alienated labor because, in a capitalist society, the means of production are privately owned and dedicated to the pursuit of profit, and because they consider the market the sole legitimate mechanism for determining what is to be produced, for assigning work, and for distributing commodities. But Marx argued that the free market relationship with respect to employment conceals an underlying struggle between worker and employer. The worker is at a considerable disadvantage in this struggle because he or she is always driven by the specter of starvation to seek a new labor contract (a job), whereas the capitalist has the choice of hiring a different worker, redeploying his capital, or hiring no one at all and simply living on his capital. Unlike his employees, the capitalist possesses sufficient wealth to refrain from capitulating to his workers' demands since, by definition, capital is that portion of his wealth over and above what he needs to satisfy his needs, however lavishly he may conceive these. His goal as a businessman is simply to augment his capital. As Marx puts it, "it is the ability of the capitalist to put his capital to other uses which subjects the worker, who is limited to one employment of labor [because commonly he has only one marketable skill] to starvation or forces him to accept every demand which the capitalist makes."[1]

The analysis of alienated labor Marx presented in the *Economic and Philosophical Manuscripts* of 1844 reveals five aspects, each pointing to a radical, human need to replace capitalist wage labor with a cooperative form of production:

1. The worker is *alienated from the product of his or her activity*. We have seen that capitalist production turns people into commodities. But since food, clothing, and shelter are owned by capitalists, even though they are actually made by workers, the worker must continually find employment, in the process reproducing himself or herself as a commodity. Proletarianization is thus self-perpetuating: for the vast majority it is impossible to rise from the proletariat, especially since capitalists continually introduce labor-saving machinery, thereby reducing the demand for workers and exerting downward pressure on wages. Further, the unpredictable and uncontrollable supply and demand relation for commodities, including labor power, determines not only the prices of commodities but also how many workers will be employed and what the level of their wages will be. Thus everyone, even capitalists (whose businesses are always in jeopardy of failing), is subject to this domina-

---

1. Ibid, p. 70.

tion of commodities and the ever-fluctuating supply and demand relations among them.

But the proletarian is especially vulnerable because, unlike the capitalist, he or she has no accumulated wealth on which to fall back when unemployed. This life-threatening uncertainty at the heart of wage labor points to the worker's need to become *human* again, to regain a sense of dignity and security by eliminating both his own transformation into a commodity and the domination of his or her economic activity by the commodities fellow workers produce. This is another reason the worker must destroy the capitalist system of production.

2. In carrying out an employer's orders, the worker becomes *alienated from his or her activity itself*, for the actions performed while on the job reflect the boss's, not his or her own, intelligence and will. Marx notes:

> The work is *external* to the worker, . . . it is not part of his nature; . . . consequently, he does not fulfill himself in his work but denies himself. . . . His work is not voluntary but imposed, *forced labor*. It is not the satisfaction of a need, but only a *means* for satisfying other needs.[2]

The worker, reduced from a living human (free, self-creative) subject to an economic object (a commodity), is little more than an append-age of the machinery owned by the capitalist. He or she doesn't use intelligence or capacity for judgment in work; nor is he or she involved in the decisions and responsibilities concerning the work. One is required simply to do as one is told. The lack of control over produc-tive activities indicates one's dehumanization and provides another basis for a radical need to replace capitalist production relations with ones that would place control over productive activity in the work-ers' own hands.

3. Insofar as the worker lacks any personal involvement (other than mere performance) in the production process, he or she is *alien-ated from the possibility that his or her work could be fulfilling, or use-ful toward his or her own development*. Self-actualization, the development of one's talents and abilities, and the pursuit of one's own life interests in and through one's work, counts for nothing in the capitalist marketplace, office, or workshop, according to Marx.

Because the capitalist continually restructures the work process to maximize its efficiency or profitability, there is a historical ten-dency toward an increasingly rigid division of labor and specializa-tion of tasks. The worker is thus trained in a fragmented, one-sided

---

2. Marx. "Alienated Labor." *The Essential Writings*, pp. 73–74 (some of Marx's italics deleted).

fashion that contributes nothing to their personal development. As a one-sided, underdeveloped cog in the machinery of capitalism, the worker has the radical, human need to become a whole, sensuous, sensitive, self-actualized being. For Marx, this too requires the thoroughgoing restructuring of society's productive relations.

4. The foregoing aspects of alienated labor also entail *alienated interpersonal relations*. Everyone is forced by the competitive market to adopt a selfish outlook, to become indifferent or even antagonistic toward everyone else in the work world. The capitalist's relation to his or her employees is one of hierarchical domination characterized by the constant attempt to maximize his gain at their expense (Marx's "exploitation"). Capitalists are themselves caught in deadly competition with one another. Likewise, workers compete with one another for relatively scarce jobs, which tends to reduce their wages. Thus everyone, capitalist or proletarian, finds himself trapped in an economic struggle against everyone else. The fact that acquisitive egoism and competition seem natural to people accustomed to bourgeois society is indicative of the extent of our alienation from even the awareness of the potential for cooperation and solidarity. In short, in bourgeois society, *man is radically alienated from man*, each reducing the others to mere means for his or her own success in the perpetual battle for economic survival. Thus we find still another radical, human need: to become genuinely social beings, or, as the French had expressed it, a need for "fraternity."

5. In the capitalist factory, mine, or office, the worker is *alienated from nature*. The labor process is artificial, increasingly estranged from complete, satisfying, natural tasks by the capitalist-imposed division of labor. In the factory districts thrown up helter-skelter with no money wasted on unprofitable aesthetic or environmental considerations, nature is no longer a habitat sustaining and enriching human existence but is instead reduced to an object, just as the worker is. The natural environment ceases to belong to people in common but is divided into property owned by capitalists, a storehouse of raw materials to be plundered by those who have seized or purchased "title" to a part of what today would be called the planetary ecosystem.

In sum, Marx argues that to meet all the human needs that the concept of alienated labor reveals, and to meet the physical and social needs of all, a radically new type of social organization is necessary. This is what Marx's "communism" is all about. According to Marx, only in a community of persons who hold the means of production in common, and who undertake production for its social utility (not for profit) on the basis of decisions freely made by all (not just by capitalists or their hired managers), could the productive forces created by capitalism cease to cause alienation and become instead the means of liberation and personal fulfillment. For such an "association"[3] to work, it is necessary that no individuals or group acquire exclusive control over the means of production. Marxian communism would thus have to be classless.[4] A "free association" marked by a rational, voluntary allocation of work could transform labor into the primary means of self-realization rather than a curse borne only grudgingly. The ravages of scarcity dictated by uncontrollable market fluctuations could be replaced by the personal security generated by assured rights to work and to share in the social product. (Marx assumes, of course, that a fully developed capitalism would have created the material preconditions to provide everyone with the necessities and comforts of life.) One's chosen work could be a creative expression of one's personality and reflect the "fraternity" of the associated producers, thereby meeting their human needs along with their physical and social needs. Marx outlines the positive consequences of such "freely associated" production as follows:

Suppose we had produced things as human beings— . . .
1. In my production, I would have objectified my individuality and its particularity, and in the course of the activity I would have enjoyed an individual life. In viewing the [product of my labor], I would have experienced the individual joy of knowing my personality as an objective, sensuously perceptible and indubitable power.
2. In your satisfaction and use of my product, I would have had the direct and conscious satisfaction that my work satisfied a human need . . . and that it created an object appropriate to the need of another human being.
3. I would have been the mediator between you and the species and you would have experienced me as a [complement] of your own nature and a necessary part of your self. . . .
4. In my individual life, I would have directly created your life; in my individual activity I would have immediately confirmed and realized my true *human* and *social* nature.[5]

The satisfactions possible under such a system, assuming a minimal requirement for all to share equally in the undesirable work, could include the chance for citizens to choose their work and participate in the social decision-making process concerning economic activity. Each person could become an *end* of the production process rather than being merely its *means*. The personality-stunting effects of the

3. Marx and Engels, "The German Ideology," *The Essential Writings*, p. 205.
4. Ibid., p. 201.
5. Marx, "Notebook on Mill," *The Essential Writings*, pp. 124–25 (some of Marx's italics deleted).

capitalist division of labor might be ameliorated by allowing everyone the opportunity to perform an equal amount of labor service at tasks chosen by each (subject to fairness for all) or by obligating everyone to accept labor service of differing types over the course of a year. Qualification for specialized roles could be obtained by guaranteeing the opportunity to acquire specialized training at certain periods of one's working life. The possibilities are endless, and Marx certainly never spent much time specifying them; in fact, his remarks on the possibilities in a future communist society amount to nothing more than mere hints.[6] Marx's point was that it is possible to create a more just and more fulfilling economic system than capitalism.

It follows that such an "authentic common life" could not be imposed by the state, for any such imposition would demonstrate that authority, rather than reason and common consent, remained the ruling social force. A communist society lacking a state apparatus could function only if all (or nearly all) its members internalized the priority of the common good, in contrast to the acquisitive egoistic ethos fostered by bourgeois society. Note that Marx is not concerned here with how people who were raised in a capitalist society and have internalized its egoistic values could be transformed so radically into communal beings. His answer, perhaps an inadequate one, became explicit only in *The German Ideology* (1845–46) and *The Poverty of Philosophy* (1847). Here Marx held that proletarians, and possibly others (like Engels and himself) who accepted the proletarian outlook, could be transformed in this way only through participation in revolutionary struggle, for only the risking of one's life for the cause of human emancipation demonstrates that one is no longer egoistically motivated.[7]

For Marx, "communist" society aimed primarily to overcome alienated labor, create free relations of associated production, and actualize the human abundance of its members. As the free association of all workers, communist society would extend democracy from political to economic aspects of life. Decisions about alternative economic priorities and about how to meet these priorities, which liberal theorists regard as private business affairs outside politics, would be made by the workers involved.

These proposals, or visions, take us far from capitalist economic theory and bourgeois political democracy, in which political decisions are made by a few officials (only some of whom are elected),

---

6. Besides the "Manuscripts" of 1844, fragments of Marx's communist vision can be found in "The German Ideology" and "Critique of the Gotha Program," *The Essential Writings*, pp. 201–7, 279–81.
7. Marx and Engels, "The German Ideology" and Marx, "The Poverty of Philosophy," *The Essential Writings*, pp. 198–201, 238–39.

while economic decisions are made by capitalists (or their hired managers) with no responsibility to society. The immediate tendency of people whose social consciousness has been molded within bourgeois society is to dismiss proposals for a more just socialist society as utopian and impractical. What distinguished Marx from the utopian theorists with whom he shared aspects of the socialist vision was that he *also* tried to show that the revolutionary overthrow of capitalism was being prepared by a real historical process within capitalism itself—indeed through capitalism's very success. That is, the struggle for communism was for Marx not something to be undertaken simply because such a society might be more desirable, but because communism represented the goal of the real historical movement arising from the proletariat's alienation. The struggle to form the proletariat into a revolutionary movement was the *Manifesto*'s purpose; indeed it was the chief purpose of Marx's life. For this reason, we now turn to Marx's theory of social structure and revolutionary change: "historical materialism."

Historical Materialism

One of the most striking things about the *Communist Manifesto* is the sweeping historical claim with which it begins: "All previous history is the history of class struggles." The materialist interpretation of history, or "historical materialism" as it was called after Marx's death, on which this claim is based, was created jointly by Marx and Engels in the mid-1840s, most importantly in *The German Ideology* (1845–46). In their view, the fundamental basis of history is material production, and social life in general depends finally on the class dynamics of the production process.

The practical purpose of historical materialism is to analyze the proletariat's social/political situation and guide it in its struggle against the bourgeoisie. Marx's goal was to relate all social phenomena in a coherent way, to see the myriad, seemingly unconnected, facts of social life as inhering in a totality defined by covert or overt class antagonism, whether consciously understood as such or not by the participants. Marx believed that the concept of such underlying class antagonism inherently lies beyond the understanding of the bourgeoisie and its social science. Liberal theorists depicted bourgeois society as morally legitimate; for them, alienation and dehumanization could not be acknowledged. For the bourgeoisie,

> it is a matter of life and death to understand its own system of production in terms of eternally valid categories: it must think of capitalism as being predestined to eternal survival by the eternal laws of nature and reason. Conversely, contradictions

that cannot be ignored must be shown to be purely surface phenomena, unrelated to this mode of production.[8]

In contrast, Marx's method is essentially one of *critique*, whether directed at the institutions of bourgeois society or at their attempted theoretical justification in the social sciences or philosophy.

PRODUCTION AND MATERIAL LIFE

In adopting a "materialist" position, Marx and Engels emphasized the differences between their conception of history and society and "idealist" conceptions based on a fixed idea of human nature. They declare that

> the premises from which we begin are not arbitrary ones, not dogmas, but real premises from which abstraction can only be made in the imagination. They are the real individuals, their activity and the material conditions under which they live, both those which they find already existing and those produced by their activity.[9]

In every known instance, some sort of production, and therefore labor, has been necessary for social groups to survive and reproduce themselves. Marx and Engels designate as "material" those needs without which social groups could not survive:

> life involves before everything else eating and drinking, a habitation, clothing and many other things. The first historical act is thus the production of the means to satisfy these needs, the production of material life itself. . . . [I]n any interpretation of history one has first of all to observe this fundamental fact in all its significance.[1]

These material needs impose upon any group the necessity of organizing and carrying out material production. But in any society production acquires a specific form according to existing natural and social conditions and the actions of the people involved:

> at each stage there is found a material result: a sum of productive forces, a historically created relation of individuals to nature and to one another, which is handed down to each generation from its predecessor; a mass of productive forces, capital funds and conditions, which, on the one hand, is indeed modified by the new generation, but also on the other prescribes for it its

8. Georg Lukács, *History and Class Consciousness* (London: Merlin, 1971), pp. 10–11.
9. Marx and Engels, "The German Ideology," p. 164.
1. Ibid., p. 172.

conditions of life and gives it a definite development, a special character.[2]

In other words, the sum of available productive forces *and* the social and natural world in which they are put to use determine the specific way in which production takes place, which in turn shapes what Marx later would call the "superstructure" of society: its politics, laws, religion, philosophy, and so on. The most important characteristics of a society, according to Marx and Engels, "coincide with their production, both with *what* they produce and with *how* they produce. The [social] nature of individuals thus depends on the material conditions determining their [social] production."[3] Yet, "circumstances make men just as much as men make circumstances."[4]

It is perhaps worthwhile to dwell a few moments on the words *just as much* in this last sentence. In *The German Ideology*, Marx and Engels were criticizing certain idealist views of history, according to which people are viewed as spiritual beings who, by acting on nature, create society and make history simply as they will. Although they were quite well aware that people are active, social beings, and thereby "make circumstances," Marx and Engels were at pains to emphasize the *interaction* of people and nature by means of material production, such that "circumstances" *also* "make humans." Human existence, which is always social (this is the one "essential" human characteristic Marx and Engels did assume), is always fundamentally dependent on the ways in which humans and nature interact.

Historical change, however, is not determined merely by changes in the physical forces of production or productive technology, as many vulgar Marxists and anti-Marxists have maintained. Nor is historical change determined by sheer will. Rather, societies continually modify both external nature and their own social relations through their productive activities. History is neither the "self-creation" of humankind through will alone (because there are always natural and social conditions limiting human action) nor a natural, economic, or technological determinism (because production and the means of production are continually being modified by the decisions and actions of groups).

CLASSES

In its earliest phases, social life took the form of the extended family, the clan, and the tribe. Although little ethnological data were

2. Ibid., p. 181.
3. Ibid., p. 165.
4. Ibid., p. 181.

available in the 1840s, Marx and Engels held that such societies, in which production usually involved gathering plants, hunting, fishing, domestication of animals, primitive agriculture, hand weaving, and the like, were characterized by an elementary division of labor on the bases of age and sex. That is, the division of labor derived originally from the hierarchical form of the extended family. Engels would later call this stage "primitive communism" because, although there was already a hierarchical division of labor, there were as yet no possessing and propertyless classes. All members of the family, clan, or tribe shared in the common stock of food, land, herds, and goods.

The situation changed drastically, however, once there were slaves, who were originally captives of war. According to Marx and Engels, slaves were held at first, like other tribal property, in common. Subsequent social forms, among which Marx included the "oriental empire," the "ancient commune" (the early city-state), feudalism, and capitalism, featured an increasingly complex social division of labor. But all these societies harbored at least one propertyless class (slaves, serfs, or proletarians) dominated by a property-owning class (monarch, nobility, or capitalists). This division of labor, of course, was accompanied by an unequal distribution of labor's products and other social goods.

Opposing classes fostered distinctive class interests. Once the state came into existence (whether by conquest or agreement), political life became chiefly the expression of the conflict of these class interests. Classes dominated by others fought for improvements in their conditions and, sometimes, for the opportunity to displace the dominant classes. One very powerful weapon in these struggles was class ideology.

BASE AND SUPERSTRUCTURE

In the *Manifesto* Marx writes:

> Does it require deep intuition to comprehend that man's ideas, views and conceptions, in one word, man's consciousness, changes with every change in the conditions of his material existence, in his social relations and in his social life?
>
> What else does the history of ideas prove, than that intellectual production changes its character in proportion as material production is changed? The ruling ideas of each age have ever been the ideas of its ruling class.

This passage has been partially responsible for the widely shared perception that historical materialism is a form of economic determinism, for it seems as if Marx maintains here that every society consists of an economic, or "material," base that is the *sole* determinant of its "superstructures" (political and legal systems, philosophy, religion, social mores, and so on). Consequently, some argue that Marx held that people's ideas are produced by economic causes, that, in particular, one has only those ideas corresponding to the interests of that class of which one is a member. This is a misunderstanding that can be traced to the ambiguity of Marx's concept of "mode of production."

A "mode of production," according to Marx, consists of "material forces of production" and "social relations of production," which *correspond to* one another.[5] The relations of production are the relations existing among the persons involved in the production process,[6] in other words, relations of class domination and subordination. For example, some people typically own the means of production while others do not; some people direct production and make the relevant decisions while others merely carry out their orders; some people typically are the slaves, serfs, or hired hands of others; and so on. Insofar as Marx claims that the relations of production "constitute the economic structure of society—the real foundation on which rise . . . superstructures . . . and to which correspond definite forms of social consciousness,"[7] it is clear that he places class conflict at the center of his analysis of society. In short, any society (in the *Manifesto*'s terms, "material existence" or "social life") is fundamentally shaped by class antagonisms, which in turn shape the legal and political institutions ("superstructures") and the forms of social consciousness (ideologies) of its inhabitants.

To these class antagonisms within the social production process there correspond certain physical forces of production, which include raw materials, energy, natural resources, machinery, tools, and the knowledge necessary to organize production in a specific way. For Marx, a *mode of production* is more than the mere physical or technological forces used in the production process: it is the "correspondence" or connection of these material forces to the relations of production; that is, these material forces *as* they are used under specific relations of production. And it is the *mode* of production, not merely the physical *forces* of production, which, according to Marx, shapes[8] the general character of social life.

5. Marx, "A Contribution to the Critique of Political Economy." *The Essential Writings*, pp. 161–62.
6. For Marx, the term "production process" always includes the exchange, distribution, and consumption of goods, as well as their actual production. See "Grundrisse." *The Essential Writings*, pp. 309–19.
7. Marx. "A Contribution," p. 161.
8. Marx's word is *bedingt*, which equally means "determines" or "conditions." The former is the stronger relation.

For this reason it is false to attribute to Marx the view that social structure and historical change derive from changes in the tools, machinery, or other physical forces of production. Marx's view is clear in the following passage from *Capital* (1867), in which he discusses how the prevailing relations of production (in this case, slavery in the antebellum South) determine the concrete significance both of workers and of machinery:

> A Negro is a Negro. He only becomes a slave in certain relations. A cotton-spinning jenny is a machine for spinning cotton. It becomes *capital* only in certain relations. Torn from those relationships it is no more capital than *gold* in itself is *money* or sugar the *price* of sugar.[9]

In sum, Marx's historical materialist method involves (1) understanding society in terms of its mode of production, especially its class structure; (2) identifying the influence of class conflicts on the prevailing political institutions and ideologies (including law, religion, and philosophy); and (3) using this "scientific" understanding of society to assess the prospects for historical change, especially for proletarian revolution.

IDEOLOGY

Now we can understand Marx's conception of "consciousness," or ideology. In the passage from the *Manifesto* cited on page 30, Marx claims that "ideas, views and conceptions" change as aspects of social life or material existence change. Marx of course did not have in mind here such ideas as "2 + 2 = 4" or "my cat is black." Rather, he had in mind what he elsewhere terms "social consciousness": the *conceptual frameworks*, or "ideologies," such as socially recognized religious, philosophical, political, and even scientific viewpoints, which we use to think about human life, the world, and society. These ideological frameworks, Marx argues, "correspond" to the relations of production; that is, they "reflect" the alternative interests and viewpoints that derive from class divisions and oppositions.

For this reason, it commonly occurs that the "same" object appears to be quite different to members of different classes. For example, a machine that a capitalist introduces into his factory seems to him to be a beneficial advance in production technology, an aid to lowering his costs of production, raising productivity, and thereby increasing his sales and profits. But to a worker, the new machine may be a threat to his livelihood (since it may result in his being thrown out of work), or an inhuman taskmaster (if it demands that he work

9. Marx, "Wage Labor and Capital," *Marx-Engels Collected Works* (New York: International Publishers, 1977) 9, p. 211.

faster than the rate to which he has been accustomed). Which is it? Since people's ideological consciousness, according to Marx, is shaped by social relations—in the last analysis by the class struggle created by the relations of production—the answer depends on one's position in relation to the mode of production.

Marx did not, however, believe that everyone in a society, or even everyone within a certain class, thinks within the framework of a single ideology, even the framework of that ideology that best reflects the situation of his or her class. Indeed, it was of the greatest practical importance to Marx that most members of the proletariat did *not* have a "proletarian" outlook. (It would otherwise have been a simple matter to organize them politically, which it was not.) Rather, most proletarians had a bourgeois or petit bourgeois class outlook, in many cases combined with acceptance of a traditional religious ideology. Most considered their chief personal interest to be rising out of the proletariat into the petit bourgeoisie, or at least helping their children to do so. Most did not consider revolution to be in their interest. Marx saw that this egoistic ideology only maintains the capitalist relations of production. It was thus crucial to create proletarian solidarity by helping workers to see that they also have fundamental *class* interests, which should override their egoistic impulses.

Having explored Marx's concept of ideology, or social consciousness, we can now return to Marx's claim in the *Manifesto* that in any epoch "the ruling ideas are the ideas of the ruling class." Marx argued that the ideology best expressing the interests of the ruling class always prevails in a society's morality, legal system, education, politics, and economic life. Ideologies legitimate and perpetuate the rule of a dominant class, which must convince its own members as well as the rest of society that its social hegemony is justified. A dominant class must therefore meet any ideological challenges to its hegemony. If it allows its legitimacy to be shaken, then its only option is to use force to maintain its power, even at the risk of provoking a revolutionary response.

Proletarian Revolution

Marx and Engels were always careful to distinguish political from social revolution. They conceived merely political revolutions as those in which a society's relations of production remain unchanged despite changes in political institutions or in political leadership. A social revolution, on the other hand, is one in which social relations, including the underlying mode of production, political life, and prevailing ideologies are all altered more or less simultaneously. It is a transition to a new *type* of society. Marx argued that social revolution occurs when a subordinate class uses political force to expel a ruling class from power and to reorganize society—beginning with the relations of production—in accordance with its own interest. The political success of the rising class must be preceded by a lengthy struggle in which the hitherto prevailing ideology, the political and legal superstructures, and the relations of production themselves become widely perceived as obstacles to progress. Frustrated by these "fetters" imposed by the hegemony of the ruling class, the rising class undertakes political action (revolution) to remove them and give birth to a new society in which it becomes the dominant class. In Marx's words,

> At a certain stage of their development, the material forces of production in society [which are increasing under the influence of the rising class] come in[to] conflict with the existing relations of production [which correspond to the older forces of production], or—what is but a legal expression for the same thing—with the property relations within which they had been at work before. From forms of development of the forces of production these [established] relations turn into their fetters. Then comes the period of social revolution. With the change of the economic foundation the entire immense superstructure is more or less rapidly transformed.[1]

That is, an established mode of production (feudalism, for example) manifests itself throughout social life: in production (the manorial and guild systems), politics (monarchy, the power of the landed aristocracy), and ideology (the cult of chivalry). Now, when a rising class (in this case the bourgeoisie) produced by this social system itself develops more advanced productive forces (banking, wage labor, the manufacturing system), it struggles to remake society in its own interest by acquiring sufficient political power (as in the English and French revolutions) to establish fully a new mode of social production (capitalism). In turn capitalism, Marx argues in the *Manifesto*, releases enormous productive forces that had previously lain dormant, but holds back the potentially more productive force of freely associated labor with which the proletariat, a creation of capitalism, can vastly increase human well-being. Under capitalism the proletariat becomes organized in the factories and acquires the know-how to operate them. The proletariat can use these skills to increase production and improve the quality of its products once capitalist fetters, especially the belief that production must be geared to profit-making, are removed.

1. Marx. "A Contribution," p. 162.

But the bourgeoisie stands in the way. It controls all centers of power—legal, ideological, political—that it can use against the proletariat. Indeed, capitalism can be expected to evolve new forms of social control as needed. As Marx put it, "no social order ever disappears before all the productive forces, for which there is room in it, have been developed; and new higher relations of production never appear before the material conditions of their existence have matured in the womb of the old society."[2] This observation implies a vast field of institutions and ideas over which the contending classes must struggle before the revolution can be victorious. The crux of the proletariat's strategy is to establish the illegitimacy of the bourgeoisie's control over social institutions—if necessary, one by one.

A crucial factor in the social struggle is the self-consciousness of the revolutionary class, in this case that of the proletariat. Workers must at some point realize that their masters are responsible for holding back the birth of more advanced and more desirable relations of production. Workers must realize that they *can* remake society in accordance with their class interest in this progress. The proletariat must persuade other classes that they too will benefit by the coming social emancipation and should join the struggle. Members of the ruling class—such as Marx and Engels themselves—might decide to join with the proletariat. Part one of the *Manifesto* shows that the bourgeoisie indeed did all this at the close of the feudal era. Part two argues that the proletariat must do this in turn; for only by transforming itself from a slavish class incapable of ruling even itself into one capable of ruling society can the proletariat become capable of its historical mission. For, as Marx and Engels once said in summing up the aims of the proletarian revolution:

> the communist revolution is directed against the preceding *mode* of activity, does away with [alienated] *labor*, and abolishes the rule of all classes with the classes themselves, because it is carried through by the class which no longer counts as a class in society . . . and is itself the expression of the dissolution of all classes, nationalities, etc. within present society. . . . Both for the production on a mass scale of this communist consciousness, and for the success of the cause itself, the alteration of men on a mass scale is necessary, an alteration which can only take place in a practical movement, a *revolution;* this revolution is necessary, therefore, not only because the *ruling* class cannot be overthrown in any other way, but also because the class *overthrowing* it can only in a revolution succeed in

2. Ibid., p. 162.

ridding itself of all the muck of ages and become fitted to found society anew.[3]

Thus the communist revolution is to be the remaking of man, or "human emancipation," through the abolition of alienated labor. It is to bring the abolition of all economic classes and the inauguration of a classless society with no forced division of labor. To accomplish this the proletarian masses must dare to risk all, to risk life itself. Through their struggle they will become both class-conscious and capable of their mission.

Marx also believed that "the emancipation of the workers must be the task of the workers themselves."[4] This is why Marx scorned the notion, central to Babeuf's and Blanqui's (and later, Lenin's) view, that the proletariat can become "enlightened" and capable of managing society only *after* a revolution has been accomplished and maintained indefinitely "for" it by a clique of revolutionary adventurers from the upper classes. It was Marx's view that mass revolutionary struggle is necessary to achieve a communist society, not only because it may be the only way to wrest power from the bourgeoisie, but because only in this way might the proletarians themselves undergo that trial-by-fire through which the "alteration of men on a mass scale" might occur.[5] In a passage written just six months before the *Manifesto*, Marx brings together all these aspects of the proletarian revolution quite clearly:

capital has created for [the mass of workers] a common situation, common interests. This mass is thus already a class as against capital, but not yet for itself. In the struggle . . . the mass becomes united, and constitutes itself as a class for itself. . . . For the oppressed class to emancipate itself it is necessary that the productive powers already acquired and the existing social relations should no longer be capable of existing side by side. Of all the instruments of production, the greatest productive power is the revolutionary class itself. . . .

The working class, in the course of its development, will substitute for the old civil society an association which will exclude classes and their antagonism, and there will be no

3. Marx and Engels, "The German Ideology," p. 201.
4. This was the slogan of the First International, of which Marx was one of the leaders.
5. Marx did on occasion express the view that in countries with strong democratic traditions (he mentioned the United States, Great Britain, and the Netherlands), violent revolution might not be necessary—although a protracted democratic political struggle would be (speech in Amsterdam, September 8, 1872, *The Essential Writings*, pp. 199–200). In 1895 Engels proposed that Social Democracy abandon its revolutionary strategy (in Germany) in favor of an electoral and parliamentary orientation ("Introduction." *Class Struggles in France* by Marx, ed. F. L. Bender, *The Betrayal of Marx* [New York: Harper & Row, 1975], pp. 126–33).

more political power properly so called, since political power is precisely the official expression of antagonism in civil society. . . .

. . . Till then, on the eve of every general reshuffling of society, the last word of social science will always be: "War or death; the bloody struggle or nothing."[6]

It is worth noting again here that Marx clearly did not hold a mechanistic theory of history, for his notion of proletarian revolution shows that revolutions do not happen automatically. Changes in the material forces of production create the conditions that make revolution possible; they do not automatically create a successful revolution itself. It cannot be overemphasized that Marx interpreted history in terms of classes and class struggle, not in terms of the physical forces of production or economics. As Marx put it in 1851, "men make their own history, but they do not make it just as they please; they do not make it under circumstances chosen by themselves, but under circumstances . . . given and transmitted from the past."[7] In other words, according to Marx, history is not primarily a matter of "forces," "elements," or "factors," but of the decisions and actions of human beings caught up in class-divided societies, in the context of which their actions contribute, one way or another, to the outcome of their society's central class conflict.

Having examined the historical background and central ideas on which the *Manifesto* rests—alienated labor, communism, the materialist conception of history, and proletarian revolution—let us turn next to its significance.

The Significance of the Communist Manifesto

Perhaps the greatest significance of the *Manifesto* is that, unlike any of the writings of Marx's socialist and communist predecessors, with the exception of Considérant's *Manifeste socialiste*, this little pamphlet presents a truly comprehensive vision of the immense historical significance of capitalism's rise and projected fall, drawing on studies of politics, economics, history, and philosophy. Unlike Marx, the radical English economists, even the Ricardian socialists, lacked the historical imagination and philosophical grounding to draw from their critique of capitalism its implications for fundamental social change. The French socialists and communists lacked any real understanding of the workings of the capitalist economy.

6. Marx, "The Poverty of Philosophy," pp. 238–39.
7. Marx, "The Eighteenth Brumaire of Louis Bonaparte," *The Essential Writings*, pp. 227n–28n.

Likewise, the French Restoration historians understood the historical role of class struggle, but, since they were exponents of the rising bourgeoisie against the feudal nobility, they ceased to emphasize the historical role of class struggle once bourgeois power was consolidated by the 1830s.[8] The *Manifesto*'s great significance is that in it Marx wove all these themes into a coherent and dramatic whole. What the *Manifesto* lacks in detail and analytic precision it more than makes up in breadth of vision and inspiring prose. The painstaking analyses and arguments on which Marx's outlook rests and on which the *Manifesto* is built can be found in Marx's and Engels's works of the 1840s.

A second source of the *Manifesto*'s lasting significance is the symbolic importance of its acceptance by the Communist League at the outset of 1848, signifying a decisive break with the artisan-oriented outlook that had previously predominated in the workers' movement. In accepting the arguments of the *Manifesto*, the German workers' leadership finally recognized that industrialization could not be thwarted, that their own fate was to become proletarians, and that the eventual revolution against capitalism would have to be a proletarian revolution.

After 1848 the *Manifesto* lay forgotten for two decades until the rising of the Paris Commune (1871) once again placed the workers' movements at the center of European politics. With the *Manifesto*'s first reprinting in 1872, it became the most important document with which the worldwide Social Democratic movement spread its basic doctrines. Since 1872 the *Communist Manifesto* has appeared in thousands of editions, in hundreds of languages. Regardless of its textual shortcomings, the *Manifesto* has become unquestionably Marx's most influential work.

The *Manifesto* succeeds as a piece of prose as did nothing else Marx ever wrote. Its rich imagery and the underlying symbolism of the proletariat's struggle for the redemption of humankind give the *Manifesto* an emotional appeal that lasts to this day. Let us consider just a few of the *Manifesto*'s more incisive images.

The *Manifesto* declares in the prologue that all European powers trembled at the "spectre of communism." This claim is pure hyper-

---

8. Marx freely acknowledged his debt to Ricardo and to the French Restoration historians F.-A. M. Mignet (1796–1884). A. Thierry (1795–1856), and F. P.-C. Cuizot (1787–1874) for the concept of class struggle: "As now to myself, no credit is due to me for discovering the existence of classes in modern society or the struggle between them. Long before me bourgeois historians had described the historical development of this class struggle and bourgeois economists the economic anatomy of the classes. What I did that was new was to prove: (1) that the *existence of classes is* only bound up with *particular historical phases in the development of production,* (2) that the class struggle necessarily leads to the *dictatorship of the proletariat,* (3) that this dictatorship itself only constitutes the transition to the *abolition of all classes* and to a *classless society.*" Marx to J. Weydemeyer, March 5, 1852. *Selected Correspondence,* p. 69.

bole. Europe's governments were far more frightened of their own bourgeoisies, which were indeed at the point of insurrection, than of motley bands of workers, whom they knew quite well were divided and disorganized. The image of the specter is borrowed from the early German sociologist Lorenz von Stein (1815–1890), who had earlier called communism "a dark, threatening spectre, in whose reality no one wants to believe, but whose existence is yet recognized and feared by everybody,"[9] after which the image of the "specter of communism" had become quite common. In Marx's hands, however, the specter ironically loses its fearsome reality to become only a "nursery tale."

The *Manifesto*'s first part, "Bourgeois and Proletarians," is in large part a panegyric to the achievements of the bourgeoisie. But it is also an attempt to undermine the ideological self-justification with which this progress was typically viewed. Marx points out that the great advances in production, social wealth, scientific knowledge, and the elimination of feudal institutions, were accompanied by the promotion of egoism and self-interest to the detriment of other values. Traditional religious, ethical, and aristocratic values had been destroyed under the impact of industrial society and its rationalistic calculation of advantage and uninterrupted transformation of production. Social progress was accompanied, moreover, by economic crises caused by unplanned overproduction, alienated labor, the enslavement of the industrial worker to the machine, and the working class's impoverishment amid rapidly growing social wealth. Marx does not lament these effects of capitalist development, but regards them as the necessary price of historical progress. Indeed, no one has more eloquently described the bourgeoisie's triumphs. Marx has no sympathy for those romantics who wished the bourgeoisie had never had its effects, nor for the Luddites within the workers' movement who hoped to thwart progress by smashing machines. From his viewpoint of historical materialism, Marx simply sees the bourgeoisie as a class that arose within and then overthrew the feudal system, and that has created, along with all its other wonders, the class that will in turn become its "gravedigger," the proletariat.

Marx's earlier description of alienated labor is much in evidence in the *Manifesto*, although the term itself is not used. Marx does explicitly discuss the transformation of the worker into a commodity, the unsatisfying nature of industrial work, the reduction of the worker to an appendage of machinery, the relentless division of labor, the lengthening of the working day, and the perpetual introduction

9. Lorenz von Stein, *Der Sozialismus und Communismus der heutigen Frankriech* (Leipzig: Wigand, 1842), p. 4.

of new machinery. He argues that under capitalism the bourgeoisie continually undermines the existence of the middle classes, causing the vast majority of society to become proletarianized. In capitalism's periodic depressions, production is curtailed and part of society's productive capacity even destroyed. Such underproduction, which makes no sense alongside the poverty of the masses, becomes a fetter on the further development of society's productive capacities. At the same time, a large segment of the proletariat suddenly finds itself unemployed, left to its own devices in a society in which the necessities of life have become commodities. With the proletariat periodically reduced to a pauper class, Marx adds with rhetorical flourish, the bourgeoisie demonstrates its inability even to keep its slaves alive! Marx considered the proletariat permanently impoverished because it is inexorably bound to cycles of employment and unemployment. Though wages may rise in the expansionary phase of the business cycle, when the cycle begins to fall workers are threatened quite literally with starvation—an all too common occurrence in the hungry 1840s. Marx's view, of course, is that the proletariat's fundamental *class* interest is to destroy the system responsible for its plight, rather than merely to seek amelioration of its distress. Still, Marx never opposed struggles to improve the workers' lot per se. Marx believed that the limited effectiveness of these reform struggles would eventually become apparent to the workers and bring them to self-consciousness as a revolutionary class.

In discussing the economic changes the Communist League seeks, Marx makes the important point that communism seeks to abolish only *bourgeois* property—private ownership of *capital*—not private property generally, not the articles of consumption or enjoyment that a person might own as a result of his labor. This is an important point, because so many anti-Marxists have argued that communism requires having property such as one's clothing or furniture expropriated by the state. In the tradition of Babeuf, the *Manifesto* regards "economic freedom," the ownership of capital, as a specifically bourgeois freedom that must be abolished. Marx held that freedom from exploitation, freedom for equal political participation, and economic democracy are impossible unless private ownership of capital is replaced by its social control. Marx considered it self-evident that a society in which exploitation and alienated labor are abolished, and in which everyone shares in the social product, is superior to one in which nine tenths of the population owns no capital and is exploited by the privileged one tenth.

In passing, Marx refers to the objection that no one would work in a society in which everyone was guaranteed an adequate basic level of subsistence. This claim is based on the premise that it is only economic necessity that motivates people to work. Such is indeed the case in a society characterized by alienated labor: the wealthy bourgeois does not engage in any socially useful work but lives on his investments, while the proletarian, in dire need of an income, has no capital to invest and must work to survive. But, according to Marx, this is perverse, because those who work receive only a pittance compared to the vast unearned income the idle bourgeoisie gain through exploitation. The economic goal of communism, for Marx, is to reverse this: to require everyone to work an equal and minimal amount of time and to eliminate differential rewards at least as far as life's basic necessities are concerned. The motivation to perform the accepted minimum amount of work would derive from a sense of civic duty and the need to acquire life's material necessities, while motivation to perform additional work presumably would derive from the enjoyment of unalienated ("freely associated") labor or, alternatively, from its material rewards justly earned.

The reader should also note Marx's passing definition of political power as the organized power of one class to oppress another. In Marx's usage any such organized class power is a dictatorship. Thus *dictatorship* does not necessarily mean the rule of one man or one party.[1] When the bourgeoisie rules, there is "bourgeois dictatorship"; if the proletariat should someday rule, there would be a "prolatarian dictatorship." In light of his belief that the state is, at any time, more or less exclusively controlled by a single class, we can see why Marx would hold that in bourgeois society the state serves primarily to promote the general interests of the bourgeoisie. Since politics is a stage on which class conflict has been traditionally played out, Marx expects politics as known hitherto, the politics of class domination, to disappear along with the economic classes and be replaced by a "free association." In the *Manifesto*, Marx refers to a communist society only in passing, declaring that in it "the free development of each" would be "the condition of the free development of all."

The *Manifesto* criticizes several rival socialist schools. The key to grasping Marx's critique of these positions is to bear in mind that in the *Manifesto* he uses the term *socialism* pejoratively, for, as the Communist League stated in its first "credo," in the 1840s any prison reformer or almshouse builder could be called a socialist.[2] It is commonly alleged that this is today the least rele-

1. It is important to note that it is only in the twentieth century that the term *dictatorship* takes on the meaning of unlimited one-person or single-party rule. Its traditional meaning, the one used by Marx, is that of a temporary rule authorized under the constitution of the Roman republic, with strict limitations on the powers of the "dictator." See Bertram D. Wolfe, *Marxism: One Hundred Years in the Life of a Doctrine* (New York: Dell, 1965), pp. 168–70 and pp. 111–22 in this volume.
2. Carl Grünberg, "Die Londoner kommunistische Festschrift und andere Urkunden aus den Jahren 1847–1848." *Archiv für die Geschichte des Sozialismus und der Arbeiterbewegung* 9 (1921), p. 330.

vant section of the *Manifesto*, for these sects no longer exist. But even if the sects themselves no longer exist, many of their ideas survive today, if in modified form. All the literary "socialisms" that Marx attacks find *some* fault with bourgeois society. But, as Marx observes, none of them understands capitalism as a comprehensive economic system; nor does any understand the defining role within capitalist society of the struggle between bourgeoisie and proletariat.

Thus the so-called feudal socialist is a type of reactionary who criticizes capitalism because it has destroyed the supposed idyll of the small, "organic" community, defined by face-to-face relations and an accepted hierarchy of birth and rank. Marx sees this nostalgia as nothing more than a faint reflection of the aristocracy's already lost struggle against the bourgeoisie. The historical reference seems to be to those romantic writers who lamented the evils of industrialization, a theme familiar nowadays in the anti-industrial desire to restore a pristine natural environment. Marx also criticizes in passing an analogous "Christian socialism," presumably that of Weitling, which seeks in an idealized picture of the early Christian communities the goal of a pure spiritual life achieved by isolating the community of believers from the materialism of bourgeois society.

The second type of "reactionary socialism" Marx criticizes is what he calls "petit-bourgeois socialism," the opposition to large-scale capitalism represented by remnants of the medieval bourgeoisie. Among these were skilled crafts people, merchants, artisans, small peasant proprietors, and shopkeepers who faced ruin in competition with large-scale industry, commerce, and agriculture. Marx acknowledges the value of these people's insight into the tendency of capital to concentrate into a few huge holdings, but he regards their remedies as whims unsupported by the real class dynamics of capitalism.

The third form of "reactionary socialism" Marx discusses is "True Socialism," the name taken by rivals of the Communist League who were active in German literary and academic circles in the late 1840s. Marx condemns these writers as utterly divorced from actual German conditions and their imported socialist ideas as fantasies in a country only beginning its capitalist development. Lacking any social base, these thinkers drew their ideas from German philosophy, thereby restricting their potential audience to fellow intellectuals. It is interesting to note that here Marx refers derisively to the True Socialists' use of the phrase, "alienation of humanity." Marx had distinguished as early as 1844 the abstract concept of alienated humanity from his own concept of alienated labor under the historically specific social system, capitalism. The *Manifesto* does *not* reject Marx's earlier analysis of alienated labor, but mocks the *abstract*, speculative notion of the alienation of "humanity."

Marx turns next to what he terms "conservative, or bourgeois, socialism," that supposedly progressive tendency within the bourgeoisie itself that seeks to ameliorate the workers' plight. Its aim is to blunt the anger of the proletariat and bind them more tightly to their exploitation, while leaving capitalist class relations undisturbed. These "bourgeois socialists" are, from a Marxist viewpoint, the most sophisticated defenders of the existing social system. Although they tinker endlessly with the effects of capitalism, Marx believed they could never succeed in solving the problems they attack because these problems are inherent in capitalism itself.

Finally Marx discusses "critical-utopian socialism," which he finds the most acceptable to the Communist League. He begins by noting that such writers as Saint-Simon, Fourier, and Owen based their social analyses on theories of class antagonism and, unlike the other schools discussed, were aware of the necessity of transforming the class basis of bourgeois society. This alone makes the "critical-utopian" socialist school far more important in Marx's eyes than the others. But these writers appeared far in advance of the historical development of the proletariat and could not conceive, as Marx later did, of its real revolutionary potential. Therefore, they sought non-revolutionary, utopian means for establishing socialism. Because of their premature appearance, the critical-utopian socialists proclaimed a new social science, formed sects, and sought to convince men of power and wealth to undertake voluntarily the creation of a better society. These utopians had no interest in political struggle, which they regarded as sure to frighten away their potential converts.

As capitalist development accelerated and the potential for proletarian revolution took concrete shape, the utopians' proposals became, for Marx, increasingly irrelevant. In the *Manifesto* he attacks their followers for their sectarian dogmatism, for their belief that their masters' words were more important than the class struggle. Their model communities only served, as Marx saw it, to divert the proletariat's efforts from the class struggle. Nonetheless, in discussing the relation of the communists to other parties of the opposition, Marx pragmatically calls for a broad democratic coalition against the ruling monarchies and, eventually, against the bourgeoisie.

Prefaces by Marx and Engels
and
ANNOTATED TEXT OF THE
COMMUNIST MANIFESTO

Prefaces

Preface to the German Edition of 1872

The Communist League, an international association of workers, which could of course be only a secret one under the conditions obtaining at the time, commissioned the undersigned,[1] at the Congress held in London in November 1847, to draw up for publication a detailed theoretical and practical programme of the Party. Such was the origin of the following Manifesto, the manuscript of which travelled to London, to be printed, a few weeks before the February Revolution.[2] First published in German, it has been republished in that language in at least twelve different editions in Germany, England and America. It was published in English for the first time in 1850 in the *Red Republican*, London, translated by Miss Helen Macfarlane, and in 1871 in at least three different translations in America.[3] A French version first appeared in Paris shortly before the June insurrection of 1848[4] and recently in *Le Socialiste* of New York. A new translation is in the course of preparation. A Polish version appeared in London shortly after it was first published in German.[5] A Russian translation was published in Geneva in the sixties. Into Danish, too, it was translated shortly after its first appearance.[6]

However much the state of things may have altered during the last twenty-five years, the general principles laid down in this Manifesto are, on the whole, as correct today as ever. Here and there some detail might be improved. The practical application of the principles will depend, as the Manifesto itself states, everywhere and at all times, on the historical conditions for the time being existing, and, for that reason, no special stress is laid on the revolutionary measures

---

1. Implying, misleadingly, that *both* Marx and Engels were commissioned by the League to write the *Manifesto* [*Ed.*].
2. The February Revolution in France, 1848 [*Ed.*].
3. These were in reality reprints of the Macfarlane translation of 1850. See Bert Andréas, *Le Manifeste communist de Marx et Engels: Histoire et Bibliographie*, 1848–1918 (Milan: Feltrinelli, 1963), p. 59 [*Ed.*].
4. No such translation was published. See Andréas, pp. 15–16 [*Ed.*].
5. It is unlikely that such a translation appeared. See Andréas, p. 17 [*Ed.*].
6. No such translation is known. The *Manifesto* was, however, translated into Swedish in 1848. See Andréas, pp. 17–22 [*Ed.*].

proposed at the end of Section II. That passage would, in many respects, be very differently worded today. In view of the gigantic strides of Modern Industry in the last twenty-five years, and of the accompanying improved and extended party organisation of the working class, in view of the practical experience gained, first in the February Revolution, and then, still more, in the Paris Commune, where the proletariat for the first time held political power for two whole months, this programme has in some details become antiquated. One thing especially was proved by the Commune, *viz.*, that "the working class cannot simply lay hold of the ready-made State machinery, and wield it for its own purposes." (See *The Civil War in France; Address of the General Council of the International Working Men's Association*, London, Truelove, 1871, p. 15, where this point is further developed.) Further, it is self-evident that the criticism of Socialist literature is deficient in relation to the present time, because it comes down only to 1847; also, that the remarks on the relation of the Communists to the various opposition parties (Section IV), although in principle still correct, yet in practice are antiquated, because the political situation has been entirely changed, and the progress of history has swept from off the earth the greater portion of the political parties there enumerated.

But, then, the Manifesto has become a historical document which we have no longer any right to alter. A subsequent edition may perhaps appear with an introduction bridging the gap from 1847 to the present day; this reprint was too unexpected to leave us time for that.

Karl Marx   *Frederick Engels*

London, June 24, 1872

Preface to the Russian Edition of 1882

The first Russian edition of the *Manifesto of the Communist Party*, translated by Bakunin, was published early in the sixties[1] by the printing office of the *Kolokol*. Then the West could see in it (the *Russian* edition of the Manifesto) only a literary curiosity. Such a view would be impossible today.

What a limited field the proletarian movement still occupied at that time (December 1847) is most clearly shown by the last section of the Manifesto: the position of the Communists in relation to the various opposition parties in the various countries. Precisely Russia and the United States are missing here. It was the time when Rus-

1. The edition referred to appeared in 1869. In Engels's Preface to the English Edition of 1888, the publication date of this Russian translation of the *Manifesto* is also incorrectly given [*note by the editors of the Moscow edition*].

sia constituted the last great reserve of all European reaction, when the United States absorbed the surplus proletarian forces of Europe through immigration. Both countries provided Europe with raw materials and were at the same time markets for the sale of its industrial products. At that time both were, therefore, in one way or another, pillars of the existing European order.

How very different today! Precisely European immigration fitted North America for a gigantic agricultural production, whose competition is shaking the very foundations of European landed property— large and small. In addition it enabled the United States to exploit its tremendous industrial resources with an energy and on a scale that must shortly break the industrial monopoly of Western Europe, and especially of England, existing up to now. Both circumstances react in revolutionary manner upon America itself. Step by step the small and middle landownership of the farmers, the basis of the whole political constitution, is succumbing to the competition of giant farms; simultaneously, a mass proletariat and a fabulous concentration of capitals are developing for the first time in the industrial regions.

And now Russia! During the Revolution of 1848–49 not only the European princes, but the European bourgeois as well, found their only salvation from the proletariat, just beginning to awaken, in Russian intervention. The tsar was proclaimed the chief of European reaction. Today he is a prisoner of war of the revolution, in Gatchina, and Russia forms the vanguard of revolutionary action in Europe.

The Communist Manifesto had as its object the proclamation of the inevitably impending dissolution of modern bourgeois property. But in Russia we find, face to face with the rapidly developing capitalist swindle and bourgeois landed property, just beginning to develop, more than half the land owned in common by the peasants. Now the question is: can the Russian *obshchina*,[2] though greatly undermined, yet a form of the primeval common ownership of land, pass directly to the higher form of communist common ownership? Or on the contrary, must it first pass through the same process of dissolution as constitutes the historical evolution of the West?

The only answer to that possible today is this: If the Russian Revolution becomes the signal for a proletarian revolution in the West, so that both complement each other, the present Russian common ownership of land may serve as the starting point for a communist development.

Karl Marx   F. *Engels*

London, January 21, 1882

2. Village community [*note by the editors of the Moscow edition*].

Preface to the German Edition of 1883

The preface to the present edition I must, alas, sign alone. Marx, the man to whom the whole working class of Europe and America owes more than to anyone else—rests at Highgate Cemetery and over his grave the first grass is already growing. Since his death, there can be even less thought of revising or supplementing the Manifesto. All the more do I consider it necessary again to state here the following expressly:

The basic thought running through the Manifesto—that economic production and the structure of society of every historical epoch necessarily arising therefrom constitute the foundation for the political and intellectual history of that epoch; that consequently (ever since the dissolution of the primeval communal ownership of land) all history has been a history of class struggles, of struggles between exploited and exploiting, between dominated and dominating classes at various stages of social development; that this struggle, however, has now reached a stage where the exploited and oppressed class (the proletariat) can no longer emancipate itself from the class which exploits and oppresses it (the bourgeoisie), without at the same time for ever freeing the whole of society from exploitation, oppression and class struggles—this basic thought belongs solely and exclusively to Marx.[1]

I have already stated this many times; but precisely now it is necessary that it also stand in front of the Manifesto itself.

F. Engels

London, June 28, 1883

Preface to the English Edition of 1888

The Manifesto was published as the platform of the "Communist League," a working men's association, first exclusively German, later on international, and, under the political conditions of the Continent before 1848, unavoidably a secret society. At a Congress of the League, held in London in November, 1847, Marx and Engels were commissioned to prepare for publication a complete theoreti-

---

1. "This proposition," I wrote in the preface to the English translation, "which, in my opinion, is destined to do for history what Darwin's theory has done for biology, we, both of us, had been gradually approaching for some years before 1845. How far I had independently progressed towards it, is best shown by my 'Condition of the Working Class in England.' But when I again met Marx at Brussels, in spring, 1845, he had it ready worked out, and put it before me, in terms almost as clear as those in which I have stated it here" [Engels's note].

cal and practical party programme. Drawn up in German, in January, 1848, the manuscript was sent to the printer in London a few weeks before the French revolution of February 24th. A French translation was brought out in Paris, shortly before the insurrection of June, 1848. The first English translation, by Miss Helen Macfarlane, appeared in George Julian Harney's "Red Republican," London, 1850. A Danish and a Polish edition had also been published.[1]

The defeat of the Parisian insurrection of June, 1848,—the first great battle between Proletariat and Bourgeoisie—drove again into the background, for a time, the social and political aspirations of the European working class. Thenceforth, the struggle for supremacy was again, as it had been before the revolution of February, solely between different sections of the propertied class; the working class was reduced to a fight for political elbow-room, and to the position of extreme wing of the middle-class Radicals. Wherever independent proletarian movements continued to show signs of life, they were ruthlessly hunted down. Thus the Prussian police hunted out the Central Board of the Communist League, than located in Cologne. The members were arrested, and, after eighteen months' imprisonment, they were tried in October, 1852. This celebrated "Cologne Communist trial" lasted from October 4th till November 12th; seven of the prisoners were sentenced to terms of imprisonment in a fortress, varying from three to six years. Immediately after the sentence, the League was formally dissolved by the remaining members. As to the Manifesto, it seemed thenceforth to be doomed to oblivion.

When the European working class had recovered sufficient strength for another attack on the ruling classes, the International Working Men's Association sprang up. But this association, formed with the express aim of welding into one body the whole militant proletariat of Europe and America, could not at once proclaim the principles laid down in the Manifesto. The International was bound to have a programme broad enough to be acceptable to the English Trades' Unions, to the followers of Proudhon in France, Belgium, Italy, and Spain, and to the Lassalleans[2] in Germany. Marx, who drew up this programme to the satisfaction of all parties, entirely trusted to the intellectual development of the working class, which was sure to result from combined action and mutual discussion. The very events and vicissitudes of the struggle against Capital, the

---

1. On the questionable existence of the French, Danish, and Polish translations, see Bert Andréas, *Le Manifeste communiste de Marx et Engels: Histoire et Bibiliographie*, 1848–1918 (Milan: Feltrinelli, 1963), p. 17 [*Ed.*].
2. Lassalle personally, to us, always acknowledged himself to be a disciple of Marx, and, as such, stood on the ground of the Manifesto. But in his public agitation, 1862–64, he did not go beyond demanding co-operative workshops supported by State credit [*Engels's note*]

defeats even more than the victories, could not help bringing home to men's minds the insufficiency of their various favourite nostrums, and preparing the way for a more complete insight into the true conditions of working-class emancipation. And Marx was right. The International, on its breaking up in 1874, left the workers quite different men from what it had found them in 1864. Proudhonism in France, Lassalleanism in Germany were dying out, and even the conservative English Trades' Unions, though most of them had long since severed their connexion with the International, were gradually advancing towards that point at which, last year at Swansea, their President could say in their name "Continental Socialism has lost its terrors for us." In fact: the principles of the Manifesto had made considerable headway among the working men of all countries.[3]

The Manifesto itself thus came to the front again. The German text had been, since 1850, reprinted several times in Switzerland, England and America. In 1872, it was translated into English in New York, where the translation was published in "Woodhull and Claflin's Weekly." From this English version, a French one was made in *Le Socialiste* of New York. Since then at least two more English translations, more or less mutilated, have been brought out in America, and one of them has been reprinted in England. The first Russian translation, made by Bakounine, was published at Herzen's *Kolokol* office in Geneva, about 1863; a second one, by the heroic Vera Zasulich[4] also in Geneva, 1882. A new Danish edition is to be found in *Social-demokratisk Bibliothek*, Copenhagen, 1885; a fresh French translation in *Le Socialiste*, Paris, 1885. From this latter a Spanish version was prepared and published in Madrid, 1886. The German reprints are not to be counted, there have been twelve altogether at the least. An Armenian translation, which was to be published in Constantinople some months ago, did not see the light, I am told, because the publisher was afraid of bringing out a book with the name of Marx on it, while the translator declined to call it his own production. Of further translations into other languages I have heard, but have not seen them. Thus the history of the Manifesto reflects, to a great extent, the history of the modern working-class movement; at present it is undoubtedly the most widespread, the most international production of all socialist literature, the common platform acknowledged by millions of working men from Siberia to California.

3. Far from it being the case that the years of the First International marked the steady increase in the acceptance of the principles of the *Communist Manifesto*, Marx had to destroy the International in 1872 (by moving its headquarters to New York) in order to avoid its falling into the hands of the Bakuninists and Proudhonians [Ed.].
4. Later on Engels himself rightly pointed out in the afterword to the article "Social Relations in Russia," published in *Internationales aus dem Volksstaat* (1871–75), Berlin, 1894, that the actual translator was G. V. Plekhanov [note by the editors of the Moscow edition].

Yet, when it was written, we could not have called it a *Socialist* Manifesto. By Socialists, in 1847, were understood, on the one hand, the adherents of the various Utopian systems: Owenites in England, Fourierists in France, both of them already reduced to the position of mere sects, and gradually dying out; on the other hand, the most multifarious social quacks, who, by all manners of tinkering, professed to redress, without any danger to capital and profit, all sorts of social grievances, in both cases men outside the working-class movement, and looking rather to the "educated" classes for support. Whatever portion of the working class had become convinced of the insufficiency of mere political revolutions, and had proclaimed the necessity of a total social change, that portion then called itself Communist. It was a crude, rough-hewn, purely instinctive sort of Communism; still, it touched the cardinal point and was powerful enough amongst the working class to produce the Utopian Communism, in France, of Cabet, and in Germany, of Weitling. Thus, Socialism was, in 1847, a middle-class movement, Communism, a working-class movement. Socialism was, on the Continent at least, "respectable"; Communism was the very opposite. And as our notion, from the very beginning, was that "the emancipation of the working class must be the act of the working class itself," there could be no doubt as to which of the two names we must take. Moreover, we have, ever since, been far from repudiating it.

The Manifesto being our joint production, I consider myself bound to state that the fundamental proposition, which forms its nucleus, belongs to Marx. That proposition is: that in every historical epoch, the prevailing mode of economic production and exchange, and the social organisation necessarily following from it, form the basis upon which is built up, and from which alone can be explained, the political and intellectual history of that epoch; that consequently the whole history of mankind (since the dissolution of primitive tribal society, holding land in common ownership) has been a history of class struggles, contests between exploiting and exploited, ruling and oppressed classes; that the history of these class struggles forms a series of evolutions in which, now-a-days, a stage has been reached where the exploited and oppressed class—the proletariat—cannot attain its emancipation from the sway of the exploiting and ruling class—the bourgeoisie—without, at the same time, and once and for all, emancipating society at large from all exploitation, oppression, class distinctions and class struggles.

This proposition which, in my opinion, is destined to do for history what Darwin's theory has done for biology, we, both of us, had been gradually approaching for some years before 1845. How far I had independently progressed towards it, is best shown by my "Condition of the Working Class in England."[5] But when I again met Marx at Brussels, in spring, 1845, he had it ready worked out, and put it before me, in terms almost as clear as those in which I have stated it here.[6]

* * *

The present translation is by Mr. Samuel Moore, the translator of the greater portion of Marx's "Capital." We have revised it in common, and I have added a few notes explanatory of historical allusions.

Frederick Engels

London, 30th January, 1888

Preface to the German Edition of 1890

Since the above was written,[1] a new German edition of the Manifesto has again become necessary, and much has also happened to the Manifesto which should be recorded here.

A second Russian translation—by Vera Zasulich—appeared at Geneva in 1882; the preface to that edition was written by Marx and myself. Unfortunately, the original German manuscript has gone astray; I must therefore retranslate from the Russian, which will in no way improve the text.[2]

* * *

At about the same date, a new Polish version appeared in Geneva: *Manifest Komunistyczny*.

Furthermore, a new Danish translation has appeared in the *Social-demokratisk Bibliothek*, Kjöbenhavn 1885. Unfortunately it is not quite complete; certain essential passages, which seem to have presented difficulties to the translator, have been omitted, and in addition there are signs of carelessness here and there, which are all the more unpleasantly conspicuous since the translation indicates that had the translator taken a little more pains he would have done an excellent piece of work.

A new French version appeared in 1885 in *Le Socialiste* of Paris; it is the best published to date.[3]

5. "The Condition of the Working Class in England in 1844." By Frederick Engels. Translated by Florence K. Wischnewetzky, New York. Lovell—London. W. Reeves, 1888 [*Engels's note*].
6. At this point Engels quotes the second and third paragraphs of the preface to the German edition of 1872, save for omitting the last sentence of the third paragraph and making one deletion: the word *party* is removed from the clause "and of the accompanying improved and extended party organization of the working class."
1. Engels refers to his preface to the German edition of 1883 [*Ed.*].
2. Engels then repeats the preface to the Russian edition of 1882, with minor stylistic differences [*Ed.*].
3. On the questionable existence of a French translation of 1848, see Bert Andreas, *Le Manifeste communiste de Marx et Engels: Histoire et Bibliographie, 1848–1918* (Milan: Feltrinelli, 1963), pp. 15–16 [*Ed.*].

From this latter a Spanish version was published the same year, first in *El Socialista* of Madrid, and then reissued in pamphlet form: *Manifiesto del Partido Comunista* por Carlos Marx y F. Engels, Madrid, Administración de *El Socialista*, Hernán Cortés 8.

As a matter of curiosity I may also mention that in 1887 the manuscript of an Armenian translation was offered to a publisher in Constantinople. But the good man did not have the courage to publish something bearing the name of Marx and suggested that the translator set down his own name as author, which the latter, however, declined.

After one and then another of the more or less inaccurate American translations had been repeatedly reprinted in England, an authentic version at last appeared in 1888. This was by my friend Samuel Moore, and we went through it together once more before it was sent to press. It is entitled: Manifesto of the Communist Party, by Karl Marx and Frederick Engels. Authorised English Translation, edited and annotated by Frederick Engels. 1888. London, William Reeves, 185 Fleet st., E. C. I have added some of the notes of that edition to the present one.[4]

The Manifesto has had a history of its own. Greeted with enthusiasm, at the time of its appearance, by the then still not at all numerous vanguard of scientific Socialism (as is proved by the translations mentioned in the first preface), it was soon forced into the background by the reaction that began with the defeat of the Paris workers in June 1848, and was finally excommunicated "according to law" by the conviction of the Cologne communists in November 1852. With the disappearance from the public scene of the workers' movement that had begun with the February Revolution, the Manifesto too passed into the background.[5]

* * *

"Working men of all countries, unite!" But few voices responded when we proclaimed these words to the world forty-two years ago, on the eve of the first Paris Revolution in which the proletariat came out with demands of its own. On September 28, 1864, however, the proletarians of most of the Western European countries joined hands in the International Working Men's Association of glorious memory. True, the International itself lived only nine years. But that the eternal union of the proletarians of all countries created by it is still alive and lives stronger than ever, there is no better witness than this day. Because today, as I write these lines, the European and American proletariat is reviewing its fighting forces, mobilised for the first time, mobilised as *one* army, under

4. This is the English translation reprinted in this volume [*Ed.*].
5. Engels then paraphrases the preface to the English edition of 1888 [*Ed.*].

one flag, for *one* immediate aim: the standard eight-hour working day, to be established by legal enactment, as proclaimed by the Geneva Congress of the International in 1866, and again by the Paris Workers' Congress in 1889.[6] And today's spectacle will open the eyes of the capitalists and landlords of all countries to the fact that today the working men of all countries are united indeed.

If only Marx were still by my side to see this with his own eyes!

F. Engels

London, May 1, 1890

Preface to the Polish Edition of 1892[†]

The fact that a new Polish edition of the Communist Manifesto has become necessary gives rise to various thoughts.

First of all, it is noteworthy that of late the Manifesto has become an index, as it were, of the development of large-scale industry on the European continent. In proportion as large-scale industry expands in a given country, the demand grows among the workers of that country for enlightenment regarding their position as the working class in relation to the possessing classes, the socialist movement spreads among them and the demand for the Manifesto increases. Thus, not only the state of the labour movement but also the degree of development of large-scale industry can be measured with fair accuracy in every country by the number of copies of the Manifesto circulated in the language of that country.

Accordingly, the new Polish edition indicates a decided progress of Polish industry. And there can be no doubt whatever that this progress since the previous edition published ten years ago has actually taken place. Russian Poland, Congress Poland, has become the big industrial region of the Russian Empire. Whereas Russian large-scale industry is scattered sporadically—a part round the Gulf of Finland, another in the centre (Moscow and Vladimir), a third along the coasts of the Black and Azov seas, and still others elsewhere—Polish industry has been packed into a relatively small area and enjoys both the advantages and the disadvantages arising from such concentration. The competing Russian manufacturers acknowledged the advantages when they demanded protective tariffs against Poland, in spite of their ardent desire to transform the Poles into Russians. The disadvantages—for the Polish manufac-

6. This is a reference to the founding of the Second International. Note that the proletariat now seeks the legal establishment of the eight-hour day rather than social revolution! [*Ed.*].

† The translation of the Preface to the Polish edition given here is from the German original [*note by editors of the Moscow edition*].

turers and the Russian government—are manifest in the rapid spread of socialist ideas among the Polish workers and in the growing demand for the Manifesto.

But the rapid development of Polish industry, outstripping that of Russia, is in its turn a new proof of the inexhaustible vitality of the Polish people and a new guarantee of its impending national restoration. And the restoration of an independent strong Poland is a matter which concerns not only the Poles but all of us. A sincere international collaboration of the European nations is possible only if each of these nations is fully autonomous in its own house. The Revolution of 1848, which under the banner of the proletariat, after all, merely let the proletarian fighters do the work of the bourgeoisie, also secured the independence of Italy, Germany and Hungary through its testamentary executors, Louis Bonaparte and Bismarck; but Poland, which since 1792 had done more for the Revolution than all these three together, was left to its own resources when it succumbed in 1863 to a tenfold greater Russian force. The nobility could neither maintain nor regain Polish independence; today, to the bourgeoisie, this independence is, to say the least, immaterial. Nevertheless, it is a necessity for the harmonious collaboration of the European nations. It can be gained only by the young Polish proletariat, and in its hands it is secure. For the workers of all the rest of Europe need the independence of Poland just as much as the Polish workers themselves.

F. Engels

London, February 10, 1892

Preface to the Italian Edition of 1893

To the Italian Reader

Publication of the *Manifesto of the Communist Party* coincided, one may say, with March 18, 1848, the day of the revolutions in Milan and Berlin, which were armed uprisings of the two nations situated in the centre, the one, of the continent of Europe, the other, of the Mediterranean; two nations until then enfeebled by division and internal strife, and thus fallen under foreign domination. While Italy was subject to the Emperor of Austria, Germany underwent the yoke, not less effective though more indirect, of the Tsar of all the Russias. The consequences of March 18, 1848, freed both Italy and Germany from this disgrace; if from 1848 to 1871 these two great nations were reconstituted and somehow again put on their own, it was, as Karl Marx used to say, because the men who suppressed the Revolution of 1848 were, nevertheless, its testamentary executors in spite of themselves.

Everywhere that revolution was the work of the working class; it was the latter that built the barricades and paid with its lifeblood. Only the Paris workers, in overthrowing the government, had the very definite intention of overthrowing the bourgeois regime. But conscious though they were of the fatal antagonism existing between their own class and the bourgeoisie, still, neither the economic progress of the country nor the intellectual development of the mass of French workers had as yet reached the stage which would have made a social reconstruction possible. In the final analysis, therefore, the fruits of the revolution were reaped by the capitalist class. In the other countries, in Italy, in Germany, in Austria, the workers, from the very outset, did nothing but raise the bourgeoisie to power. But in any country the rule of the bourgeoisie is impossible without national independence. Therefore, the Revolution of 1848 had to bring in its train the unity and autonomy of the nations that had lacked them up to then: Italy, Germany, Hungary. Poland will follow in turn.

Thus, if the Revolution of 1848 was not a socialist revolution, it paved the way, prepared the ground for the latter. Through the impetus given to large-scale industry in all countries, the bourgeois regime during the last forty-five years has everywhere created a numerous, concentrated and powerful proletariat. It has thus raised, to use the language of the Manifesto, its own grave-diggers. Without restoring autonomy and unity to each nation, it will be impossible to achieve the international union of the proletariat, or the peaceful and intelligent co-operation of these nations toward common aims. Just imagine joint international action by the Italian, Hungarian, German, Polish and Russian workers under the political conditions preceding 1848!

The battles fought in 1848 were thus not fought in vain. Nor have the forty-five years separating us from that revolutionary epoch passed to no purpose. The fruits are ripening, and all I wish is that the publication of this Italian translation may augur as well for the victory of the Italian proletariat as the publication of the original did for the international revolution.

The Manifesto does full justice to the revolutionary part played by capitalism in the past. The first capitalist nation was Italy. The close of the feudal Middle Ages, and the opening of the modern capitalist era are marked by a colossal figure: an Italian, Dante, both the last poet of the Middle Ages and the first poet of modern times. Today, as in 1300, a new historical era is approaching. Will Italy give us the new Dante, who will mark the hour of birth of this new, proletarian era?

Frederick Engels

London, February 1, 1893

Karl Marx, Manifesto of the Communist Party[†]

A spectre is haunting Europe—the spectre of Communism.[1] All the Powers of old Europe have entered into a holy alliance to exorcise this spectre: Pope and Czar, Metternich and Guizot, French Radicals[2] and German police-spies.[3]

Where is the party in opposition that has not been decried as Communistic by its opponents in power? Where the Opposition that has not hurled back the branding reproach of Communism,

---

[†] The English text of the *Communist Manifesto* that follows was authorized by Engels in 1888. Engels himself chose the translator, Samuel Moore, who had translated volume 1 of *Capital*. The translation was based on the German editions of either 1872 or 1873, which are almost identical.

Engels played an important role in the preparation of this translation. He emphasized the importance, and the difficulties, of an English translation of the *Manifesto*, negotiated with the publisher, made numerous suggestions, added eight footnotes, and wrote the longest of the prefaces to any of the editions that appeared in his and Marx's lifetimes. Because of Engels's active role, the Moore translation has been regarded as the standard English translation since its appearance.

This was not, however, the first attempt at an English translation of the *Manifesto*. Engels himself started one in 1849 but did not complete it, and a partial translation, by Helen Macfarlane, appeared in 1850 in George Julian Harney's weekly newspaper. *The Red Republican*.

However, the Moore translation contains a great number of modifications, omissions, and minor changes from the German text. The notes to this edition distinguish these changes and other additions to the text, according to their authorship or to the person who was first to note them, as follows.

D.R. = David Riazanov, former director of the Marx-Engels-Lenin Institute (Moscow), whose annotations on textual differences are found in *MEGA* 1/6, 685–86. MEGA is the standard abbreviation for the first attempt (aborted) at an edition of Marx and Engels's collected works. The full title is *Karl Marx, Friedrich Engels historische-kritische-Gesamtausgabe*. Publication began (in the USSR) in 1927 and lasted through 1935. The first editor, D. Riazanov, was purged by Stalin in the early thirties.

B.A. = Bert Andréas, whose annotations appear in *Le Manifeste communiste de Marx et Engels, Histoire et Bibliographie, 1818–1918* (Milan: Feltrinelli. 1963), p. 371.

Ed. = the present editor.
1. Macfarlane has "A frightful hobgoblin stalks throughout Europe. . . ." [*Ed*].
2. Foremost among them were Marrast, Carnot, and Marie, prominent critics of the French Social Democrats, led by Ledru-Rollin and Flocon. In 1848 the pope was Pius IX, Russia was ruled by Czar Nicholas I; Clemens Wenzel Lothar Metternich-Winneburg, the architect of the Holy Alliance, was chancellor of the Austrian Empire; and the historian Guizot was foreign minister of France. Guizot, incidentally, had Marx expelled from France (January 16, 1845) at the request of the Prussian government [*Ed*.].
3. *Polizisten* = policemen; not "police-spies" [*D.R.*].

59

against the more advanced opposition parties, as well as against its reactionary adversaries?

Two things result from this fact.

I. Communism is already acknowledged by all European Powers to be itself a Power.[4]

II. It is high time that Communists should openly, in the face of the whole world, publish their views, their aims, their tendencies, and meet this nursery tale of the Spectre of Communism with a Manifesto of the party itself.

To this end, Communists of various nationalities have assembled in London, and sketched the following Manifesto, to be published in the English, French, German, Italian, Flemish and Danish languages.[5]

I
Bourgeois and Proletarians[1]

The history of all hitherto existing society[2] is the history of class struggles.

4. This, of course, is an exaggeration [Ed.].
5. On the question of the contemporary translations of the Communist Manifesto, see Andréas, pp. 14–27 [Ed.].
1. By bourgeoisie is meant the class of modern Capitalists, owners of the means of social production and employers of wage-labour. By proletariat, the class of modern wage-labourers who, having no means of production of their own, are reduced to selling their labour-power in order to live [Engels's note to the English edition of 1888].
2. That is, all written history. In 1847, the pre-history of society, the social organisation existing previous to recorded history, was all but unknown. Since then, Haxthausen discovered common ownership of land in Russia, Maurer proved it to be the social foundation from which all Teutonic races started in history, and by and by village communities were found to be, or to have been the primitive form of society everywhere from India to Ireland. The inner organisation of this primitive Communistic society was laid bare, in its typical form, by Morgan's crowning discovery of the true nature of the gens and its relation to the tribe. With the dissolution of these primaeval communities society begins to be differentiated into separate and finally antagonistic classes. I have attempted to retrace this process of dissolution in: The Origin of the Family, Private Property, and the State [Engels's note to the English edition of 1888].
    August von Haxthausen (1792–1866) was a Prussian baron who, at the behest of Nicholas I, investigated the land laws, agricultural conditions, and lifestyles of the peasants of the Russian Empire. His major work, A Study of the Folk Life and, more especially, the Agrarian Institutions of Russia, appeared in three volumes between 1847 and 1852. Georg Ludwig von Maurer (1790–1872) was a German historian, lawyer, statesman, and writer who studied extensively early German social institutions and the history of village and urban communal institutions in Germany. Lewis Henry Morgan (1818–1881) was an American ethnologist who lived among the Iroquois Indians and studied their manners and customs, especially their family life. Engels's book, The Origin of the Family, Private Property, and the State, is heavily indebted to Morgan's researches [Ed.].

I. BOURGEOIS AND PROLETARIANS

Freeman and slave, patrician and plebeian, lord and ser[f],
master[3] and journeyman, in a word, oppressor and oppresse[d],
in constant opposition to one another, carried on an uninter[rupted,]
now hidden, now open fight, a fight that each time ended, either in
a revolutionary re-constitution of society at large, or in the common
ruin of the contending classes.

In the earlier epochs of history, we find almost everywhere a
complicated arrangement of society into various orders, a manifold
gradation of social rank. In ancient Rome we have patricians,
knights, plebeians, slaves; in the Middle Ages, feudal lords, vassals,
guild-masters, journeymen, apprentices,[4] serfs; in almost all of these
classes, again, subordinate gradations.

The modern bourgeois society that has sprouted from the ruins
of feudal society has not done away with class antagonisms. It has
but established new classes, new conditions of oppression, new
forms of struggle in place of the old ones.

Our epoch, the epoch of the bourgeoisie, possesses, however, this
distinctive feature: it has simplified the class antagonisms. Society
as a whole is more and more splitting up into two great hostile
camps, into two great classes directly facing each other: Bourgeoisie
and Proletariat.

From the serfs of the Middle Ages sprang the chartered burghers[5]
of the earliest towns. From these burgesses the first elements of the
bourgeoisie were developed.

The discovery of America, the rounding of the Cape,[6] opened up
fresh ground for the rising bourgeoisie. The East-Indian and Chinese markers, the colonisation of America, trade with the colonies,
the increase in the means of exchange and in commodities generally, gave to commerce, to navigation, to industry, an impulse never
before known, and thereby, to the revolutionary element in the tot-
tering feudal society, a rapid development.

The feudal system of industry, under which industrial production
was monopolised by closed guilds,[7] now no longer sufficed for the
growing wants of the new markets. The manufacturing system took
its place. The guild-masters were pushed on one side by the manufacturing middle class; division of labour between the different

---

3. Guild-master, that is, a full member of a guild, a master within, not a head of a guild
   [*Engels's note to the English edition of 1888*].
4. *Gesellen* = journeymen; not "journeymen, apprentices" [*D.R.*].
5. Inhabitants of towns or boroughs possessing full municipal rights—i.e., citizens, free-
   men of a town [*Ed.*].
6. The Cape of Good Hope, at the southern end of Africa [*Ed.*].
7. *Die bisherige feudale oder zünftige Betriebsweise der Industrie* = The previous feudal or
   guild mode of industry; not: "The feudal system of industry, under which industrial
   production was monopolized by closed guilds" [*D.R.*].

corporate guilds vanished in the face of division of labour in each single workshop.

Meantime the markets kept ever growing, the demand ever rising. Even manufacture no longer sufficed. Thereupon, steam and machinery revolutionised industrial production. The place of manufacture was taken by the giant, Modern Industry, the place of the industrial middle class, by industrial millionaires, the leaders of whole industrial armies, the modern bourgeois.

Modern industry has established the world-market, for which the discovery of America paved the way. This market has given an immense development to commerce, to navigation, to communication by land. This development has, in its turn, reacted on the extension of industry; and in proportion as industry, commerce, navigation, railways extended, in the same proportion the bourgeoisie developed, increased its capital, and pushed into the background every class handed down from the Middle Ages.

We see, therefore, how the modern bourgeoisie is itself the product of a long course of development, of a series of revolutions in the modes of production and of exchange.

Each step in the development of the bourgeoisie was accompanied by a corresponding political advance of that class.[8] An oppressed class under the sway of the feudal nobility, an armed and self-governing association in the mediaeval commune;[9] here independent urban republic (as in Italy and Germany),[1] there taxable "third estate" of the monarchy (as in France),[2] afterwards, in the period of manufacture proper, serving either the semi-feudal[3] or the absolute monarchy as a counterpoise against the nobility, and, in fact, corner-stone of the great monarchies in general, the bourgeoisie has at last, since the establishment of Modern Industry and of the world-market, conquered for itself, in the modern representative State, exclusive political sway. The executive of the modern State is but a committee for managing the common affairs of the whole bourgeoisie.[4]

---

8. "of that class" added by the translator [D.R.].
9. "Commune" was the name taken, in France, by the nascent towns even before they had conquered from their feudal lords and masters local self-government and political rights as the "Third Estate." Generally speaking, for the economical development of the bourgeoisie, England is here taken as the typical country; for its political development, France [Engels's note to the English edition of 1888].
  This was the name given their urban communities by the townsmen of Italy and France, after they had purchased or wrested their initial rights of self-government from their feudal lords [Engels's note to the German edition of 1890].
  "mediaeval" added by translator [D.R.].
1. "as in Italy and Germany" added by translator [D.R.].
2. "as in France" added by translator [D.R.].
3. ständischen = belonging to the (feudal) estates, feudal; not "semi-feudal" [D.R.].
4. This noteworthy characterization of the modern i.e., liberal, state suggests that the basic function of the state is to support those endeavors that serve to sustain or

The bourgeoisie, historically, has played a most revolutionary part.

The bourgeoisie, wherever it has got the upper hand, has put an end to all feudal, patriarchal, idyllic relations. It has pitilessly torn asunder the motley feudal ties that bound man to his "natural superiors," and has left remaining no other nexus between man and man than naked self-interest, than callous "cash payment." It has drowned the most heavenly ecstasies of religious fervour, of chivalrous enthusiasm, of philistine sentimentalism, in the icy water of egotistical calculation. It has resolved personal worth into exchange value,[5] and in place of the numberless indefeasible chartered freedoms, has set up that single, unconscionable freedom—Free Trade.[6] In one word, for exploitation, veiled by religious and political illusions, it has substituted naked, shameless, direct, brutal exploitation.[7]

The bourgeoisie has stripped of its halo every occupation hitherto honoured and looked up to with reverent awe. It has converted the physician, the lawyer, the priest, the poet, the man of science, into its paid wage-labourers.

The bourgeoisie has torn away from the family its sentimental veil, and has reduced the family relation to a mere money relation.

The bourgeoisie has disclosed how it came to pass that the brutal display of vigour in the Middle Ages, which Reactionists[8] so much admire, found its fitting complement in the most slothful indolence. It has been the first to show what man's activity can bring about. It has accomplished wonders far surpassing Egyptian pyramids, Roman

---

improve the interests of the bourgeoisie as a whole, e.g., against the nobility or subordinate classes, or against the bourgeoisies of other nations. It does not intend that the interests of the bourgeoisie in any one nation are always monolithic: often the interests of various segments of the bourgeoisie in a market economy, and those of one segment must be sacrificed to those of the class as a whole [Ed.].

5. This is another way of saying that persons (workers) are reduced to commodities under capitalism. Exchange value is defined as the quantitative measure of socially necessary labor time embodied in a commodity (*Capital*, 1.1). Here in the *Manifesto*, Marx means that the "personal worth" of the commodity "worker" is reduced to the labor power that he or she embodies, which in turn equals the exchange value of all the commodities necessary to produce the worker (the value of his or her means of subsistence, housing, clothing, education, etc.) [Ed.].

6. An economic doctrine favored by the industrial bourgeoisie that would eliminate tariffs and other protectionist levies that hinder the flow of goods across national boundaries. Marx supported free trade in numerous speeches and articles in late 1847 and early 1848 as part of his support for the development of capitalism in Germany, quite often in opposition to the views of workers [Ed.].

7. That is, the bourgeoisie has replaced various feudal labor relations with that of wage labor. In 1849 Marx described the exploitation of the wage laborer in the following terms: "for a smaller sum of exchange values which he pays to the worker [wages], the latter must produce a greater amount of exchange value" ("Wage Labor and Capital," *Neue Rheinische Zeitung*, no. 267, April 8, 1849 [*Marx-Engels Collected Works* (New York: International Publishers, 1975–), pp. 9, 25] 218) [Ed.].

8. I.e., reactionaries, in present usage [Ed.].

aqueducts, and Gothic cathedrals; it has conducted expeditions that put in the shade all former Exoduses of nations and crusades.

The bourgeoisie cannot exist without constantly revolutionising the instruments of production, and thereby the relations of production, and with them the whole relations of society. Conservation of the old modes of production in unaltered form, was, on the contrary, the first condition of existence for all earlier industrial classes. Constant revolutionising of production, uninterrupted disturbance of all social conditions, everlasting uncertainty and agitation distinguish the bourgeois epoch from all earlier ones. All fixed, fast-frozen relations, with their train of ancient and venerable prejudices and opinions, are swept away, all new-formed ones become antiquated before they can ossify. All that is solid melts into air, all that is holy is profaned, and man is at last compelled to face with sober senses, his real conditions of life, and his relations with his kind.

The need of a constantly expanding market for its products chases the bourgeoisie over the whole surface of the globe. It must nestle everywhere, settle everywhere, establish connexions everywhere.

The bourgeoisie has through its exploitation of the world-market given a cosmopolitan character to production and consumption in every country. To the great chagrin of Reactionists, it has drawn from under the feet of industry the national ground on which it stood.[9] All old-established national industries have been destroyed or are daily being destroyed. They are dislodged by new industries, whose introduction becomes a life and death question for all civilised nations, by industries that no longer work up indigenous raw material, but raw material drawn from the remotest zones; industries whose products are consumed, not only at home, but in every quarter of the globe. In place of the old wants, satisfied by the productions of the country, we find new wants, requiring for their satisfaction the products of distant lands and climes. In place of the old local and national seclusion and self-sufficiency, we have intercourse in every direction, universal inter-dependence of nations. And as in material, so also in intellectual production. The intellectual creations of individual nations become common property. National one-sidedness and narrow-mindedness become more and more impossible, and from the numerous national and local literatures, there arises a world literature.

The bourgeoisie, by the rapid improvement of all instruments of production, by the immensely facilitated means of communication, draws all, even the most barbarian, nations into civilisation. The cheap prices of its commodities are the heavy artillery with which

9. "on which it stood" added by translator [D.R.].

it batters down all Chinese walls, with which it forces the barbarians' intensely obstinate hatred of foreigners to capitulate. It compels all nations, on pain of extinction, to adopt the bourgeois mode of production; it compels them to introduce what it calls civilisation into their midst, i.e., to become bourgeois themselves. In one word, it creates a world after its own image.[1]

The bourgeoisie has subjected the country to the rule of the towns. It has created enormous cities, has greatly increased the urban population as compared with the rural, and has thus rescued a considerable part of the population from the idiocy of rural life. Just as it has made the country dependent on the towns, so it has made barbarian and semi-barbarian countries dependent on the civilised ones, nations of peasants on nations of bourgeois, the East on the West.

The bourgeoisie keeps more and more doing away with the scattered state of the population, of the means of production, and of property.[2] It has agglomerated population, centralised means of production, and has concentrated property in a few hands. The necessary consequence of this was political centralisation. Independent, or but loosely connected provinces, with separate interests, laws, governments and systems of taxation, became lumped together into one nation, with one government, one code of laws, one national class-interest, one frontier[3] and one customs-tariff.

The bourgeoisie, during its rule of scarce one hundred years,[4] has created more massive and more colossal productive forces than have all preceding generations together. Subjection of Nature's forces to man, machinery, application of chemistry to industry and agriculture, steam-navigation, railways, electric telegraphs, clearing of whole continents for cultivation, canalisation of rivers, whole populations conjured out of the ground—what earlier century had even a presentiment that such productive forces slumbered in the lap of social labour?

We see then: the means of production and of exchange,[5] on whose foundation the bourgeoisie built itself up, were generated in feudal society. At a certain stage in the development of these means of production and of exchange,[6] the conditions under which feudal

---

1. The primary referent in this paragraph is the First Opium War, 1840–42 [Ed.].
2. Transposition. The original reads: ". . . doing away with the scattered state of the means of production, of property, and of the population" [B.A.].
3. "one frontier" added by translator [B.A.].
4. Marx means here the economic, not political, dominance of the bourgeoisie. In 1848 "its rule of scarce one hundred years" could have applied only to Great Britain, even in this sense [Ed.].
5. Produktions- und Verkehrsmittel = means of production and circulation; not "means of production and exchange" [B.A.].
6. See previous note [Ed.].

society produced and exchanged, the feudal organisation of agriculture and manufacturing industry, in one word, the feudal relations of property became no longer compatible with the already developed productive forces; they became so many fetters.[7] They had to be burst asunder; they were burst asunder.[8]

Into their place stepped free competition, accompanied by a social and political constitution adapted to it, and by the economical and political sway of the bourgeois class.

A similar movement is going on before our own eyes. Modern bourgeois society with its relations of production, of exchange and of property, a society that has conjured up such gigantic means of production and of exchange, is like the sorcerer, who is no longer able to control the powers of the nether world whom he has called up by his spells. For many a decade past the history of industry and commerce is but the history of the revolt of modern productive forces against modern conditions of production, against the property relations that are the conditions for the existence of the bourgeoisie and of its rule. It is enough to mention the commercial crises[9] that by their periodical return put on its trial, each time more threateningly, the existence of the entire bourgeois society. In these crises a great part not only of the existing products, but also of the previously created productive forces, are periodically destroyed. In these crises there breaks out an epidemic[1] that, in all earlier epochs, would have seemed an absurdity—the epidemic of over-production. Society suddenly finds itself put back into a state of momentary barbarism; it appears as if a famine, a universal war of devastation had cut off the supply of every means of subsistence; industry and commerce seem to be destroyed; and why? Because there is too much civilisation, too much means of subsistence, too much industry, too much commerce. The productive forces at the disposal of society[2] no longer tend to further the development of the conditions of bourgeois property; on the contrary,

7. At this point a sentence is missing from the English translation. It should read: "They hinder production instead of promoting it" [D.R.].
8. This passage suggests Marx's characteristic theory of social revolution: established property relations, which, of course, favor one class over others, block the further development of the forces of production, which development would favor another class. At some point, the pressure of the new forces of production becomes sufficient to triumph over the older system of property relations holding it in check. This is what makes social revolution possible; it remains for the revolutionary class to carry the revolution to successful completion, e.g., the English bourgeoisie in 1688, the French bourgeoisie in the period from 1789 to 1830 [Ed.].
9. The older term for what today are called *depressions*. The first general crisis occurred in 1825–26, the second in 1836–37, and the third in 1847 [Ed.].
1. The original reads "a social epidemic," not "an epidemic" [D.R.].
2. *bürgerlichen Zivilisation* = bourgeois civilization; not "society" [D.R.].

they have become too powerful for these conditions, by which they are fettered, and so soon as they overcome these fetters, they bring disorder into the whole of bourgeois society, endanger the existence of bourgeois property. The conditions of bourgeois society are too narrow to comprise the wealth created by them. And how does the bourgeoisie get over these crises? On the one hand by enforced destruction of a mass of productive forces; on the other, by the conquest of new markets, and by the more thorough exploitation of the old ones.[3] That is to say, by paving the way for more extensive and more destructive crises, and by diminishing the means whereby crises are prevented.

The weapons with which the bourgeoisie felled feudalism to the ground are now turned against the bourgeoisie itself.

But not only has the bourgeoisie forged the weapons that bring death to itself; it has also called into existence the men who are to wield those weapons—the modern working class[4]—the proletarians.

In proportion as the bourgeoisie, *i.e.*, capital, is developed, in the same proportion is the proletariat, the modern working class, developed—a class of labourers, who live only so long as they find work, and who find work only so long as their labour increases capital. These labourers, who must sell themselves piecemeal, are a commodity, like every other article of commerce, and are consequently[5] exposed to all the vicissitudes of competition, to all the fluctuations of the market.[6]

Owing to the extensive use of machinery and to division of labour, the work of the proletarians has lost all individual character, and, consequently, all charm for the workman. He becomes an appendage of the machine, and it is only the most simple, most monotonous, and most easily acquired knack, that is required of him. Hence, the cost of production of a workman is restricted, almost entirely, to the means of subsistence that he requires for his maintenance, and for the propagation of his race. But the price of a commodity, and therefore also of labour, is equal to its cost of production. In proportion, therefore, as the repulsiveness of the work increases, the wage decreases.[7] Nay more, in proportion as the use

3. At this point the original has the sentence: "And so how does it do that?" [*D.R.*].
4. *Arbeiter* = workers; not "working class" [*D.R.*].
5. *daher gleichmäßig* = consequently equally; not "consequently" [*D.R.*].
6. The transformation of the worker into a commodity, whose livelihood is exposed to the fluctuations of the market, and his or her reduction to an appendage of the machine (in the following paragraph) recalls the concept of alienated labor so prominent in the "Manuscripts" of 1844 [*Ed.*].
7. This and the preceding two sentences express Marx's theory of the subsistence cost of labor (wages), which has been subject to much critical scrutiny. For further discussion, see Ernest Mandel, pp. 161–65 in this volume. [*Ed.*].

of machinery and division of labour increases, in the same proportion the burden of toil[8] also increases, whether by prolongation of
the working hours, by increase of the work exacted in a given time
or by increased speed of the machinery, etc.

Modern industry has converted the little workshop of the patriarchal master into the great factory of the industrial capitalist.
Masses of labourers, crowded into the factory, are organised like
soldiers. As privates of the industrial army they are placed under the
command of a perfect hierarchy of officers and sergeants. Not only
are they slaves of the bourgeois class, and of the bourgeois State;
they are daily and hourly enslaved by the machine, by the overlooker,
and, above all, by the individual bourgeois manufacturer himself.
The more openly this despotism proclaims gain to be its end and
aim, the more petty, the more hateful and the more embittering
it is.

The less the skill and exertion of strength implied in manual
labour, in other words, the more modern industry becomes developed,
the more is the labour of men superseded by that of women.[9] Differences of age and sex have no longer any distinctive social validity
for the working class. All are instruments of labour, more or less
expensive to use, according to their age and sex.

No sooner is the exploitation of the labourer by the manufacturer, so far, at an end, and he receives his wages in cash, than he
is set upon by the other portions of the bourgeoisie, the landlord,
the shopkeeper, the pawnbroker, etc.

The[1] lower strata of the middle class—the small tradespeople,
shopkeepers, and retired tradesmen generally,[2] the handicraftsmen
and peasants—all these sink gradually[3] into the proletariat, partly
because their diminutive capital does not suffice for the scale on
which Modern Industry is carried on, and is swamped in the competition with the large capitalists, partly because their specialised
skill is rendered worthless by new methods of production. Thus the
proletariat is recruited from all classes of the population.

The proletariat goes through various stages of development. With
its birth begins its struggle with the bourgeoisie. At first the contest
is carried on by individual labourers, then by the workpeople of a
factory, then by the operatives of one trade, in one locality, against

---

8. *Masse der Arbeit* = amount of work; not "burden of toil" [*D.R.*].
9. At this point the words "and children" appeared in the first German edition but were
   removed from the second. All subsequent German editions, and the authorized English
   translation, are based upon the latter [*D.R.*].
1. *Die bisherige* = The previous; not merely "The" [*D.R.*].
2. *Rentiers* = men of private means; not "retired tradesmen generally" [*D.R.*].
3. "gradually" added by the translator [*D.R.*].

the individual bourgeois who directly exploits them. They direct their attacks not[4] against the bourgeois conditions of production, but against the instruments of production themselves; they destroy imported wares that compete with their labour, they smash to pieces machinery, they set factories ablaze, they seek to restore by force the vanished status of the workman of the Middle Ages.

At this stage the labourers still form an incoherent[5] mass scattered over the whole country, and broken up by their mutual competition. If anywhere they unite to form more compact bodies, this is not yet the consequence of their own active union, but of the union of the bourgeoisie, which class, in order to attain its own political ends, is compelled to set the whole proletariat in motion, and is moreover yet, for a time, able to do so. At this stage, therefore, the proletarians do not fight their enemies, but the enemies of their enemies, the remnants of absolute monarchy, the landowners, the non-industrial bourgeois, the petty bourgeoisie. Thus the whole historical movement is concentrated in the hands of the bourgeoisie; every victory so obtained is a victory for the bourgeoisie.

But with the development of industry the proletariat not only increases in number; it becomes concentrated in greater masses, its strength grows, and it feels that strength more. The various interests and conditions of life within the ranks of the proletariat are more and more equalised, in proportion as machinery obliterates all distinctions of labour, and nearly everywhere reduces wages to the same low level. The growing competition among the bourgeois, and the resulting commercial crises, make the wages of the workers ever more fluctuating.[6] The unceasing improvement of machinery, ever more rapidly developing, makes their livelihood more and more precarious; the collisions between individual workmen and individual bourgeois take more and more the character of collisions between two classes. Thereupon the workers begin to form combinations[7] (Trades' Unions) against the bourgeois; they club together in order to keep up the rate of wages; they found[8] permanent associations in order to make provision beforehand for these occasional revolts.[9] Here and there the contest breaks out into riots.

---

4. *nicht nur* = not only; not "not" [D.R.].
5. "incoherent" added by the translator [D.R.].
6. Note that Marx states here that wages fluctuate throughout the business cycle with changing relations between the supply of workers and capitalists' demand for their labor power. This is not a theory of inevitably increasing absolute impoverishment of the proletarian [Ed.].
7. *Koalitionen* = coalitions; not "combinations" [B.A.].
8. *Sie stiften selbst* = They themselves found; not "They found" [B.A.]
9. Note that Marx, contrary to a prevailing myth, was neither ignorant of trade unions nor opposed to their development [Ed.].

nd then the workers are victorious, but only for a time. The
t of their battles lies, not in the immediate result, but in the
anding union of the workers. This union is helped on by
the improved means of communication that are created by modern
industry and that place the workers of different localities in contact
with one another. It was just this contact that was needed to centralise the numerous local struggles, all of the same character, into
one national struggle between classes. But every class struggle is a
political struggle.[1] And that union, to attain which the burghers of
the Middle Ages, with their miserable highways,[2] required centuries,
the modern proletarians, thanks to railways, achieve in a few years.

This organisation of the proletarians into a class, and consequently into a political party, is continually being upset again by the
competition between the workers themselves.[3] But it ever rises up
again, stronger, firmer, mightier. It compels legislative recognition
of particular interests of the workers, by taking advantage of the
divisions among the bourgeoisie itself. Thus the ten-hours' bill[4] in
England was carried.

Altogether collisions between the classes of the old society further, in many ways, the course of development of the proletariat.
The bourgeoisie finds itself involved in a constant battle. At first
with the aristocracy; later on, with those portions of the bourgeoisie itself, whose interests have become antagonistic to the progress
of industry; at all times, with the bourgeoisie of foreign countries.
In all these battles it sees itself compelled to appeal to the proletariat, to ask for its help, and thus, to drag it into the political
arena. The bourgeoisie itself, therefore, supplies the proletariat
with its own elements of political and general education,[5] in other
words, it furnishes the proletariat with weapons for fighting the
bourgeoisie.

Further, as we have already seen, entire sections of the ruling
classes are, by the advance of industry, precipitated into the proletariat, or are at least threatened in their conditions of existence.

1. This has ceased to be true, to the extent that labor unions have substituted strictly
   economic demands (for higher wages, better working conditions, etc.) for political ones
   (control over production, reduction of the bourgeoisie's power over the state, etc.). Yet
   it always remains a possibility for the labor movement [Ed.].
2. *Vizinalwegen* = local routes; not "miserable highways" [B.A.]. In this play on words
   Marx is both contrasting local (or branch) roads to railways and suggesting that
   whereas the burghers could struggle only locally because there was no national forum
   for their struggle, the proletariat is fortunate that its struggle can succeed all the more
   rapidly due to vastly improved means of communication [Ed.].
3. Note that Marx assumes that the trade union movement leads directly ("consequently")
   to the formation of a workers political party. This has proven to be the case in nearly all
   industrialized capitalist nations, the United States being the major exception [Ed.].
4. Enacted in 1847 [Ed.].
5. *ihre eigenen Bildungselemente* = with elements of its own development; not "its own
   elements of political and general education" [D.R.].

These also supply the proletariat with fresh elements of enlightenment and progress.[6]

Finally, in times when the class struggle nears the decisive hour, the process of dissolution going on within the ruling class, in fact within the whole range of old society, assumes such a violent, glaring character, that a small section of the ruling class cuts itself adrift, and joins the revolutionary class, the class that holds the future in its hands. Just as, therefore, at an earlier period, a section of the nobility went over to the bourgeoisie, so now a portion of the bourgeoisie goes over to the proletariat, and in particular, a portion of the bourgeois ideologists, who have raised themselves to the level of comprehending theoretically the historical movement as a whole.[7]

Of all the classes that stand face to face with the bourgeoisie today, the proletariat alone is a really revolutionary class. The other classes decay and finally disappear in the face of Modern Industry; the proletariat is its special and essential product.[8]

The lower middle class,[9] the small manufacturer, the shopkeeper, the artisan, the peasant, all these fight against the bourgeoisie, to save from extinction their existence as fractions of the middle class.[1] They are therefore not revolutionary, but conservative. Nay more, they are reactionary, for they try to roll back the wheel of history. If by chance they are revolutionary, they are so only in view of their impending transfer into the proletariat, they thus defend not their present, but their future interests, they desert their own standpoint to place themselves at that of the proletariat.[2]

The "dangerous class," the social scum,[3] that passively rotting mass thrown off by the lowest layers of old society, may, here and there, be swept into the movement by a proletarian revolution, its conditions of life, however, prepare it far more for the part of a bribed tool of reactionary intrigue.

6. *eine Masse Bildungselemente* = with a number of elements of its own development; not "with fresh elements of enlightenment and progress" [*D.R.*].
7. Such as Marx and Engels themselves [*Ed.*].
8. "Capital can only increase by exchanging itself for labor, by calling wage labor to life. Wage labor can only be exchanged for capital by increasing capital, by strengthening the power whose slave it is. *Hence, increase of capital is increase of the proletariat, that is, of the working class*" (Marx, "Wage Labor and Capital," *Neue Rheinische Zeitung*, no. 266, April 7, 1849 [*Marx-Engels Collected Works* 9, p. 214]) [*Ed.*].
9. *Die Mittelstände* = The middle classes: not "The lower middle class" [*D.R.*].
1. *als Mittelstände* = as middle classes; not "as fractions of the middle class" [*D.R.*].
2. Marx is referring here to the spread of revolutionary ideas among classes displaced by the advance of capitalist industrialization [*Ed.*].
3. *Das Lumpenproletariat* = an untranslatable term, meaning literally "the rag-proletariat," or the proletariat in rags and tatters, ragamuffins created by capitalist relations of production, not "the 'dangerous class,' the social scum." The latter phrase is misleading because it is unspecific. Marx is referring here to beggars, thieves, criminals, drifters, bohemians, etc., all of whom he excluded from the concept of the proletariat, despite their poverty, because they lack the proletarians' specific relation to the means of production: wage labor [*Ed.*].

In the conditions of the proletariat, those of old society at large are already virtually swamped. The proletarian is without property; his relation to his wife and children has no longer anything in common with the bourgeois family-relations; modern industrial labour, modern subjection to capital, the same in England as in France, in America as in Germany, has stripped him of every trace of national character. Law, morality, religion, are to him so many bourgeois prejudices, behind which lurk in ambush just as many bourgeois interests.

All the preceding classes that got the upper hand, sought to fortify their already acquired status by subjecting society at large to their conditions of appropriation. The proletarians cannot become masters of the productive forces of society, except by abolishing their own previous mode of appropriation,[4] and thereby also every other previous mode of appropriation. They have nothing of their own to secure and to fortify,[5] their mission is to destroy all previous securities for, and insurances of, individual property.[6]

All previous historical[7] movements were movements of minorities, or in the interests of minorities. The proletarian movement is the self-conscious,[8] independent movement of the immense majority, in the interests of the immense majority. The proletariat, the lowest stratum of our present society,[9] cannot stir, cannot raise itself up, without the whole superincumbent strata of official society being sprung into the air.

Though not in substance, yet in form, the struggle of the proletariat with the bourgeoisie is at first a national struggle. The proletariat of each country must, of course, first of all settle matters with its own bourgeoisie.

In depicting the most general phases of the development of the proletariat, we traced the more or less veiled civil war, raging within existing society, up to the point where that war breaks out into open revolution, and where the violent overthrow of the bourgeoisie lays the foundation for the sway of the proletariat.

Hitherto, every form of society has been based, as we have already seen, on the antagonism of oppressing and oppressed classes. But in order to oppress a class, certain conditions must be assured to it

4. I.e., wage labor and the private ownership of the means of production [*Ed.*].
5. "and to fortify" added by the translator [*D.R.*].
6. *Privatsicherheit und Privatsicherungen* = private security and private protection; not "securities for, and insurances of, individual property" [*D.R.*].
7. "historical" added by the translator [*D.R.*].
8. *selbständige* = independent; not "self-conscious, independent" [*D.R.*].
9. The *Lumpenproletariat*, by definition, is not a stratum of society, but is utterly outside it. Note that it is precisely these elements outside society who appeared to Bakunin to be the revolutionary class *par excellence*, while the proletariat seemed to him already bourgeois by virtue of its willingness to labor under the domination of the bourgeoisie. For Marx, on the other hand, the *Lumpenproletariat* is politically unreliable, more likely to support the quick "solutions" of reactionary politicians ("Bonapartism") than the long struggle of proletarian revolution [*Ed.*].

under which it can, at least, continue its slavish existence. The serf, in the period of serfdom, raised himself to membership in the commune, just as the petty bourgeois, under the yoke of feudal absolutism, managed to develop into a bourgeois. The modern labourer, on the contrary, instead of rising with the progress of industry, sinks deeper and deeper below the conditions of existence of his own class. He becomes a pauper, and pauperism develops more rapidly than population and wealth.[1] And here it becomes evident, that the bourgeoisie is unfit any longer to be the ruling class in society, and to impose its conditions of existence upon society as an over-riding law. It is unfit to rule because it is incompetent to assure an existence to its slave within his slavery, because it cannot help letting him sink into such a state, that it has to feed him, instead of being fed by him. Society can no longer live under this bourgeoisie, in other words, its existence is no longer compatible with society.

The essential condition for the existence, and for the sway of the bourgeois class, is[2] the formation and augmentation of capital; the condition for capital is wage-labour. Wage-labour rests exclusively on competition between the labourers. The advance of industry, whose involuntary[3] promoter is the bourgeoisie, replaces the isolation of the labourers, due to competition, by their revolutionary combination, due to association. The development of Modern Industry, therefore, cuts from under its feet the very foundation on which the bourgeoisie produces and appropriates products. What the bourgeoisie, therefore, produces, above all, is its own grave-diggers. Its fall and the victory of the proletariat are equally inevitable.[4]

II
Proletarians and Communists[1]

In what relation do the Communists stand to the proletarians as a whole?

1. This suggests that Marx here held to the theory of the absolute impoverishment of the proletariat [Ed.].
2. At this point the original has the phrase "the piling up of wealth in the hands of private individuals," which has been omitted from the authorized translation [D.R.].
3. *willenlosen und widerstandslosen* = involuntary and unresisting; not "involuntary" [D.R.].
4. Marx's meaning evidently is that the advance of capitalism necessarily produces an ever-growing, organized class in opposition to the bourgeoisie. At best, this is a necessary, but not sufficient, condition for the revolutionary victory of the proletariat. Note that the creation of a revolutionary proletariat is assumed to be the byproduct of the work of the bourgeoisie itself. There is no mention as yet of the role to be played by the Communist League [Ed.].
1. A reference, of course, to the Communist League, for which this *Manifesto* was written, not to communism in general nor to other communist sects or theories, e.g., those of Morelly, Mably, et al. [Ed.].

ommunists do not form a separate party opposed to other
class parties.

have no interests separate and apart from those of the proletariat as a whole.

They do not set up any sectarian principles of their own, by which
to shape and mould the proletarian movement.

The Communists are distinguished from the other working-class
parties by this only: 1. In the national struggles of the proletarians
of the different countries, they point out and bring to the front the
common interests of the entire proletariat, independently of all
nationality. 2. In the various stages of development which the struggle
of the working class against the bourgeoisie has to pass through,
they always and everywhere represent the interests of the movement
as a whole.

The Communists, therefore, are on the one hand, practically, the
most advanced and resolute[2] section of the working-class parties of
every country, that section which pushes forward all others; on the
other hand, theoretically, they have over the great mass of the proletariat the advantage of clearly understanding the line of march,
the conditions, and the ultimate general results of the proletarian
movement.

The immediate aim of the Communists is the same as that of all
the other proletarian parties: formation of the proletariat into a class,
overthrow of the bourgeois supremacy, conquest of political power by
the proletariat.[3]

The theoretical conclusions of the Communists are in no way
based on ideas or principles that have been invented, or discovered,
by this or that would-be universal reformer.

They merely express, in general terms, actual relations springing
from an existing class struggle, from a historical movement going
on under our very eyes. The abolition of existing property relations
is not at all a distinctive feature of Communism.

All property relations in the past have continually been subject
to historical change consequent upon the change in historical
conditions.[4]

---

2. *entschiedenste* = most resolute; not "most advanced and resolute" [*D.R.*].
3. Note Marx's insistence on the conquest of political power (the state), a point of contention for the remainder of his career between him and the anarchists (who emphasized
seizure of factories, establishment of communes, rooting out of bourgeois values and
attitudes among the workers, etc., rather than seizure of the state, which they viewed as
merely recreating class domination over society). "A class": i.e., not merely the sociological category of wage labor but a class "for itself," fully conscious of its status, its antagonistic relation to the bourgeoisie, and its revolutionary mission [*Ed.*].
4. *einem beständigen geschichtlichen Wechsel, einer beständigen geschichtlichen Veände-
rung unterworfen* = subject to a continual historical change, to a continual historical
transformation; not "continually been subject to historical change consequent upon
the change in historical conditions" [*D.R.*].

II. Proletarians and Communists

The French Revolution, for example, abolished feudal pro̲ favour of bourgeois property.

The distinguishing feature of Communism is not the abolition ̲ property generally, but the abolition of bourgeois property. But modern bourgeois private property is the final and most complete expression of the system of producing and appropriating products, that is based on class antagonisms, on the exploitation of the many by the few.[5]

In this sense, the theory of the Communists may be summed up in the single sentence: Abolition of private property.[6]

We Communists have been reproached with the desire of abolishing the right of personally acquiring property as the fruit of a man's own labour, which property is alleged to be the groundwork of all personal freedom, activity and independence.

Hard-won, self-acquired, self-earned property! Do you mean the property of the petty artisan[7] and of the small peasant, a form of property that preceded the bourgeois form? There is no need to abolish that, the development of industry has to a great extent already[8] destroyed it, and is still destroying it daily.

Or do you mean modern bourgeois private property?

But does wage-labour[9] create any property for the labourer? Not a bit. It creates capital, *i.e.*, that kind of property which exploits wage-labour, and which cannot increase except upon condition of begetting a new supply of wage-labour for fresh exploitation. Property, in its present form, is based on[1] the antagonism of capital and wage-labour. Let us examine both sides of this antagonism.

To be a capitalist, is to have not only a purely personal, but a social *status* in production. Capital is a collective product, and only by the united action of many members, nay, in the last resort, only by the united action of all members of society, can it be set in motion.

Capital is, therefore, not a personal, it is a social power.

When, therefore, capital is converted into common property, into the property of all members of society, personal property is not thereby transformed into social property. It is only the social character of the property that is changed. It loses its class-character.

Let us now take wage-labour.

The average price of wage-labour is the minimum wage, *i.e.*, that quantum of the means of subsistence, which is absolutely requisite

---

5. *der Einen durch der Andern* = of everyone by the others; not "of the many by the few" [D.R.].
6. Specifically bourgeois private property *in the means of production*, e.g., capital, factories, power machines [Ed.].
7. *keinbürgerlichen* = petty bourgeois; not "petty artisan" [D.R.].
8. "to a great extent already" added by the translator [B.A.].
9. *die Lohnarbeit, die Arbeit des Proletariers* = wage labor, the labor of proletarians; not "wage labor" [B.A.].
1. *bewegt sich in* = moves within; not "is based on" [D.R.].

to keep the labourer in bare existence as a labourer. What, therefore, the wage-labourer appropriates by means of his labour, merely suffices to prolong[2] and reproduce a bare existence.[3] We by no means intend to abolish this personal appropriation of the products of labour, an appropriation that is made for the maintenance and reproduction of human life,[4] and that leaves no surplus wherewith to command the labour of others.[5] All that we want to do away with, is the miserable character of this appropriation, under which the labourer lives merely to increase capital, and is allowed to live only in so far as the interest of the ruling class requires it.

In bourgeois society, living labour[6] is but a means to increase accumulated labour. In Communist society, accumulated labour[7] is but a means to widen, to enrich, to promote the existence of the labourer.

In bourgeois society, therefore, the past dominates the present; in Communist society, the present dominates the past. In bourgeois society capital is independent and has individuality, while the living person is dependent and has no individuality.

And the abolition of this state of things is called by the bourgeois, abolition of individuality and freedom! And rightly so. The abolition of bourgeois individuality, bourgeois independence, and bourgeois freedom is undoubtedly aimed at.

By freedom is meant, under the present bourgeois conditions of production, free trade, free selling and buying.

But if selling and buying disappears, free selling and buying disappears also. This talk about free selling and buying, and all the other "brave words" of our bourgeoisie about freedom in general, have a meaning, if any, only in contrast with restricted selling and buying, with the fettered traders of the Middle Ages, but have no meaning when opposed to the Communistic abolition of buying and selling, of the bourgeois conditions of production, and of the bourgeoisie itself.

You are horrified at our intending to do away with private property. But in your existing society, private property is already done

2. "to prolong" added by the translator [B.A.].
3. The assumption behind this thesis is that the supply of workers always exceeds capitalists' demand for their labor power. Thus wages cannot rise. But Marx has already shown that wages fluctuate throughout the business cycle, rising during the expansionary phase and falling during the phase of contraction. Marx would appear to hold here that although average wages may rise temporarily in booms (as most or all workers find employment), they may fall below the subsistence minimum in periods of bust (the unemployed receive wages of zero), so that average wages averaged over a full business cycle can be said to fluctuate around the subsistence minimum, sometimes above it, sometimes below [Ed.].
4. *Wiedererzeugung des unmittelbaren Lebens* here = reproduction of life itself: not "maintenance and reproduction of human life" [B.A.].
5. This clarifies that "the abolition of private property" refers to capital, i.e., productive property, not to private property for consumption [Ed.].
6. The labor power of living workers actually employed [Ed.].
7. Capital, whether in the form of machines, investment funds, etc. [Ed.].

away with for nine-tenths of the population; its existence for the few is solely due to its non-existence in the hands of those nine-tenths.[8] You reproach us, therefore, with intending to do away with a form of property, the necessary condition for whose existence is the non-existence of any property for the immense majority of society.

In one word, you reproach us with intending to do away with your property. Precisely so; that is just what we intend.

From the moment when labour can no longer be converted into capital, money, or rent, into a social power capable of being monopolised, *i.e.*, from the moment when individual property can no longer be transformed into bourgeois property, into capital,[9] from that moment, you say, individuality vanishes.

You must, therefore, confess that by "individual" you mean no other person than the bourgeois, than the middle-class[1] owner of property. This person must, indeed, be swept out of the way, and made impossible.[2]

Communism deprives no man of the power to appropriate the products of society; all that it does is to deprive him of the power to subjugate the labour of others by means of such appropriation.

It has been objected that upon the abolition of private property all work will cease, and universal laziness will overtake us.

According to this, bourgeois society ought long ago to have gone to the dogs through sheer idleness; for those of its members who work, acquire nothing, and those who acquire anything, do not work. The whole of this objection is but another expression of the tautology: that there can no longer be any wage-labour when there is no longer any capital.

8. *I.e.*, Marx holds that nine-tenths of society own no capital while one-tenth owns (nearly) all the means of production. Incidentally, by 1980, the United States' labor force had the following composition: salaried managers and administrators (bourgeoisie) 8.6 percent; self-employed (petty bourgeoisie) 10.8 percent; wage and salaried employees (proletariat) 81 percent; while, in 1962, 17.4 percent of all households held 90.9 percent of income-producing wealth (from Michael Reich, "The Development of the Wage-Labor Force," and Frank Ackerman and Andrew Zimbalist, "Capitalism and Inequality in the United States," *The Capitalist System*, 3rd ed. [Englewood Cliffs: Prentice-Hall, 1978], pp. 124, 220). Perhaps Marx's "nine-tenths" was not such a bad estimate, after all [*Ed.*].
9. "into capital" added by the translator [*B.A.*].
1. The bourgeoisie, owners of capital. In the European context of the time, the landed nobility was the upper class. By contrast, in the present American context, the bourgeoisie is the upper class and the petty bourgeoisie the middle class [*Ed.*].
2. *aufgehoben* = untranslatable dialectical term meaning at the same time abolition, transcendence, and preservation, not "be swept out of the way, and made impossible." In this context, Marx's meaning is that bourgeois property ownership will be abolished (by the victorious proletarian state), transcended (in the sense that communal property relations will replace those of private property), and yet "preserved" (in the sense that all property will be everyone's property and each individual in communist society will share in the common ownership of all social property). This change in the social relation to property (from its ownership by a few, with everyone else dependent on the bourgeois property holder, to common—and equal—ownership) in turn, would replace the bourgeois "egoist" as a character-type with an "individual" possessing new and different personality characteristics [*Ed.*].

78   COMMUNIST MANIFESTO

All objections urged against the Communistic mode of producing and appropriating material products, have, in the same way, been urged against the Communistic modes of producing and appropriating intellectual products. Just as, to the bourgeois, the disappearance of class property is the disappearance of production itself, so the disappearance of class culture is to him identical with the disappearance of all culture.

That culture, the loss of which he laments, is, for the enormous majority, a mere training to act as a machine.

But don't wrangle with us so long as you apply, to our intended abolition[3] of bourgeois property, the standard of your bourgeois notions of freedom, culture, law, &c. Your very ideas are but the outgrowth of the conditions of your bourgeois production and bourgeois property, just as your jurisprudence is but the will of your class made into a law for all, a will, whose essential character and direction[4] are determined by the economical[5] conditions of existence of your class.

The selfish misconception[6] that induces you to transform into eternal laws of nature and of reason, the social forms springing from your present mode of production and form of property[7]—historical relations that rise and disappear in the progress of production—this misconception you share with every ruling class that has preceded you. What you see clearly in the case of ancient property, what you admit in the case of feudal property you are of course forbidden to admit in the case of your own[8] bourgeois form of property.

Abolition of the family! Even the most radical flare up at this infamous proposal of the Communists.

On what foundation is the present family, the bourgeois family, based? On capital, on private gain. In its completely developed form this family exists only among the bourgeoisie. But this state of things finds its complement in the practical absence of the family among the proletarians, and in public prostitution.

The bourgeois family will vanish as a matter of course when its complement vanishes, and both will vanish with the vanishing of capital.

3. *die Abschaffung* = the abolition; not "our intended abolition" [D.R.].
4. *Inhalt* = contents; not "essential character and direction" [D.R.].
5. *materiellen* = material; not "economical" [D.R.].
6. *interessierte Vorstellung* = interested idea; not "selfish misconception" [D.R.]. Marx's meaning here seems to be that the interests of the bourgeois class shape its ideas, such that people looking at things from the bourgeois viewpoint *see* what are merely contingent social forms springing from bourgeois relations of production and therefore subject to change, *as if they were* eternal laws of nature and reason [Ed.].
7. *Eure Produktions- und Eigentumsverhältnisse* = your relations of production and property relations; not "your present mode of production and forms of property" [D.R.]. "Mode of production" and "relations of production" are two technical terms, with quite different meanings, in the Marxist lexicon [Ed.].
8. *für das* = for the; not "in the case of your own" [D.R.].

Do you charge us with wanting to stop the exploitation of children by their parents? To this crime we plead guilty.

But, you will say, we destroy the most hallowed of relations, when we replace home education by social.

And your education! Is not that also social, and determined by the social conditions under which you educate, by the intervention, direct or indirect, of society, by means of schools, &c.? The Communists have not invented the intervention of society in education; they do but seek to alter the character of that intervention, and to rescue education from the influence of the ruling class.

The bourgeois clap-trap about the family and education, about the hallowed co-relation of parent and child, becomes all the more disgusting, the more, by the action of Modern Industry, all family ties among the proletarians are torn asunder, and their children transformed into simple articles of commerce and instruments of labour.[9]

But you Communists would introduce community of women, screams the whole bourgeoisie in chorus.

The bourgeois sees in his wife a mere instrument of production. He hears that the instruments of production are to be exploited in common, and, naturally, can come to no other conclusion than that the lot of being common to all will likewise fall to the women.

He has not even a suspicion that the real point aimed at is to do away with the status of women as mere instruments of production.

For the rest, nothing is more ridiculous than the virtuous indignation of our bourgeois at the community of women which, they pretend, is to be openly and officially established by the Communists.[1] The Communists have no need to introduce community of women; it has existed almost from time immemorial.

Our bourgeois, not content with having the wives and daughters of their proletarians at their disposal,[2] not to speak of common

9. In order to reform such conditions, "the [English] Factory Act of 1833 forbade the employment of children under nine years of age (except in silk mills), limited the working hours of children between 9–13 years to 48 per week . . . ; that of young persons from 14–18 years of age to 69 per week. . . . [Factory] Inspectors reports for October and December 1844 state that, in a number of branches in which the employment of children can be dispensed with or superseded by that of adults, the working day is still fourteen to sixteen hours, or even longer. . . . Many employers disregard the law, shorten the meal times, work children longer than is permitted, and risk prosecution, knowing that the possible fines are trifling in comparison with the certain profits derivable from the offence" (Engels, *The Condition of the Working Class in England in 1844*, in *Marx-Engels Collected Works* 4, pp. 461–63) [*Ed.*].
1. *über die angebliche offizielle Weibergemeinschaft der Kommunisten* = at the alleged official community of women of the Communists; not "at the community of women which, they pretend, is to be openly and officially established by the Communists" [*D.R.*].
2. "It is, besides, a matter of course that factory servitude, like any other, and to an even higher degree, confers the *jus primae noctis* [right of the first night] upon the master. In this respect also the employer is sovereign over the persons and charms of his

prostitutes, take the greatest pleasure in seducing each other's wives.

Bourgeois marriage is in reality a system of wives in common and thus, at the most, what the Communists might possibly be reproached with, is that they desire to introduce, in substitution for a hypocritically concealed, an openly legalised[3] community of women. For the rest, it is self-evident that the abolition of the present system of production must bring with it the abolition of the community of women springing from that system, i.e., of prostitution both public and private.[4]

The Communists are further reproached with desiring to abolish countries and nationality.

The working men have no country. We cannot take from them what they have not got. Since the proletariat must first of all acquire political supremacy, must rise to be the leading class of the nation, must constitute itself the nation,[5] it is, so far, itself national, though not in the bourgeois sense of the word.

National differences[6] and antagonisms between peoples are daily more and more vanishing, owing to the development of the bourgeoisie, to freedom of commerce, to the world-market, to uniformity in the mode of production and in the conditions of life corresponding thereto.

The supremacy of the proletariat will cause them to vanish still faster. United action, of the leading civilised countries at least, is one of the first conditions for the emancipation of the proletariat.

In proportion as the exploitation of one individual by another is put an end to, the exploitation of one nation by another will also be put an end to. In proportion as the antagonism between classes within the nation vanishes, the hostility of one nation to another will come to an end.

The charges against Communism made from a religious, a philosophical, and, generally, from an ideological standpoint, are not deserving of serious examination.

Does it require deep intuition to comprehend that man's ideas, views and conceptions, in one word, man's consciousness, changes

---

employees. The threat of discharge suffices to overcome all resistance in nine cases out of ten. . . . If the master is mean enough, and the official [Factory Inquiry Commission] report mentions several such cases, his mill is also his harem; and the fact that not all manufacturers use their power, does not in the least change the position of the girls" (Engels, *Condition of the Working Class*, pp. 441–42) [*Ed.*].

3. *offizielle, offenherzige* = official, candid; not "an openly legalized" [*B.A.*].

4. *offizielle und nichtoffizielle* = official and unofficial; not "both public and private" [*B.A.*].

5. *als Nation* = as the nation; not "*the* nation" [*D.R.*].

6. *Die nationalen Absonderungen* = National divisions; not "National differences" [*B.A.*].

with every change in the conditions of his material existence, in his social relations and in his social life?

What else does the history of ideas prove, than that intellectual production changes its character in proportion as material production is changed? The ruling ideas of each age have ever been the ideas of its ruling class.

When people speak of ideas that revolutionise society,[7] they do but express the fact, that within the old society, the elements of a new one have been created, and that the dissolution of the old ideas keeps even pace with the dissolution of the old conditions of existence.

When the ancient world was in its last throes, the ancient religions were overcome by Christianity. When Christian ideas succumbed in the 18th century to rationalist ideas, feudal society fought its death battle with the then revolutionary bourgeoisie. The ideas of religious liberty and freedom of conscience merely gave expression to the sway of free competition within the domain of knowledge.

"Undoubtedly," it will be said, "religious, moral, philosophical[8] and juridical ideas have been modified in the course of historical development. But religion, morality, philosophy, political science,[9] and law, constantly survived this change."

"There are, besides, eternal truths, such as Freedom, Justice, etc., that are common to all states of society. But Communism abolishes eternal truths, it abolishes all religion, and all morality, instead of constituting them on a new basis; it therefore acts in contradiction to all past historical experience."

What does this accusation reduce itself to? The history of all past society has consisted in the development of class antagonisms,[1] antagonisms that assumed different forms at different epochs.

But whatever form they may have taken, one fact is common to all past ages, viz., the exploitation of one part of society by the other. No wonder, then, that the social consciousness of past ages, despite all the multiplicity and variety it displays, moves within certain common forms, or general ideas,[2] which cannot completely vanish except with the total disappearance of class antagonisms.

The Communist revolution is the most radical rupture with traditional property relations; no wonder that its development involves the most radical rupture with traditional ideas.

---

7. *eine ganze Gesellschaft* = an entire society; not merely "society" [B.A.].
8. The original text reads here: philosophical, political, and juridical [D.R.].
9. *die Politik* = politics; not "political science" [D.R.].
1. *bewegte sich in Klassengegensätzen* = developed through class antagonisms; not "has consisted in development of class antagonisms" [B.A.].
2. *Bewußtseinsformen* = forms of consciousness; not "or general ideas" [D.R.].

But let us have done with the bourgeois objections to Communism.

We have seen above, that the first step in the revolution by the working class, is to raise the proletariat to the position of ruling class, to win the battle of democracy.[3]

The proletariat will use its political supremacy to wrest, by degrees, all capital from the bourgeoisie, to centralise all instruments of production in the hands of the State, i.e., of the proletariat organised as the ruling class; and to increase the total of productive forces as rapidly as possible.

Of course, in the beginning, this cannot be effected except by means of despotic inroads on the rights of property, and on the conditions of bourgeois production; by means of measures, therefore, which appear economically insufficient and untenable, but which, in the course of the movement, outstrip themselves, necessitate further inroads upon the old social order,[4] and are unavoidable as a means of entirely revolutionising the mode of production.

These measures will of course be different in different countries.

Nevertheless in the most advanced countries, the following will be pretty generally applicable.

1. Abolition[5] of property in land and application of all rents of land to public purposes.

2. A heavy progressive or graduated income tax.[6]

3. Abolition of all right of inheritance.

4. Confiscation of the property of all emigrants and rebels.

5. Centralisation of credit in the hands of the State, by means of a national bank with State capital and an exclusive monopoly.

6. Centralisation of the means of communication and transport in the hands of the State.

7. Extension of factories and instruments of production owned by the State,[7] the bringing into cultivation of waste-lands, and the improvement of the soil generally in accordance with a common plan.

8. Equal liability of all to labour. Establishment of industrial armies, especially for agriculture.

---

3. *die Erkämpfung der Demokratie* = which is the struggle of democracy; not "to win the battle of democracy" [D.R.]. Marx means the raising of the proletariat to the position of the ruling class is the whole point of the democratic struggle, i.e., the struggle for the real rule of the majority [Ed.].
4. *über sich selbst hinaustreiben* = carry beyond themselves; not "outstrip themselves, necessitate further inroads upon the old social order" [B.A.].
5. *Expropriation* = expropriation; not "abolition" [D.R.].
6. *Steuer* = taxation; not "income tax" [D.R.].
7. *Vermehrung der Nationalfabriken, Produktionsinstrumente* = Increase of national factories, instruments of production; not "Extension of factories and instruments of production owned by the State" [B.A.].

9. Combination of agriculture with manufacturing industries; gradual abolition of the distinction between town and country, by a more equable distribution of the population over the country.[8]

10. Free education for all children in public schools. Abolition of children's factory labour in its present form. Combination of education with industrial production, &c., &c.

When, in the course of development, class distinctions have disappeared, and all production has been concentrated in the hands of a vast association of the whole nation,[9] the public power will lose its political character. Political power, properly so called, is merely the organised power of one class for oppressing another. If the proletariat during its contest with the bourgeoisie is compelled, by the force of circumstances, to organise itself as a class, if, by means of a revolution, it makes itself the ruling class, and, as such, sweeps away by force[1] the old conditions of production, then it will, along with these conditions, have swept away the conditions for the existence of class antagonisms and of classes generally, and will thereby have abolished its own supremacy as a class.

In place of the old bourgeois society, with its classes and class antagonisms, we shall have an association, in which the free development of each is the condition for the free development of all.

III
Socialist and Communist Literature

1. Reactionary Socialism

A. FEUDAL SOCIALISM

Owing to their historical position, it became the vocation of the aristocracies of France and England to write pamphlets against modern bourgeois society. In the French revolution of July 1830, and in the English reform agitation,[1] these aristocracies again succumbed to the hateful upstart. Thenceforth, a serious political

---

8. "by a more equable distribution of the population over the country" added by the translator [D.R.].
9. *der assozierten Individuen* = the associated individuals; not "a vast association of the whole nation" [D.R.]. Marx's meaning is that the voluntary "association" of individuals is to replace the coercion of class-society to the extent that market relations are replaced by the common ownership of the means of social production. In Marx's lexicon, *association* is by definition "the realm of freedom," while *bourgeois civil society* is by sociological observation and by philosophical and economic analysis coercive, "the realm of necessity" [Ed.].
1. *aufhebt* = abolishes, transcends, and preserves; not "sweeps away by force" [Ed.].
1. The Reform Act of 1832 extended the franchise to property owners and leaseholders with a minimum annual income of £10. The proletariat and petty bourgeoisie were unable to meet this qualification and remained disenfranchised [Ed.].

contest was altogether out of question. A literary battle alone remained possible. But even in the domain of literature the old cries of the restoration period[2] had become impossible.

In order to arouse sympathy, the aristocracy were obliged to lose sight, apparently, of their own interests, and to formulate their indictment against the bourgeoisie in the interest of the exploited working class alone. Thus the aristocracy took their revenge by singing lampoons on their new master, and whispering in his ears sinister prophecies of coming catastrophe.

In this way arose Feudal Socialism: half lamentation, half lampoon; half echo of the past, half menace of the future; at times, by its bitter, witty and incisive criticism, striking the bourgeoisie to the very heart's core; but always ludicrous in its effect, through total incapacity to comprehend the march of modern history.

The aristocracy, in order to rally the people to them, waved the proletarian alms-bag in front for a banner. But the people, so often as it joined them, saw on their hindquarters the old feudal coats of arms, and deserted with loud and irreverent laughter.

One section of the French Legitimists and "Young England"[3] exhibited this spectacle.

In pointing out that their mode of exploitation was different to[4] that of the bourgeoisie, the feudalists forget that they exploited under circumstances and conditions that were quite different, and that are now antiquated. In showing that, under their rule, the modern proletariat never existed, they forget that the modern bourgeoisie is the necessary offspring of their own form of society.

For the rest, so little do they conceal the reactionary character of their criticism that their chief accusation against the bourgeoisie amounts to this, that under the bourgeois *régime* a class is being developed, which is destined to cut up root and branch the old order of society.

What they upbraid the bourgeoisie with is not so much that it creates a proletariat, as that it creates a *revolutionary* proletariat.

2. Not the English Restoration 1660 to 1689, but the French Restoration 1814 to 1830 [*Engels's note to the English edition of 1888*].
3. A group of British Conservatives—aristocrats and men of politics and literature—formed about 1842. Prominent among them were Disraeli, Carlyle, and Lord Ashley (later Lord Shaftesbury). They opposed free trade and the development of industrial capitalism while they dreamed of the restoration of the political supremacy of the aristocracy. Disraeli and Carlyle came to the defense of the Chartists when the latter were under attack by the Whigs, and Lord Ashley played a prominent part in the history of British factory legislation. Engels was particularly impressed by Carlyle's *Chartism* (1839) and *Past and Present* (1843), both of which are cited repeatedly in *The Condition of the Working Class in England*. "French Legitimists": the party of the landed nobility, who advocated the restoration of the Bourbon dynasty, consequently attacking the bourgeois July monarchy of Louis Phillipe. That "section" Marx has in mind here evidently included Lamennais and Montalembert, both of whom sought to win the sympathies of the "common people" by criticizing the bourgeoisie, the introduction of the manufacturing system, child labor, etc. [*Ed.*].
4. *anders* = different from; not "different to" [*D.R.*].

In political practice, therefore, they join in all coercive measures against the working class; and in ordinary life, despite their high-falutin phrases, they stoop to pick up the golden apples dropped from the tree of industry, and to barter truth, love, and honour for traffic in wool, beetroot-sugar, and potato spirits.[5]

As the parson has ever gone hand in hand with the landlord,[6] so has Clerical Socialism with Feudal Socialism.

Nothing is easier than to give Christian asceticism a Socialist tinge. Has not Christianity declaimed against private property, against marriage, against the State? Has it not preached in the place of these, charity and poverty, celibacy and mortification of the flesh, monastic life and Mother Church? Christian Socialism[7] is but the holy water with which the priest consecrates the heart-burnings of the aristocrat.

B. PETTY-BOURGEOIS SOCIALISM

The feudal aristocracy was not the only class that was ruined by the bourgeoisie, not the only class whose conditions of existence pined

5. This applies chiefly to Germany where the landed aristocracy and squirearchy have large portions of their estates cultivated for their own account by stewards, and are, moreover, extensive beetroot-sugar manufacturers and distillers of potato spirits. The wealthier British aristocracy are, as yet, rather above that; but they, too, know how to make up for declining rents by lending their names to floaters of more or less shady joint-stock companies [*Engels's note to the English edition of 1888*].
6. *Feudalen* here = feudal nobility; not "landlord" [*D.R.*].
7. Group that sought to reconcile socialism with Christianity by turning the latter back to a primitive Christianity that stood for the abolition of private property and the state and espoused asceticism and poverty. Lamennais, after breaking with the Legitimists in 1837, was a leading spokesman for this school, as was Philipe Buchez, French author and statesman. They advocated the replacement of capitalism with productive associations of workers and a guaranteed minimum subsistence for the poor. Weitling was the most prominent representative of this tendency in Germany. Marx, in 1847, rejected the view that communism is merely a late expression of the social theories underlying Christianity in the following passage:

   The social principles of Christianity have now had eighteen hundred years to be developed, and need no further development by Prussian Consistorial Counsellors.

   The social principles of Christianity justified the slavery of antiquity, glorified the serfdom of the Middle Ages and are capable, in case of need, of defending the oppression of the proletariat, even if with somewhat doleful grimaces.

   The social principles of Christianity preach the necessity of a ruling and an oppressed class, and for the latter all they have to offer is the pious wish that the former may be charitable.

   The social principles of Christianity place the Consistorial Counsellor's compensation for all infamies in heaven, and thereby justify the continuation of these infamies on earth.

   The social principles of Christianity declare all the vile acts of the oppressors against the oppressed to be either a just punishment for original sin and other sins, or trials which the Lord, in his infinite wisdom, ordains for the redeemed.

   The social principles of Christianity preach cowardice, self-contempt, abasement, submissiveness and humbleness, in short, all the qualities of the rabble, and the proletariat, which will not permit itself to be treated as rabble, needs its courage, its self-confidence, its pride and its sense of independence even more than its bread.

and perished in the atmosphere of modern bourgeois society. The mediaeval burgesses and the small peasant proprietors were the precursors of the modern bourgeoisie. In those countries which are but little developed, industrially and commercially, these two classes[8] still vegetate side by side with the rising bourgeoisie.

In countries where modern civilisation has become fully developed, a new class of petty bourgeois has been formed, fluctuating between proletariat and bourgeoisie and ever renewing itself as a supplementary part of bourgeois society. The individual members of this class, however, are being constantly hurled down into the proletariat by the action of competition, and, as modern industry develops, they even see the moment approaching when they will completely disappear as an independent section of modern society, to be replaced, in manufactures, agriculture and commerce, by overlookers, bailiffs and shopmen.[9]

In countries like France, where the peasants constitute far more than half of the population, it was natural that writers who sided with the proletariat against the bourgeoisie, should use, in their criticism of the bourgeois *régime*, the standard of the peasant and petty bourgeois, and from the standpoint of these intermediate classes should take up the cudgels for the working class.[1] Thus arose petty-bourgeois Socialism. Sismondi[2] was[3] the head of this school, not only in France but also in England.

This school of Socialism dissected with great acuteness the contradictions in the conditions of modern production. It laid bare the hypocritical apologies of economists. It proved, incontrovertibly, the disastrous effects of machinery and division of labour; the concentration of capital and land in a few hands;[4] overproduction and crises; it pointed out the inevitable ruin of the petty bourgeois and peasant, the misery of the proletariat, the anarchy in production, the crying inequalities in the distribution of wealth, the industrial

---

The social principles of Christianity are sneaking and hypocritical, and the proletariat is revolutionary.

So much for the social principles of Christianity (Marx "The Communism of the *Rheinische Beobachter*," written on September 5, 1847, published on September 12, 1847 [*Marx-Engels Collected Works*, 6, p. 231]) [*Ed.*].

8. *diese Klasse* = this class; not "these two classes" [*B.A.*].
9. *und Domestiken* = and domestics; not "bailiffs and shopmen" [*B.A.*].
1. *und die Partei der Arbeiter vom Standpunkt des Kleinbürgertums ergriffen* = and should make use of the workers' party from the standpoint of the petty bourgeoisie; not "from the standpoint of these intermediate classes should take up the cudgels for the working class" [*D.R.*].
2. Jean Charles Léonard de Sismondi (1773–1842), French economist who was regarded highly by Marx for his criticisms of capitalism, although from a petty-bourgeois, petty-peasant standpoint. Sismondi is mentioned with respect in the *Grundrisse*, *A Contribution to the Critique of Political Economy*, and in all three volumes of *Capital* [*Ed.*].
3. *ist* = is; not "was" [*B.A.*].
4. "in a few hands" added by the translator [*B.A.*].

war of extermination between nations, the dissolution of old moral bonds, of the old family relations, of the old nationalities.

In its positive aims, however, this form of Socialism aspires either to restoring the old means of production and of exchange,[5] and with them the old property relations, and the old society, or to cramping the modern means of production and of exchange, within the framework of the old property relations that have been, and were bound to be, exploded by those means. In either case, it is both reactionary and Utopian.

Its last words are: corporate guilds for manufacture, patriarchal relations in agriculture.

Ultimately, when stubborn historical facts had dispersed all intoxicating effects of self-deception, this form of Socialism ended in a miserable fit of the blues.[6]

C. GERMAN, OR "TRUE," SOCIALISM[7]

The Socialist and Communist literature of France, a literature that originated under the pressure of a bourgeoisie in power, and that was[8] the expression[9] of the struggle against this power, was introduced into Germany at a time when the bourgeoisie, in that country, had just begun its contest with feudal absolutism.

German philosophers, would-be philosophers, and *beaux esprits*, eagerly seized on this literature, only forgetting, that when these writings immigrated from France into Germany, French social conditions had not immigrated along with them. In contact with German social conditions, this French literature lost all its immediate practical significance, and assumed a purely literary aspect.[1] Thus, to the German philosophers of the eighteenth century, the demands of the first French Revolution were nothing more than the demands of "Practical Reason" in general,[2] and the utterance of the will of the revolutionary French bourgeoisie signified in their eyes the laws of pure Will, of Will as it was bound to be, of true human Will generally.

The work of the German *literati* consisted solely in bringing the new French ideas into harmony with their ancient philosophical

---

5. *Produktions- und Verkehrsverhältnisse* = relations of production and circulation; not "means of production and of exchange" [*B.A.*].
6. *In ihrer weitern Entwicklung hat sich diese Richtung in einen feigen Katzenjammer verlaufen* = In its further development this tendency lost itself in pangs of cowardice; not "Ultimately, when stubborn historical facts had dispersed all intoxicating effects of self-deception, this form of Socialism ended in a miserable fit of the blues" [*D.R.*].
7. This school was criticized at length by Marx and Engels in *The German Ideology* [*Ed.*].
8. *ist* = is; not "was" [*B.A.*].
9. *literarische Ausdruck* = literary expression; not "expression" [*D.R.*].
1. At this point the sentence "These had to appear as ideal speculations on the true society, on the realization of the human essence" is omitted from the English translation [*D.R.*].
2. A reference to the philosophy of Immanuel Kant (1724–1804) [*Ed.*].

conscience, or rather, in annexing the French ideas without desert-
ing their own philosophic point of view.

This annexation took place in the same way in which a foreign
language is appropriated, namely, by translation.

It is well known how the monks wrote silly lives of Catholic
Saints *over* the manuscripts on which the classical works of ancient
heathendom had been written. The German *literati* reversed this
process with the profane French literature. They wrote their philosophical nonsense beneath the French original. For instance,
beneath the French criticism of the economic functions of money,[3]
they wrote "Alienation of Humanity,"[4] and beneath the French criticism of the bourgeois State they wrote "Dethronement of the Category of the General,"[5] and so forth.

The introduction of these philosophical phrases at the back of the
French historical criticisms[6] they dubbed "Philosophy of Action,"
"True Socialism," "German Science of Socialism," "Philosophical
Foundation of Socialism," and so on.

The French Socialist and Communist literature was thus completely emasculated. And, since it ceased in the hands of the German to express the struggle of one class with the other, he felt
conscious of having overcome "French one-sidedness" and of repre-
senting, not true requirements, but the requirements of Truth; not
the interests of the proletariat, but the interests of Human Nature,
of Man in general, who belongs to no class, has no reality, who
exists only in the misty realm of philosophical fantasy.

This German Socialism, which took its schoolboy task[7] so seriously
and solemnly, and extolled its poor stock-in-trade in such mounte-
bank fashion, meanwhile gradually lost its pedantic innocence.

The fight of the German, and, especially, of the Prussian bourgeoisie, against feudal aristocracy and absolute monarchy, in other
words, the liberal movement, became more earnest.

By this, the long wished-for opportunity was offered to "True"
Socialism of confronting the political movement with the Socialist
demands, of hurling the traditional anathemas against liberalism,
against representative government, against bourgeois competition,
bourgeois freedom of the press, bourgeois legislation, bourgeois

3. *Geldverhältnisse* = monetary relations; not "the economic functions of money" [D.R.].
4. Note that Marx's concept of "alienated labor" *does* express "the struggle of one class
with the other" (see two paragraphs below) [Ed.].
5. *"Aufhebung der Herrschaft des abstrakt Allgemeinen"* = "Abolition, transcendence, preservation of the rule of abstract Universality"; not "Dethronement of the Category of the
General" [D.R.]. Marx's meaning here is that the "True Socialists" sought to "go beyond"
the liberal conception of society, "the rule of abstract Universality," i.e., the abstract
equality of all citizens both in the market and before the law, regardless of other
aspects of their social condition. *Aufhebung*, as always, is untranslatable [Ed.].
6. *Entwicklungen* = developments; not "historical criticisms" [D.R.].
7. *unbeholfenen Schulübungen* = clumsy schoolboy tasks; not "schoolboy task" [B.A.].

liberty and equality, and of preaching to the masses that they had nothing to gain, and everything to lose, by this bourgeois movement. German Socialism forgot, in the nick of time, that the French criticism, whose silly echo it was, presupposed the existence of modern bourgeois society, with its corresponding economic conditions of existence, and the political constitution adapted thereto, the very things whose attainment was the object of the pending struggle in Germany.

To the absolute governments,[8] with their following of parsons, professors, country squires and officials, it served as a welcome scarecrow against the threatening bourgeoisie.

It was a sweet finish after the bitter pills of floggings and bullets with which these same governments, just at that time, dosed the German working-class risings.

While this "True" Socialism thus served the governments as a weapon for fighting the German bourgeoisie, it, at the same time, directly represented a reactionary interest, the interest of the German Philistines.[9] In Germany, the *petty-bourgeois* class, a relic of the sixteenth century, and since then constantly cropping up again under various forms, is the real social basis of the existing state of things.

To preserve this class is to preserve the existing state of things in Germany. The industrial and political supremacy of the bourgeoisie threatens it with certain destruction; on the one hand, from the concentration of capital; on the other, from the rise of a revolutionary proletariat. "True" Socialism appeared to kill these two birds with one stone. It spread like an epidemic.

The robe of speculative cobwebs, embroidered with flowers of rhetoric, steeped in the dew of sickly sentiment, this transcendental robe in which the German Socialists wrapped their sorry "eternal truths," all skin and bone, served to wonderfully increase the sale of their goods amongst such a public.

And on its part, German Socialism recognised, more and more, its own calling as the bombastic representative of the petty-bourgeois Philistine.[1]

It proclaimed the German nation to be the model nation, and the German petty Philistine[2] to be the typical man. To every villainous meanness of this model man it gave a hidden, higher, Socialistic interpretation, the exact contrary of its real character. It went to

8. *I.e.,* absolutist governments [*Ed.*].
9. *der deutschen Pfahlbürgerschaft* = of German Philistinism; not "of the German Philistines" [*D.R.*]. "Philistine" is a pejorative term for unenlightened, unimaginative small-town dwellers, the typical petty bourgeois in Germany in Marx's day [*Ed.*].
1. *Pfahlbürgerschaft* = Philistinism; not "the petty-bourgeois Philistine" [*D.R.*].
2. *Spießbürger* = narrowminded townsman or Philistine; not "petty Philistine" [*D.R.*]. *Spießbürger* and *Pfahlbürger* are nearly interchangeable [*Ed.*].

the extreme length of directly opposing the "brutally destructive"[3] tendency of Communism, and of proclaiming its supreme and impartial contempt of all class struggles. With very few exceptions, all the so-called Socialist and Communist publications that now (1847)[4] circulate in Germany belong to the domain of this foul and enervating literature.[5]

2. Conservative, or Bourgeois, Socialism

A part of the bourgeoisie is desirous of redressing social grievances, in order to secure the continued existence of bourgeois society.[6]

To this section belong economists, philanthropists, humanitarians, improvers of the condition of the working class, organisers of charity, members of societies for the prevention of cruelty to animals, temperance fanatics, hole-and-corner reformers of every imaginable kind. This form of Socialism has, moreover, been worked out into complete systems.

We may cite Proudhon's *Philosophie de la Misère*[7] as an example of this form.

The Socialistic bourgeois[8] want all the advantages[9] of modern social conditions without the struggles and dangers necessarily resulting therefrom. They desire the existing state of society minus its revolutionary and disintegrating elements. They wish for a bourgeoisie without a proletariat. The bourgeoisie naturally conceives the world in which it is supreme to be the best; and bourgeois Socialism develops this comfortable conception into various more or less complete systems. In requiring the proletariat to carry out such a system, and thereby to march straightway into the social New Jerusalem,[1] it but requires in reality, that the proletariat should remain within the bounds of existing society, but should cast away all its hateful ideas concerning the bourgeoisie.[2]

A second and more practical, but less systematic, form of this Socialism sought to depreciate every revolutionary movement in the

---

3. Quotation marks added by the translator [B.A.].
4. "now (1847)" added by the translator [B.A.].
5. The revolutionary storm of 1848 swept away this whole shabby tendency and cured its protagonists of the desire to dabble further in Socialism. The chief representative and classical type of this tendency is Herr Karl Grün [*Engels's note to the German edition of 1890*].
6. *I.e.*, the "socialism" under consideration here refused to attack the bourgeoisie's economic and political rule over the rest of society, merely offering palliative reforms to redress the most glaring excesses of this rule—the better to forestall revolutionary uprisings [*Ed.*].
7. In English, *The Philosophy of Poverty*, published in 1846. Marx's polemical reply, *The Poverty of Philosophy*, appeared the following year [*Ed.*].
8. *I.e.*, the reform-oriented segment of the bourgeois class [*Ed.*].
9. *Lebensbedingungen* = vitally essential conditions; not "advantages" [*D.R.*].
1. *das neue Jerusalem* = the new Jerusalem; not "the social new Jerusalem" [*D.R.*].
2. *von derselben* = it (presently existing society); not "the bourgeoisie" [*D.R.*].

eyes of the working class, by showing that no mere political reform, but only a change in the material conditions of existence, in economical relations, could be of any advantage to them. By changes in the material conditions of existence, this form of Socialism, however, by no means understands abolition of the bourgeois relations of production,[3] an abolition that can be effected only by a revolution, but administrative reforms, based on the continued existence of these relations; reforms, therefore, that in no respect affect the relations between capital and labour, but, at the best, lessen the cost, and simplify the administrative work, of bourgeois government.

Bourgeois Socialism attains adequate expression, when, and only when, it becomes a mere figure of speech.

Free trade: for the benefit of the working class. Protective duties: for the benefit of the working class. Prison Reform: for the benefit of the working class. This is the last word and the only seriously meant word of bourgeois Socialism.

It is summed up in the phrase: the bourgeois is a bourgeois—for the benefit of the working class.

3. Critical-Utopian Socialism and Communism

We do not here refer to that literature which, in every great modern revolution, has always given voice to the demands of the proletariat, such as the writings of Babeuf and others.

The first direct attempts of the proletariat to attain its own ends, made in times of universal excitement, when feudal society was being overthrown, these attempts necessarily failed, owing to the then undeveloped state of the proletariat, as well as to the absence of the economic conditions for its emancipation, conditions that had yet to be produced, and could be produced by the impending bourgeois epoch alone.[4] The revolutionary literature that accompanied these first movements of the proletariat had necessarily a reactionary character. It inculcated universal asceticism and social levelling in its crudest form.

The Socialist and Communist systems properly so called, those of Saint-Simon, Fourier, Owen and others, spring into existence in the early undeveloped period, described above, of the struggle between proletariat and bourgeoisie (see Section I. Bourgeoisie and Proletariat).

The founders of these systems see, indeed, the class antagonisms, as well as the action of the decomposing elements, in the

---

3. *I.e.*, the ownership (and control) of the social means of production by the bourgeois class, its control over wage labor, and its consequent domination of the proletariat [*Ed.*].
4. *die eben erst das Produkt der bürgerlichen Epoche sind* = which could only be the products of the bourgeois epoch; not "and could be produced by the impending bourgeois epoch alone" [*D.R.*].

prevailing form of society. But the proletariat, as yet in its infancy,[5] offers to them the spectacle of a class without any historical initiative or any independent political movement.

Since the development of class antagonism keeps even pace with the development of industry, the economic situation, as they find it, does not as yet offer to them the material conditions,[6] for the emancipation of the proletariat. They therefore search after a new social[7] science, after new social laws, that are to create these conditions.

Historical action is to yield to their personal inventive action, historically created conditions of emancipation to fantastic ones,[8] and the gradual, spontaneous class-organisation of the proletariat[9] to an organisation of society specially contrived by these inventors. Future history resolves itself, in their eyes, into the propaganda and the practical carrying out of their social plans.

In the formation of their plans they are conscious of caring chiefly for the interests of the working class, as being the most suffering class. Only from the point of view of being the most suffering class does the proletariat exist for them.

The undeveloped state of the class struggle, as well as their own surroundings, causes Socialists of this kind to consider themselves far superior to all class antagonisms. They want to improve the condition of every member of society, even that of the most favoured. Hence, they habitually appeal to society at large, without distinction of class; nay, by preference, to the ruling class. For how can people, when once they understand their system, fail to see in it the best possible plan of the best possible state of society?

Hence, they reject all political, and especially all revolutionary, action; they wish to attain their ends by peaceful means, and endeavour, by small experiments, necessarily doomed to failure, and by the force of example, to pave the way for the new social Gospel.

Such fantastic pictures of future society, painted at a time when the proletariat is still in a very undeveloped state and has but a fantastic conception of its own position, correspond with the first instinctive yearnings of that class for a general reconstruction of society.

5. "as yet in its infancy" added by the translator [D.R.].
6. *finden sie eben so wenig die materiellen Bedingungen* = they find the material conditions precisely too little; not "the economic situation as they find it, does not as yet offer to them the material conditions" [D.R.].
7. *sozialen* = social; not "new social" [B.A.].
8. *I.e.*, to conditions of emancipation created (only) in fantasy [Ed.].
9. *der allmälig vor sich gehenden Organization des Proletariats zur Klasse* = the gradually proceeding organization of the proletariat into a class; not "the gradual, spontaneous class organization of the proletariat" [D.R.].

But these[1] Socialist and Communist publications contain also a critical element. They attack every principle of existing society. Hence they are full of the most valuable materials for the enlightenment of the working class. The practical measures proposed in them[2]—such as the abolition of the distinction between town and country, of the family, of the carrying on of industries for the account of private individuals, and of the wage system, the proclamation of social harmony, the conversion of the functions of the State into a mere superintendence of production, all these proposals point solely to the disappearance of class antagonisms which were, at that time, only just cropping up, and which, in these publications, are recognised in their earliest, indistinct and undefined forms only. These proposals, therefore, are of a purely Utopian character.

The significance of Critical-Utopian Socialism and Communism bears an inverse relation to historical development. In proportion as the modern class struggle[3] develops and takes definite shape, this fantastic standing apart from the contest, these fantastic attacks on it, lose all practical value and all theoretical justification. Therefore, although the originators of these systems were, in many respects, revolutionary, their disciples have, in every case, formed mere reactionary sects. They hold fast by the original views of their masters, in opposition to the progressive historical development of the proletariat. They, therefore, endeavour, and that consistently, to deaden the class struggle and to reconcile the class antagonisms. They still dream of experimental realisation of their social Utopias, of founding isolated "*phalanstères*," of establishing "Home Colonies," of setting up a "Little Icaria"[4]—duodecimo editions[5] of the New Jerusalem—and to realise all these castles in the air, they are compelled to appeal to the feelings and purses of the bourgeois. By degrees they sink into the category of the reactionary conservative Socialists depicted above, differing from these only by more systematic pedantry, and by their fanati-

1. *Die* = the; not "these" [*D.R.*].
2. *Ihre positiven Sätze über die zukünftige Gesellschaft* = Their positive propositions on the future society; not "The practical measures proposed in them" [*D.R.*].
3. *der Klassenkampf* = the class struggle; not "the modern class struggle" [*D.R.*].
4. *Phalanstères* were Socialist colonies on the plan of Charles Fourier: *Icaria* was the name given by Cabet to his Utopia and, later on, to his American Communist colony [*Engels's note to the English edition of 1888*].

    "Home colonies" were what Owen called his Communist model societies. *Phalanstères* was the name of the public palaces planned by Fourier. *Icaria* was the name given to the Utopian land of fancy, whose Communist institutions Cabet portrayed [*Engels's note to the German edition of 1890*].
5. Of minute or diminutive size [*Ed.*].

cal and superstitious belief in the miraculous effects of their social science.

They, therefore, violently oppose all political action on the part of the working class; such action, according to them, can only result from blind unbelief in the new Gospel.

The Owenites in England, and the Fourierists in France, respectively, oppose the Chartists and the *Réformistes*.[6]

IV
Position of the Communists in Relation to the Various Existing Opposition Parties

Section II has made clear the relations of the Communists to the existing working-class parties, such as the Chartists in England and the Agrarian Reformers in America.[1]

The Communists[2] fight for the attainment of the immediate aims, for the enforcement of the momentary[3] interests of the working class; but in the movement of the present, they also represent and take care of[4] the future of that movement. In France the Communists ally themselves with the Social-Democrats,[5] against the conservative and radical bourgeoisie, reserving, however, the right to take up a critical position in regard to phrases and illusions traditionally handed down from the great Revolution.[6]

6. Republican democrat and petty-bourgeois socialist adherents of the newspaper *La Réforme*, organ of radical opposition to the July monarchy, which was published in Paris from 1843 to 1850. Ledru-Rollin and Louis Blanc were among the leaders of the *Réforme* party. Engels made the acquaintance of the leaders of this group, contributed articles to the newspaper, and eventually joined its staff. "Chartists": in the view of Marx and Engels, authentic proletarians who really represented the interests of the working class, albeit often only crudely. As early as 1845, Engels considered it essential that the communists in England link up with Chartism. The Chartist leader George Julian Harney published many of Engels's early articles in *The Northern Star* and the first English translation of the *Communist Manifesto* in *The Red Republican* [Ed.].

1. Reference to the movement in the late 1840s of the National Reform Association on behalf of small American farmers, first, for no rents (the Anti-Rent League), and, then, for distribution of small holdings sufficient for each farmer to maintain himself and his dependents, with a limitation of the size of farms to 160 acres. Marx supported this movement to free the land from large-scale private ownership only to the extent that it might become a preliminary form of an American proletarian movement [Ed.].

2. *Sie* = They; not "The Communists" [D.R.].

3. "for the enforcement of the momentary" added by the translator [B.A.].

4. "and take care of" added by the translator [D.R.].

5. The party then represented in Parliament by Ledru-Rollin, in literature by Louis Blanc, in the daily press by the *Réforme*. The name of Social Democracy signified, with these its inventors, a section of the Democratic or Republican party more or less tinged with Socialism [Engels's note to the English edition of 1888].

The party in France which at that time called itself Socialist-Democratic was represented in political life by Ledru-Rollin and in literature by Louis Blanc; thus it differed immeasurably from present-day German Social-Democracy [Engels's note to the German edition of 1890].

6. *aus der revolutionären Überlieferung* = from the revolutionary tradition; not "traditionally handed down from the great Revolution" [B.A.].

In Switzerland they support the Radicals,[7] without losing sight of the fact that this party consists of antagonistic elements, partly of Democratic Socialists, in the French sense, partly of radical bourgeois.

In Poland they support the party that insists on an agrarian revolution as the prime condition for national emancipation, that party which fomented the insurrection of Cracow in 1846.[8]

In Germany they fight with the bourgeoisie whenever it acts in a revolutionary way, against the absolute monarchy, the feudal squirearchy,[9] and the petty bourgeoisie.

But they never cease, for a single instant, to instil into the working class the clearest possible recognition of the hostile antagonism between bourgeoisie and proletariat, in order that the German workers may straightway use, as so many weapons against the bourgeoisie, the social and political conditions that the bourgeoisie must necessarily introduce along with its supremacy, and in order that, after the fall of the reactionary classes in Germany, the fight against the bourgeoisie itself may immediately begin.

The Communists turn their attention chiefly to Germany, because that country is on the eve of a bourgeois revolution that is bound to be carried out under more advanced conditions of European civilisation, and with a much more developed proletariat, than that of England was in the seventeenth, and of France in the eighteenth century, and because the bourgeois revolution in Germany will be but the prelude to an immediately following proletarian revolution.

In short, the Communists everywhere support every revolutionary movement against the existing social and political order of things.

In all these movements they bring to the front, as the leading question in each, the property question, no matter what its degree of development at the time.

Finally, they labour everywhere for the union and agreement of the democratic parties of all countries.

The Communists disdain to conceal their views and aims. They openly declare that their ends can be attained only by the forcible

7. In 1847 and 1848 the Swiss Radicals were concentrated mainly in the French-speaking cantons of Geneva and Vaud. They took a prominent part in the *Sonderbund* war and brought about the defeat and destruction of the *Sonderbund*, a special alliance of reactionary, Catholic cantons. By 1849, however, the Radicals refused asylum to fleeing German revolutionaries [*Ed.*].

8. The party that sought an agrarian and democratic revolution in Poland was the Polish Democratic Society, founded in 1832 to counterbalance the aristocrats who had led the insurrection of 1830. In its appeals to the peasants, the Society advocated equality of rights for the peasantry and free possession of the lands cultivated by them. The abortive Cracow uprising of January 24, 1846, aroused widespread sympathy among democrats and communists throughout Europe, for its awareness that national liberation in agrarian countries dominated by outside powers (in this case, Russia) must also be democratic, i.e., must include the liberation of the oppressed peasantry [*Ed.*].

9. *das feudale Grundeigentum* = feudal landed property; not "the feudal squirearchy" [*D.R.*].

overthrow of all existing social conditions.[1] Let the ruling classes tremble at a Communistic revolution. The proletarians have nothing to lose[2] but their chains. They have a world to win.

WORKING MEN OF ALL COUNTRIES, UNITE!

---

1. *aller bisherigen Gesellschaftsordnung[en]* = of all social order[s] up to now; not "of all existing social conditions" [*D.R.*].
2. *nichts in ihr zu verlieren* = nothing to lose in this [the revolution]; meaning "nothing to lose from it" [*D.R.*].

SOURCES AND
BACKGROUNDS

BERT ANDRÉAS

A Note on Sources[†]

* * * The *Manifesto* is equally the spiritual property of Marx and Engels * * * as they have attested several times. * * * It is certain, however, that Marx alone is responsible for the definitive literary form. After having received a mandate to draw up the *Manifesto*, Marx and Engels were together only a few days in London [immediately after the second Congress of the Communist League] and afterward a dozen days in Brussels. From the end of December 1847 to January 29, 1848, Engels was in Paris, and he returned to Brussels only on January 31. The only sign of a draft of the *Manifesto* is a plan of section 3, the date of the writing of which is probably in December 1847; the outline—an outline of some general terms in Marx's handwriting—is found on the cover of a notebook of Marx's bearing the inscription "Brussels. December 1847" and including some notes for his lectures before the German Workers' Educational Society in Brussels on "Wage Labor and Capital." On January 26, 1848, the manuscript was not yet in the possession of the Central Committee in London, which communicated that day to the leading circle in Brussels its decision of January 24, in accordance with which it was necessary to pressure Marx into giving them a manuscript ready for printing before February 1; otherwise, he would have to return the documents that had been put at his disposal.[1] As the measures announced in case of delay were apparently not put into effect, one may presume that the manuscript reached London about February 1, and, consequently, the month of January 1848 may be considered as the period of its writing.

For composition, Marx used the documents that the Central Committee had placed at his disposal; one may suppose that [these included] the messages of the Central Committee of the League of the Just of November 1846 and February 1847, the discussion pro-

---

† From *Le Manifeste communiste de Marx et Engels: Histoire et Bibliographie, 1848–1918* (Milan: Feltrinelli, 1963) 1–4. Excerpts reprinted by permission of the publisher. These pages have been translated from the French by Frederic L. Bender for this volume. All notes are Andréas's unless otherwise indicated.
1. Pp. 15–16 in this volume [*Editor*].

gram of the League Congress of June 1847, and the outline program of the League's Circles in Paris, drawn up by Engels.[2]

For the writing of sections 1 and 2 of the *Manifesto*, Marx relied in part upon *The Poverty of Philosophy*[3] and his notes on wage labor;[4] it is on the cover of the notebook that contains these notes that Marx sketched his outline.[5] For the writing of sections 1–3, Max relied in very large measure on the manuscript that he had, in 1845–46, drawn up together with Engels, *The German Ideology*, which was not printed in his lifetime; he took from there ideas and expressions, above all from chapters 1 ("Feuerbach"),[6] 3 ("Saint Max"),[7] and [volume 2:] "True Socialism."[8] Engels's manuscript "The Status Quo in Germany," written in March 1847 but also not published at that time, was probably also among the works utilized by Marx; one finds there already, for example, the turn of phrase used in the Preamble: "It is high time that the Communists . . .";[9] Engels accuses the rabble of venality (it is the first time that the expression *Lumpenproletariat* figures in a writing of Marx or Engels); the petit bourgeoisie is characterized as the natural class of Germany;[1] the application of a military image to an economic process (*Manifesto*: "the cheap prices of their commodities are the heavy artillery . . .") is found also in Engels's manuscript.[2] Engels's book, *The Condition of the Working Class in England* (Leipzig, 1845), was also utilized by Marx, and several times he used its characteristic expressions: "his 'natural superiors,'" "no other nexus between man and man . . . than callous 'cash

---

2. The last-mentioned document is presumably Engels's "Principles of Communism" [*Editor*].
3. E.g., MEGA I/6, p. 123, lines 35–39: ". . . to make a marketable value out of virtue, love, etc., to raise exchange value to its third and last power. We see that M. Proudhon's 'historical and descriptive method' is applicable to everything, it answers everything, explains everything." [For MEGA, see p. 59, dagger note—*Editor*.]
4. E.g., ibid., p. 454, lines 21–23: "General principle of modern industry: to replace adults by children, skilled laborers by unskilled ones, men by women"; ibid., p. 471, line 35–p. 472, line 6: "*First*: by this everything patriarchal fell away, as just the haggling, purchase and sale, remains the only connection, the monetary relation the only relation, between employer and worker. *Second*: The glory fell generally from all relations of the old society, as they were dissolved into purely monetary relations. In the same way, all so-called higher labors, spiritual, artistic, etc., were turned into articles of commerce and thereby lost their old inspiration. What great progress it was, that the whole regiment of priests, doctors, judges, etc., hence religion, jurisprudence, etc., were assigned just their market value."
5. The outline of section 3 of the *Manifesto* is meant [*Editor*.]
6. MEGA I/5, p. 23, lines 22–24: "every class which is struggling for mastery . . . as is the case with the proletariat, postulates the abolition of the old form of society in its entirety and of domination in general, must first conquer political power for itself", ibid., p. 35, lines 30–31: "The ideas of the ruling class are in every era the ruling ideas"; ibid., p. 60, lines 15–18: "Communism differs from all previous movements in that it overturns the basis of all earlier relations of production and intercourse (*Verkehr*). . . ."
7. Ibid., pp. 97–428; e.g., p. 162, passim.
8. Ibid., pp. 435–37, passim.
9. MEGA. I/6, p. 233, line 24.
1. Ibid., p. 241, lines 4, 19–20: p. 242, line 32.
2. Ibid., p. 239, line 28.

payment,'" and "these laborers, who must sell themselves piece-meal."[3] The developments borrowed from the [Economic and Philo-sophical] Manuscripts of 1844 are indicated in MEGA, as follows:

> Marx speaks [in the 1844 Manuscripts] of the industrial bourgeoisie, who stand at the head of entire industrial armies (p. 51). He emphasizes the fact that now "on the whole, there are only two classes in the population, the working class and the class of capitalists" (p. 75). The workers are, in this social sys-tem, reduced to the status of commodities. "The worker becomes a cheaper commodity the more commodities he produces" (p. 82). The worker is "himself capital, a commodity" (p. 103).
>
> To the same extent as production develops itself higher and the pile of riches grows, the standard of living of the workers sinks: "the worker becomes the poorer, the more wealth he produces, the more his production takes on power and size" (p. 82). "The more labor the worker gives—long, painful, loathe-some—so much less will he be repaid" (p. 51).[4]

[Andréas then lists references to five passages in Engels's "Principles of Communism" that parallel the *Manifesto*].[5] The twelve demands enumerated by Engels, except for numbers 10 and 11, are picked

---

3. MECA I/4, p. 78, lines 17–18, qualified by "favorite expression of the English manufac-turers"; ibid., p. 262, lines 24–26; ibid., p. 81, lines 15–18, respectively.
4. MEGA I/3, p. xiii—page references for the Paris Manuscripts are to the same volume.
5. The passages from Engels's "Principles" are as follows:

> The price of a commodity under the dominion of large-scale industry or of free competition, which, as we shall see, means the same thing, is on the average always equal to the cost of production of that commodity. The price of labour, is, therefore, likewise equal to the cost of production of labour. The latter cost consists precisely of that sum of the means of subsistence which is needed to make the worker fit to perform the labour and to prevent the working class from dying out. Thus, the worker will not receive more for his labour than is necessary for that purpose; the price of labour, or wages, will be the lowest, the minimum required to maintain a livelihood." [MEGA I/6, p. 505, lines 14–22.]
>
> *In the first place*, since owing to machine labour the prices of industrial products constantly decreased, the old system of manufacture or industry founded upon manual labour was completely destroyed in all countries of the world. All semibar-barian countries, which had hitherto been more or less cut off from historical development and whose industry had until then been based on manufacture, were thus forcibly dragged out of their isolation. They brought the cheaper commodities of the English and allowed their own manufactory workers to perish. Thus it was that countries which had stagnated for millennia, India for example, were revolu-tionised from top to base and even China is now marching towards a revolution." [Ibid., p. 507. line 30–p. 508, line 3.]
>
> "*First*, that although in the initial stage of its development large-scale industry itself created free competition, it now has outgrown free competition; that competi-tion and in general the carrying on of industrial production by individuals have become fetters upon large-scale industry. . . ." [Ibid., p. 510, lines 17–21.]
>
> "In the Middle Ages, which were dependent upon agriculture, we find the lord and the serf; the towns of the later Middle Ages provide us with the master guilds-man and his apprentices and day-labourers; the seventeenth century has manufac-turers and manufactory workers; the nineteenth century—the big factory owner and the proletarian." [Ibid., p. 512, line 21–p. 513, line 1.]

up, in a different order, in the ten demands at the end of section 2 of the *Manifesto*.[6]

The questions posed in the "Credo" of the League of the Just of November 1846 are taken up in section 4 of the *Manifesto*, and the critique of the different socialist schools and systems, contained in the "Credo" of February 1847, is pursued in section 3. In its structure, the *Manifesto* follows Engels's "Principles of Communism"; it develops them and presents them under a different form in four sections. The historical sections 1 and 2 ("Bourgeois and Proletarians"

Democracy would be quite useless to the proletariat if it were not immediately utilised as a means of accomplishing further measures directly attacking private ownership and securing the existence of the proletariat. Principal among these measures, already now consequent upon the existing relations, are the following:

1. Restriction of private ownership by means of progressive income taxes, high inheritance taxes, abolition of inheritance by collateral lines (brothers, nephews, etc.), compulsory loans, and so forth.

2. Gradual expropriation of landed proprietors, factory owners, railway and shipping magnates, partly through competition on the part of state industry and partly directly through the payment of compensation in currency notes.

3. Confiscation of the property of all emigrants and rebels against the majority of the people.

4. Organisation of the labour or occupation of the proletarians on national estates, in national factories and workshops, thereby putting an end to competition among the workers themselves and compelling the factory owners, as long as they still exist, to pay the same high wages as those paid by the State.

5. Equal liability to work for all members of society until the abolition of private ownership is completed. Formation of industrial armies, especially for agriculture.

6. Centralisation of the credit and banking systems in the hands of the State, by means of a national bank with state capital and the suppression of all private banks and bankers.

7. Increase of national factories, workshops, railways, and ships, cultivation of all uncultivated land and improvement of the already cultivated land in the same proportion in which the capital and workers at the disposal of the nation are increasing.

8. Education of all children, as soon as they are old enough to dispense with maternal care, in national institutions and at the charge of the nation. Education combined with production.

9. The erection of large palaces on national estates as common dwellings for communities of citizens carrying on industry as well as agriculture, and combining the advantages of urban and rural life without the citizens having to suffer from the onesidedness and the disadvantages of either.

10. The demolition of all insanitary and badly built houses and blocks of flats.

11. Equal right of inheritance to be enjoyed by illegitimate and legitimate children.

12. Concentration of all means of transport in the hands of the nation.

Of course, all these measures cannot be introduced at once. But one will always lead to the other. Once the first radical onslaught upon private ownership has been made, the proletariat will be compelled to go further, and more and more to concentrate in the hands of the State all capital, all agriculture, all industry, all transport, and all means of exchange. All these measures work towards such results; and they will become realisable and their centralising consequences will develop in the same proportion in which the productive forces of the country will multiply through the labour of the proletariat. Finally, when all capital, all production, and all exchange are concentrated in the hands of the nation, private ownership will automatically have ceased to exist, money will have become superfluous, and production will have so increased and men will have so changed that the last forms of the old social relations will also be able to fall away. [Ibid., p. 514, line 9–p. 515, line 40.]

6. "Principles" #1 = *Manifesto* #2 & 3; 2 = 1; 3 = 4; 4 & 7 = 7; 5 = 8; 6 = 5; 8 = 10; 9 = 9; 12 = 6.

and "Proletarians and Communists") correspond to points 1 to 23 of the "Principles," while section 3 ("Socialist and Communist Literature") discusses point 24, and section 4 ("The Position of the Communists in Relation to the Various Existing Opposition Parties") discusses point 25.

The title of the *Manifesto* was suggested by Engels,[7] one finds it, possibly for the first time, as the title of a series of articles that appeared without signature in *La Phalange* in 1841.[8] Marx and Engels "could not have called it a *Socialist Manifesto.* . . . Socialism in 1847 signified a bourgeois movement, Communism, a working-class movement. Socialism was . . . quite respectable, whereas Communism was the very opposite."[9]

Of the first phrase of the *Manifesto*, "a spectre is haunting Europe—the spectre of Communism," it has been affirmed[1] that Marx had borrowed it from Lorenz von Stein's book on communism in France.[2] However, the image was quite widespread at that time.[3] It seems to us more likely that Marx, in using the image of the spectre, refers to the article on communism that appeared in the *Staatslexikon,*[4] of which the first phrase reads: "In Germany there has been talk for the past few years of Communism, and already it has become a threatening spectre before which some people are frightened, and which others seek to frighten away." Of all the passages known to us, [appearing] before the *Manifesto*, which applied the image of the spectre of communism, it is only to the passage

7. "This Congress must be decisive, *as this time we shall have it all our own way.* . . .
    "Think over the Confession of Faith a bit. I believe we had better drop the catechism form and call the thing: Communist *Manifesto*. As more or less history has got to be related in it the form it has been in hitherto is quite unsuitable. I am bringing what I have done here with me: it is in simple narrative form, but miserably worded, in fearful haste. I begin: What is Communism? And then straight to the proletariat—history of its origin, difference from former labourers, development of the antithesis between proletariat and bourgeoisie, crises, conclusions. In between this all sorts of secondary matters and in conclusion the Party policy of the Communists, in so far as it should be made public." [Engels to Marx, November 23–24, 1847.]
8. Cf. *La Phalange* (Paris), May 19, 1841, no. 8, p. 122; May 26, no. 11, p. 169; June 11, no. 18, p. 282; *Manifeste des communistes.* It was Moses Hess who pointed out this *Manifeste des communistes* to Marx, in his second article, *Die Communisten in Frankreich*, in the *Rheinische Zeitung* (Cologne), April 21, 1842, no. 111 (Supplement), p. 1. Marx and Engels certainly knew Hess's articles.
9. Engels's preface to the German edition of the *Manifesto* of 1890.
1. See Arnold Winkler: *Die Entstehung des "Kommunistischen Manifests"* (Vienna, 1936), pp. 121–27.
2. "Communism, a dark, threatening spectre, in whose actuality no one wants to believe, and whose existence is yet recognized and feared by everybody." Lorenz von Stein, *Der Sozialismus und Communismus des heutigen Frankreich: Ein Beitrag zur Zeitgeschichte* (Leipzig: Otto Wigand, 1842), p. 4.
3. It is found, e.g., in 1842 in Stein (see n. 2, above); in 1846 in Wilhelm Schulz: "Communismus"; in Carl von Rotteck and C. Welker: *Supplemente zur ersten Auflage des Staatslexikons oder der Encyklopädie der Staatswissenschaften, in Verbindung mit vielen der angesehensten Publicisten Deutschlands herausgegeben: Zweiter Band* (Altona, 1846), pp. 23–94; and in the anonymous *Der Pauperismus und die Volksschule: Ein ernestes Wort über die wichstigsten Fragen unserer Zeit* (Leipzig: Barth and Schulze, 1847), pp. 1–2.
4. Schulz, loc. cit.

cited from the *Staatslexikon* that the qualification of "nursery tale of the Spectre of Communism" also corresponds.[5]

The motto: "Proletarians of all countries, unite!" appeared for the first time[6] in the masthead of the specimen number of the *Kommunistische Zeitschrift*, published in London, in September 1847. * * * The review, of which this was the only number, was to have become the organ of the Communist League. The new watchword replaced the old formula of the League of the Just: "All men are brothers!" Engels, earlier than Marx, had maintained relations with the revolutionaries of various countries, and he had called for the international unification of communists; he had had a major part in the preparation and execution of the fusion of the League of the Just and the Communist Correspondence Committees; he probably wrote one of the articles that appeared in the *Kommunistische Zeitschrift*;[7] we believe it therefore possible to attribute to Engels the authorship of the new motto.

The manuscript of the *Manifesto* has not been preserved.

* * *

MICHAEL HARRINGTON

The Democratic Essence of Socialism[†]

* * *

In the 1840s * * * Marx and Engels became socialists and what set them off from all other radicals of the time was their insistence upon the democratic character of the coming revolution. This fact is sometimes conceded by the Communist inventors of the totalitarian Marx, but it is explained away as a youthful exuberance and naiveté. That is not true.

The commitment to democracy dominates Marx's whole life; it can be found in *The Communist Manifesto* and, above all, in *Das Kapital*, and not just in the early writings.

Between 1848 and 1850 Marx and Engels changed their minds about their basic political orientation no less than three times. *The*

---

5. MEGA I/6, p. 525, lines 19–22. In order to explain this expression of the *Manifesto*, Winkler needs to presume a mistake by Marx, who would have had to misunderstand the sense of the word *Gespenst* ("spectre") in Stein (see Winkler, op. cit., pp. 125–26).
6. It is also found in a toast pronounced on September 20, 1847, in London at the meeting of the German, French, and English Communists: "May the proletarians of all countries unite themselves in common for the vindication of their rights!" See *Telegraph für Deutschland* (Hamburg), November 1847, no. 176, p. 703/1.
7. "Der preussische Landtag und das Proletariat in Pruessen, wie überhaupt in Deutschland," in *Kommunistische Zeitschrift* (London), September 1847, no. 1, pp. 8–14.
† From *Socialism* (New York: Saturday Review Press, 1972), pp. 42–53. Reprinted by permission of Skyhorse Publishing, Inc.

Communist Manifesto was a great, and contradictory, document which advocated an alliance with the very bourgeoisie whose death sentence it pronounced. When the course of action derived from this ambiguous analysis proved a failure, Marx became a disillusioned and bitter ultra-Leftist. But then in 1850 reality forced itself upon him and he once more turned to the work of elaborating a tactic for the mass movement.

The two years between 1848 and 1850 were the period of Marx's antidemocratic temptation, and the dictatorial Marxists have celebrated them ever since. In fact, he never did become a partisan of revolution from above, even in his angriest hours, and by late 1850 he had begun to deepen his democratic strategy for socialist revolution. So if Marx's memory is to be saved from the totalitarians and restored to the future, these developments must be seen in detail.

The opening sentence of the preface of the *Manifesto*—"A spectre is haunting Europe, the spectre of Communism"—was wrong.

England, the most industrialized nation of the time, had a mass working-class movement in Chartism, but this movement did not go beyond the struggle for democratic freedoms. In France there were indeed socialist political groupings, but the country was overwhelmingly peasant and those rural millions were to applaud the bloody suppression of the proletariat in June, 1848.

In Germany the bourgeois revolution had not even taken place and the bourgeoisie itself was already giving signs of the timidity it was to show in the coming upheavals. On the rest of the continent conditions were, politically and economically, even more backward than in these three countries.

In one mood—but not in all their moods, for they contradicted themselves on this count—Marx and Engels pictured reality as much more radical than it was. *"Democracy is today Communism,"* Engels proclaimed at a London meeting in 1845. "Democracy has become the proletarian principle, the principle of the masses. The masses may be more or less clear about the unique and true significance of democracy, but there is still a feeling that the basis of social equality is in democracy. . . . With insignificant exceptions, all European democrats in 1846 are more or less clear Communists."[1] This is in the all-or-nothing spirit of Marx's view in 1843 that the bourgeoisie no longer had a role to play and that the proletariat and the philosophers would soon jointly realize the millennium.

But in another mood Marx and Engels knew the truth: that in most of the countries of Europe it was only the conquest of bourgeois freedoms, not socialism, that was on the agenda. In 1847 Marx

1. Marx and Engels, *Werke*, ed. Institute for Marxism-Lenism of the Central Committee of the Socialist Unity ["Communist"] Party of the German Democratic Republic (Berlin: Dietz, 1956–68) II, p. 613.

wrote with considerable realism, ". . . the aristocracy can only be overthrown when the bourgeoisie and the people join together. To advocate the rule of the people in a land in which the aristocracy and the bourgeoisie are still allies is sheer madness."[2] And in the same year Engels took much the same line: "The Communists are far from starting useless fights with the democrats under present circumstances. Moreover, in all practical party questions the Communists appear as democrats. . . . So long as the democracy has not yet conquered, so long do the Communists and democrats struggle together, so long are the interests of the democrats also those of the Communists."[3]

This contradiction between a sense of imminent proletarian revolution on the one hand, and the sober knowledge that the coming battle would seek only democratic freedoms on the other, can be found within the *Manifesto* itself.

* * *

Thus the *Manifesto* is a schizophrenic statement. Its dialectical and historical method, its definition of socialism and identification of the historic tendencies of capitalism, represented an incomparable advance for a confused socialist movement. Its overestimation of both capitalism and Communism and its assertion that society was rapidly polarizing into two, and only two, significant classes were misleading. And, as it turned out, its tactics were much too soft on bourgeois democracy. This last, rather bizarre, fact is worth examining for two reasons: it emphasizes that Marx and Engels' democratic commitment was so serious that, far from being crypto-totalitarians, they were too uncritical of the bourgeois democrats; and it helps us to understand the bitterness of their disillusionment which came at the end of this tumultuous period.

Perhaps the most telling summary of their participation in these events was made by David Riazanov, a great Communist scholar who was purged by Stalin. In 1848, Riazanov points out, Marx and Engels refused to organize a separate proletarian party.[4] Basing himself upon the experience of the French Revolution with its long, drawn-out movement to the Left, Marx wanted the workers to fight as a part of the bourgeois democratic forces. Indeed, when Stephen Born, a member of the Communist League, actually organized the workers in Berlin on a class basis during that period, Marx and Engels turned on him bitterly.

So it is incredible, but true, that Karl Marx's *Neue Rheinische Zeitung* was attacked during the Revolution of 1848 for not paying

2. *Werke*, IV, p. 202.
3. Ibid., p. 317.
4. Riazanov, *Marx et Engels* (Paris: Editions Sociales Internationales, n.d.), pp. 88ff.

enough attention to economics and to the working class. Marx admitted the charge: "From all sides people reproach us that we have not described the *economic relations* that form the basis of the current class and national struggles. We purposely only touched on those relations when they actually intruded immediately into the political battle."[5] But by March–April, 1848, Marx continued, the bourgeoisie had triumphed in France and feudalism was victorious everywhere in Europe. In a sharp *volte face* he drew a conclusion diametrically opposed to the theory he had been acting upon for several years: "any social reform remains a utopia until the proletarian revolution and the feudal counterrevolution take each other's measure in a world war."[6]

These events are important for both scholarly and political reasons. In the last, tactical section of the *Manifesto*, even as Marx advocated an alliance with the bourgeois democrats, he warned the workers of their basic hostility to the capitalists alongside of whom they were to fight. In Germany, he comments, "the bourgeois revolution can only be the immediate prelude to a proletarian revolution." So E. H. Carr can argue that the *Manifesto* had "announced the prospect in Germany of an immediate transition from bourgeois revolution to proletarian revolution without the intervening period of bourgeois rule."[7] But if that is indeed the case, then the *Manifesto* also anticipated, and legitimated, the Marxism of both V. I. Lenin and Joseph Stalin, for that is exactly the kind of revolution they claimed to make in Russia. * * * Carr's reading of a seemingly abstruse point of history and doctrine has the very political result "that the Russian Revolution can claim to be a legitimate child of *The Communist Manifesto*."[8] And that is an important step in making Marx the father of totalitarianism.

Carr is wrong. Insofar as the *Manifesto* was interpreted by Marx and Engels themselves, they read it as committing them to a long-term alliance with bourgeois democracy, not as urging a Bolshevik-like leap from an unripe capitalism to a revolutionary socialism. This is clearly the premise of their actions in 1848. It was only when Marx turned his back on the strategy of the *Manifesto* in late 1848 that there is even a hint of the view that Carr ascribes to the *Manifesto* itself. For two bitter disillusioned years after that turning point, Marx was indeed in a sullen, ultra-Leftist mood, and this period is a classic source for the Bolshevik, and then the Stalinist, version of Marxism. Even then, however, Marx never became dictatorial, much less totalitarian. But in any case, the

5. *Werke*, VI, p. 397.
6. Ibid.
7. E. H. Carr, *Studies in Revolution* (New York: Grosset and Dunlap, 1964), pp. 22 ff.
8. Ibid., p. 36.

crucial moment in that period was his decisive rejection of anti-democratic politics.

* * *

This new analysis required a new strategy. By March of 1850 Marx and Engels, who had refused to build a workers' party only two years before, were calling upon the proletarians to set up their own fiercely independent organizations. When it was necessary, they were to march together with the petty-bourgeois democrats, but in any case, they must form secret, armed groups. And then, in a passage that prefigures some of the tactics of the Russian Revolution of 1917, Marx and Engels wrote, "The workers must set up their own revolutionary proletarian regime alongside the new official government, whether in the form of local boards, councils, clubs, or committees of workers. . . .

"From the very first moment of the victory, the workers must distrust not only the defeated reactionary party, but its former comrades as well, and fight that party which will try to exploit the common victory on its own." And the conclusion—which clearly echoed in the mind of Leon Trotsky in the Petrograd Soviet of 1917: "The battle cry must be: Permanent Revolution.[9] (Die Revolution in Permanenz)

This mood lasted for about two years, from the fall of 1848 to the middle of 1850. It brought Marx as close to anti-democracy as he ever came.

It was during this ultra-Leftist period that Marx used the fateful phrase "dictatorship of the proletariat."[1]

It is, alas, of little political moment that it can be demonstrated that when Marx wrote this phrase, he did not mean "dictatorship," at least as the word is now commonly employed. Nor does it matter to posterity that the phrase is used only a few times in the writings of Marx and Engels and at one point describes anarchist libertarianism rather than violent suppression. Nevertheless, the phrase provided a certain semantic legitimacy for the anti-socialist totalitarians who were to inscribe the slogan on their banners. * * *

It was in April of 1850 that Marx and Engels met with some Blanquists and Left-wing Chartists in London. There they signed the statutes of the World Society of Revolutionary Communists. Article I declared: "The aim of the association is the overthrow of all privileged classes, their subjugation by the dictatorship of the proletariat which will maintain the revolution in permanence until

9. *Werke*, VI, pp. 421 ff, 440
1. On Marx and Engels's use of "dictatorship of the proletariat," see Hal Draper, "Marx and the Dictatorship of the Proletariat," *New Politics* (Vol. 1, 1962) p. 73.

communism, the last organizational form of the human family, will be constructed."[2] The organization was stillborn. The Blanquists sided with the anti-Marxist minority within the Communist League and Marx and Engels (and the Chartist Harney) denounced the statutes in October, 1850.[3] But the phrase "dictatorship of the proletariat" had now been identified with Karl Marx and his ideas.

The problem is Marx did not mean dictatorship when he said dictatorship. Even in his *Class Struggles in France*, which was written during the bitter months in early 1850, the term is used so as to be compatible, even identified, with democracy. "The *constitutional republic*,"[4] Marx wrote of the peasants, "is the dictatorship of their united exploiters; the *social democratic* red republic is the dictatorship of their allies."[5] In each case, it is possible to have a republic, and in the latter instance, a social democratic republic, which is also a dictatorship.

Such a paradoxical definition makes no sense in contemporary vocabulary. It makes, however, a good deal of sense when it is understood within the framework of Marx's thought. Sidney Hook brilliantly clarified this point in *Towards the Understanding of Karl Marx*. In Marx, Hook writes, "wherever we find a state we find a dictatorship."[6] In the Marxian analysis, the state is necessary only in a class society of inequality where the struggle over scarce resources is organized—by force, if necessary—to favor the ruling class. Therefore the most libertarian of bourgeois democracies is a dictatorship in the sense that the economic wealth and power of the rich contradicts the theoretical political equality of all citizens. For economic power is political power, and under capitalism, the means of production are always concentrating and falling under the control of an ever smaller elite. "Dictatorship" then defined the class basis of a society, not its political forms, and it did not necessarily imply the repression of civil liberties.

Thus it was that Engels, who also proclaimed his belief in the dictatorship of the proletariat, was against any form of minority rule. In 1874 he analyzed the French ultra-Leftists: "Given Blanqui's conception of the revolution as the work of a small, revolutionary minority, it followed necessarily that there would be a dictatorship after the revolution; *not, to be sure, the dictatorship of the entire class of the proletariat*, but of that small number who made the surprise attack and who are themselves organized under the dictatorship of

2. *Werke*, VII, p. 553.
3. Ibid., p. 45.
4. *Werke*, VII, p. 33.
5. Ibid., p. 84.
6. Sidney Hook, *Towards the Understanding of Karl Marx* (New York: The John Day Company, 1933), pp. 300ff.

one individual or of a few members of a small group."[7] (Emphasis added.)

But it was in Marx's and Engels' description of the Paris Commune as a dictatorship that the uniqueness of their definition is most apparent. As Engels put it, "In opposition to the changes that had taken place under all previous forms of the state, where the servants of the society become its master, the Commune had two weapons. First of all, every position, be it administrative, judicial or educational, was filled by universal suffrage of the people and was subject to immediate recall by the same people. And secondly, all official jobs, high or low, were paid at the same wages as the workers received."[8] Thus "dictatorship" equals universal suffrage, immediate recallability of all officials and a working-class wage for the bureaucracy. What is "dictatorial" about the situation is that the property forms of the society now systematically favor the workers as they once—even in democratic republics—discriminated on behalf of the bourgeoisie.

So "dictatorship" does not mean dictatorship but the fulfillment of democracy. The tragic problem is that the scholar can follow the subtlety of the Marxian analysis, but the activist in the street—and the dictator occupying the seat of power—tend to take the word at its most obvious, and brutal, meaning. It is in this way that Marxism has become identified with anti-democratic repression.

* * *

It was in the fall of 1850 that events forced Marx and Engels to reverse themselves once again. They abandoned that ultra-Leftist intransigence that had led them to their brief flirtation with Blanqui's conspiratorial ideas. But even more important, they had made a decisive turn toward deepening their democratic vision of socialism.

The Revolution of 1848, Marx argued, had been created by the depression of 1837–1842, the speculative crisis of 1846 and the failure of the potato harvest and the consequent hunger in Ireland. Prosperity had returned to England in 1848, and in 1849 there was a great spurt in the cotton industry. This helped the Germans and the French as well as the English, and the discovery of gold in California gave even more encouragement to the system. Marx concluded, "Given this general prosperity in which the productive power of bourgeois society develops itself as much as it can within the framework of bourgeois relations, there can be no talk of revolution."[9]

7. *Werke,* XVIII, p. 529.
8. *Werke,* XVII, p. 624.
9. *Werke,* VIII, pp. 412–13.

The Communist League split over Marx's new analysis. Two leaders of the organization, Willich and Schapper, continued to defend the old position. Marx charged, "In the place of critical analysis, the minority is dogmatic. It is idealist, not materialist. Instead of making living relationships the driving force of the revolution, they appeal to *pure will.* While we say to the workers, 'You have fifteen, twenty, or fifty years of civil war and popular struggle to carry out, not only to change the relationships but to change yourself and enable yourself to rule politically,' they say 'We must either come to power or we might as well go to sleep.'"[1]

In March, 1850, Marx had called for insurrection and "permanent revolution."[2] Six months later he stoically contemplated the possibility that it would take half a century of struggle before socialism would triumph and insisted, in profound contrast to the Blanquists and other conspirators, that the workers had to change not only political and economic relationships, but themselves as well. * * *

BERTRAM D. WOLFE

Democracy and Dictatorship in 1848†

Marx and Engels became revolutionists in Germany under the influence of the ideas of the French Revolution, which they devoutly hoped was about to repeat itself on a more advanced scale. Their hearts were possessed by the dream of Babeuf: "The French Revolution is the precursor of another, more significant revolution, which will be the last." It was through the distorting prism and many-colored spectrum of that dream that Marx beheld the uprisings of 1848. He was, so to speak, an advocate of a French Revolution for Germany, and then, for all Europe. * * *

When Marx got to Paris in 1844, the word *dictatorship* itself was a term in flux, being used in various contexts with varying meanings. Today we have tended to settle on one of those meanings: we regard dictatorship as a synonym for permanent dictatorship, personal dictatorship, autocracy, despotism, tyranny, absolutism, authoritarianism, or totalitarianism. That is a wide range, yet all these uses imply some form of permanent and uncontrolled autocratic rule, a meaning quite different from that which prevailed throughout much of recorded history.

1. *Werke*, VIII, p. 575.
2. *Werke*, VIII, pp. 589–90.
† From *Marxism: One Hundred Years in the Life of a Doctrine* (New York: Dial Press, 1965), pp. 168–82.

"Dictatorship," Lenin said on December 5, 1919, in a moment of frankness, "is a harsh, heavy, and even bloody word." He did not shrink from exercising it in that spirit. When he wrote from the vantage point of power (on October 20, 1920), "the scientific concept *dictatorship* means nothing more nor less than unrestricted power, not limited by anything, not restrained by any laws, nor by any absolute rules, and resting directly upon force, *that, and nothing else but that,* is the meaning of the concept, dictatorship,"—Lenin may not have been as "scientific" as he thought, but he was fully in accord with the semantic uses of our day, expressing them with marvelous precision and clarity. But the usage of our day, as I have suggested, is one quite different from that which prevailed when the term was first conceived, and throughout much of its subsequent history.

The term *dictatura* is of course Latin. It originated in the early Roman Republic, where it had a long and honorable life as a way of designating a temporary-emergency delegation of power by the Republic to a trusted servant, to meet a crisis requiring special unity, unusual energy, and exceptionally complete mobilization of the forces of the Republic. The dictatorship of the Roman Republic was distinguished by a number of features which our present usage has lost, features which make it in many ways the direct opposite of Lenin's "scientific" definition:

(1) It was constitutional. The constitution provided for this office in emergencies, defined the qualifications of those who might be chosen and the limits of their powers.

(2) It was temporary. The period of a dictatorship was a maximum of six months, but the dictator surrendered his powers earlier if the emergency ended.

(3) The dictator had control of the army, and the power of life and death. He could abrogate the laws and the ordinary rights of citizens, as Lincoln did the right of *habeas corpus* during the Civil War. But he could not make *new* laws, alter the constitution permanently, or even touch the treasury, without the authorization of the proper constitutional body.

(4) When he surrendered his powers he was accountable for any arbitrary and unjust use he might have made of them.

(5) The dictatorship system worked for three centuries—until it was abolished by that permanent and self-chosen dictator, the Roman imperator or emperor, raised to absolute power on the shields of his legions. With its death died the Republic. But as long as the Republic lived, dictatorship stayed within the republican, constitutional, legal framework, and did not degenerate into tyranny.

Thus the classic Roman Republican *dictatura* corresponds not to the modern dictatorial régime, but to the modern institutions of temporary *state of siege*, proclamation of *martial law* in a distress area, or some other form of *crisis-and-emergency government.* These make the same constitutional assumptions as the *dictatura* of the Roman Republic, namely, that they can abrogate certain rights for an emergency period, but can neither make new law nor destroy these rights permanently. "Not only is this consistent with democracy, but when directed against a power conceived of as threatening liberty, it appears as the very shield and buckler of democracy."[1]

When the French revolutionists, both those of 1789 and those of 1848, wrapped themselves in Roman togas, it was in this sense that they at first used the term, *dictatura.* But, in an age of continuous revolution, terms and institutions change continually, acquiring ever new meanings. Alongside of, and displacing each other, arose the *dictatorship of the Convention*, the *dictatorship of the Commune of Paris*, the *dictatorship of the Committee of Public Safety*, and the *dictatorship of Robespierre.* * * *

Marx first used the term *dictatorship of the proletariat* * * * in March 1850 in his *Class Struggles in France 1848–50.* In that work, and the next one, *The Eighteenth Brumaire of Louis Napoleon*, he also uses the term dictatorship in five other contexts and different senses. He speaks of the dictatorship delegated temporarily to Cavaignac to crush the insurrection of the workingmen of Paris in June 1848. This is a temporary, military, or state-of-siege dictatorship exercised *by* bourgeois society "by means of the saber," but not a dictatorship "by the saber" *over* bourgeois society. It is also a dictatorship of a representative body, namely of the Constituent Assembly, which has delegated this power to Cavaignac. Next, Marx speaks of the successive stages in the dictatorship of Louis Napoleon. When he is elected President, he represents "the legislative dictatorship of the united royalists . . . the parliamentary dictatorship of the Party of Order," *and* "the dictatorship of the bourgeoisie." When the bourgeoisie, however, repudiates universal suffrage, it openly confesses, according to Marx, that:

> Our dictatorship has hitherto existed by the will of the people; it must now be consolidated against the will of the people.[2]

Thereby, the dictatorship of the bourgeoisie brings about its own downfall; the Emperor becomes an irresponsible dictator *over society and over the bourgeoisie.*

1. H. Draper, *Marx and the Dictatorship of the Proletariat*, in *Etudes de Marxicologie* no. 6 p. 7. On the nature of the Roman Republican dictatorship see any standard history of Rome.
2. Marx and Engels, *Werke*, ed. Institute for Marxism-Lennism of the Central Committee of the Socialist Unity [Communist] Party of the German Democratic Republic (Berlin: Dietz, 1956–68) Vol. VII, p. 93.

Thus Marx has successively recognized that there is the possibility of *a class* dictatorship, of the dictatorship of *a representative institution*, and of the dictatorship of *an individual*, which may be delegated, temporary and limited, or may be permanent and unlimited. It is only in this last case that it becomes a true despotism, raising the state over society and the autocracy of the Emperor over the class or classes that raised him to power, and over society as a whole.

If we turn from Marx's use of the term dictatorship in general to his use of the term in connection with his predilect class, the proletariat, we find that Marx, and with him Engels, normally use not dictatorship (*Diktatur*) but rule (*Herrschaft*). There are two brief periods in Marx's life, 1850–51, and 1872–75, when Marx several times replaces *Herrschaft* by *Diktatur*. And there is a third period, long after Marx's death, when Engels employs the word *Diktatur* in 1890–91 in some retrospective musings on the period from 1872–75. This substitution of one term for the other or their simultaneous use for short periods raises a number of ambiguities for us and for the heirs.

Are the terms synonymous? Were there any special reasons for using one term in preference to the other several times during two brief periods of their lives? Did the term come into Marx's vocabulary from his association with Blanqui? Was it Blanqui's term or Marx's? Was *Diktatur des Proletariats* the dictatorship of a class? of a party claiming to speak for that class? of a conspirative élite?

Was it merely a *Woertchen*, an unimportant little word that Marx let slip once or twice, as Kautsky maintained? Or was it what he meant all along, but only occasionally translated from German into Latin, as Lenin maintained? Is it a synonym for the "democratic rule of the immense majority in the interests of the immense majority," a synonym which, however, puts emphasis on the *energetic character* of the measures taken by that rule to maintain itself and to establish a new political constitution, or a "new social order"? Or is it the dictatorship of a single party, then of its leading committee, then of a single infallible interpreter of its infallible doctrine, as Lenin, Stalin, and Khrushchev have conceived it?

In the earliest of their joint political writings, the "German Ideology," 1845–46, Marx and Engels wrote:

> . . . every class which is struggling for rule (*Herrschaft*), even when its rule, as in the case of the proletariat, postulates the abolition of the old form of society in its entirety and the abolition of *Herrschaft* itself, must first conquer for itself political power. . . . [3]

3. MEGA. I/5, p. 23. It is interesting to note how the word *Herrschaft* has been translated in this passage by R. Pascal for the International Publishers translation, New York, 1947, p. 23: ". . . every class which is struggling for *mastery*, even when its *domination*, as is the case with the proletariat, postulates the abolition of *mastery* itself, must first

A year before the *Communist Manifesto* was published, Engels wrote for a German-language journal in Brussels:

> The Communists, far from starting useless quarrels with the Democrats . . . themselves prefer at present to take a stand as democrats in all practical party matters. Democracy brings with it in all civilized lands the political rule (*Herrschaft*) of the proletariat as a necessary consequence, and the political rule of the proletariat is the first prerequisite for all Communist measures. As long as democracy has not been won therefore, Communists and Democrats fight side by side, and the interests of the Democrats are also the interests of the Communists.[4]

This conviction that universal suffrage and other democratic institutions would inevitably mean the victory of the proletariat or the Communists in their struggle for power, was to remain with Marx and Engels all their lives, growing stronger in their last years. It was inconceivable to them that the proletariat, once it had the vote and formed the majority of the population, should fail to vote for the dismantling of the existing order and its replacement by a new *system* called socialism.

When Marx and Engels were working on the *Communist Manifesto*, Engels's main contribution was a rough draft in the form of a Communist Catechism, known as *Grundsätze des Kommunismus* (Principles of Communism). The eighteenth question reads: "What will be the course of development of this revolution?" Engels answers:

> First of all it will establish a *democratic constitution*, and thereby, directly or indirectly, the rule of the proletariat. Directly in England, where the proletariat are already a majority of the population. Indirectly in France and Germany, where the majority of the people consists not of proletarians alone, but also of small peasants and petty bourgeois, who are just beginning to be caught up in a transition to proletarians and to become more and more dependent on the proletariat in all their political interests, and must therefore soon adapt themselves to the demands of the proletariat. Perhaps this may cost a second struggle, which however can only end with the victory of the proletariat.
>
> Democracy will be useless to the proletariat if it does not use it immediately as a means to the realization of measures directly attacking private property and making secure the existence of the proletariat.[5]

---

conquer for itself political power. . . ." Each of the three terms I have italicized is expressed in German by the word *Herrschaft*. [For MEGA, see p. 59, dagger note—*Editor*.]

4. MEGA. I/6, p. 289.

5. Ibid., p. 514. See also pp. 101–102, n. 5 in this volume [*Editor*].

Clearly, then, the word *Herrschaft*, or rule, of the proletariat, signifies to Marx and Engels a democratic government of the working class, or the working class and those small proprietors, etc. who are being driven into the ranks. Further, it is a government which will be *energetic* in its own defense, in its attacks upon private property and on the existence of the old "ruling classes." It is, moreover, given the limited suffrage of that day, a government not likely to be achieved by democratic process but by a pro-democratic revolution.

In the *Communist Manifesto* this proposition is expressed by Marx in the following language:

> All previous historical movements were movements of minorities, or in the interest of minorities. The proletarian movement is the self-conscious, independent movement of the immense majority. The proletariat, the lowest stratum of our present society, cannot stir, cannot raise itself up, without the whole superincumbent strata of official society being sprung into air.
> . . . the first step in the revolution by the working class is to raise the proletariat to the position of the ruling class, to win the battle of democracy.

When Marx and Engels got back to Germany in 1848, although it was a Germany in insurrection, they did not find it ripe for the rule of the working class. Hence, when Marx put on the masthead of the *Neue Rheinische Zeitung* the words, "Organ of Democracy," he was not merely trying to conciliate his financial backers and stockholders. He was also, he thought, adjusting his aim to the realities and possibilities of the moment, which obliged him and his handful of disciples to conceal the "proletarian" program he had just drafted, and to back, encourage, and drive forward, the "bourgeois" democratic movement then on the march in Germany. So far did this concealment or tactical reticence go that he made no reference to and used no formulation from the *Communist Manifesto*, and made no use either of sixteen of the seventeen points contained in a circular just drafted by him as an address of the Communist League to the German workingmen. Only the first point, "All Germany is declared a single, indivisible republic," was of any use to him as the editor of the German "Organ of Democracy." When Engels wrote him from Barmen:

> The mood of the bourgeoisie is really despicable. The workers are beginning to move a little, still very crudely, but on a mass scale. They immediately formed unions. But that certainly doesn't suit *us*.[6]

---

6. Engels to Marx, April 25, 1848. *Collected Works*, volume 38, p. 173 [*Editor*].

Marx agreed. In fact, the NRZ published no reports whatsoever about the labor movement and its activities.[7]

To have called then for the as yet unformed German working class to take power, Marx felt, would be a fruitless exercise in self-isolation, and a way of frightening the bourgeoisie away from the revolutionary role history had assigned to it.[8] Hence he called on the liberal and democratic "middle class" to take power and use their rule energetically to make a clean sweep of the old régime, to make a French Revolution in Germany.

What infuriated Marx, and rightly so, was the lack of energy, courage, and understanding of what to destroy and what to build, shown by the majority of the democratic Frankfurt Assembly, which the insurrections of 1848 had called into being. The Assembly suffered from "parliamentary cretinism," timid constitutional prejudices and illusions. It was voluntarily donning the straitjacket of the old constitution which reaction and counterrevolution were using to prepare the dispersal of the new Assembly itself. What was needed, Marx wrote, was "a revolution which had first to establish constitutional principles of its own."

> Every provisional state set up after a revolution requires a dictatorship and an energetic dictatorship at that. From the beginning we have reproached Camphausen [the Premier designated by the Frankfurt Assembly] for not acting dictatorially, for not immediately shattering and eliminating the remnants of old institutions.[9]

Thus once more Marx speaks of, and calls for, a "revolutionary dictatorship" of a democratic institution, a representative body, to be exercised by an agent responsible to it. Once more dictatorship and democracy are not opposites but dictatorship is an energetic way of action by the new democratic institutions to abolish the old undemocratic ones, and to safeguard the new democracy's own existence and extension. Only a dictatorship of "the bourgeoisie" and of its democratic representative assembly could save democracy and the

7. The letter of Engels is *MEGA*, III/1, p. 100. The authority for the statement that NRZ published nothing about the labor movement is Franz Mehring, both in his biography of Marx, p. 189, and in a special study for *Archiv für die Geschichte des Sozialismus und der Arbeiterbewegung*, Vol. 1, p. 119, where he explains that "Socialist theory and even the proletarian class struggle still greatly receded behind the revolutionary struggle of the German nation against the reactionary classes." His "German nation" or "German people" (*Volk*) gives a sounder picture of the variegated movement than does Marx's class term, *bourgeoisie*.
8. Marx was inclined to distinguish between a class which exists *in itself* (*an sich*) and the same class as existing *for itself* (*für sich*). The first was a physical or objective fact, the second a matter of the class having become conscious of its existence, its interests, and its role in history. See *The Essential Writings*, pp. 238–39. In 1848 Marx found the German working class unformed even in the first sense.
9. *MEGA*, I/7, pp. 361–62.

German Revolution. Since such energy was lacking, the revolution failed.

With these uses of the word dictatorship in mind—as the dictatorship of a class, as the dictatorship of a democratic assembly, as a dictatorship temporarily entrusted to its commissioners, as energetic rule consistent with Marx's idea of democracy—we can now examine his use of the term in connection with the proletariat.

All through the stormy years 1848 and '49, Marx continued to speak of the rule (*Herrschaft*) of the proletariat. Only in March 1850 . . . , when the tide had ebbed but Marx would not admit it to himself, did he for the first time employ the term *dictatorship of the proletariat*. And the first use of *Diktatur* was in a passage dedicated to Blanqui as the incarnation of revolutionary socialism. Let us examine more closely the passage in *Class Struggles in France* in which this seeming identification of the name of Blanqui with the dictatorship of the proletariat occurs:

> the proletariat groups itself more and more around *revolutionary socialism*, around *communism*, for which the bourgeoisie itself has invented the name *Blanqui*. This socialism is the *declaration of the revolution in permanence*, the *class dictatorship* of the proletariat as a necessary transition point to the *abolition of class differences altogether*, to the abolition of all the productive relations on which they rest, of all social relations which correspond to these production relationships, the transformation of all ideas which arise from these social relationships.

*   *   *

[W]hen Marx wrote it, he was entering into his *Association* with the Blanquists; he was agreeing to, or more probably he was writing, virtually the same formula into the joint statement of principles; he was issuing his peculiarly "Blanquist" *Circular*; and he was using Blanquist conspirators as emissaries to the branches of the Communist League.

On the other hand * * * even at his most "Blanquist," Marx was not for the revolutionary dictatorship of a conspirative élite of professional revolutionaries, but, as he himself underlines, for a "*class dictatorship* of the proletariat."

But at the moment the two formulas looked suspiciously alike. The proletariat in Paris was beaten. The proletariat in Germany was unformed, so that Marx had worked there with the Liberals and Democrats of other classes. The "Universal Association" in practice looked more like a Blanquist conspiracy than like the rising of a class. It was led by a conspiratorial elite of self-chosen "professional revolutionaries," for, though they did not use the word, that is what they were. Blanqui was indifferent to the workers' organizations as such while there were elements of Marx's doctrinal theories which even then pointed at the future labor movement and the working class as the repositories of socialist doctrine, as the class destined to rule, and by its revolutionary dictatorship, to keep the revolution going in permanence until society had been completely transformed.

Thus at the moment when Marx was joining forces with the Blanquists and proclaiming his unstinting admiration for the old conspirator, there were two things they possessed in common and one which separated them: Marx had acquired from Blanqui his formula of the "revolution in permanence" and an intensification of his penchant for a "revolutionary dictatorship." But he was not able then, nor during their second united front after the Paris Commune, to persuade the Blanquists of the importance of the working class or the need for the revolutionary dictatorship to be a class dictatorship of the proletariat. As a matter of fact, in 1872 Marx was to spend many days and nights expounding this idea to the Blanquists in London. His lectures briefly "infected" their proclamations, but then for the second time he broke with Blanquist formulas for the social revolution, and they dropped their interest, always superficial, in the working-class movement and the formula of the dictatorship of the proletariat. The formula disappeared from his writings and from theirs within a year or a little more.

Neither united front with the Blanquists lasted very long. Actually, the "Universal Association" never really got going in 1850; within a few months Marx quarreled both with the Blanquists and with the spirit of "the permanent revolution" in his own organization. By September he had come to the conclusion, although he never acknowledged it as his own error, that the Communist League was living in a dream world and playing with conspiracies to bring back the revolutionary atmosphere that fresh winds of prosperity had blown away.

In place of repudiating his own erroneous estimate he made the sharp attack on Willich and Schapper which we have already quoted, charging them with "dogmatism," an "idealistic" refusal to take account of "the real facts of the situation," a reliance on "naked revolutionary will," a refusal to wait for the working class to mature and a new objective revolutionary situation to ripen. It is this utterance of Marx that is the take-off point for "mature Marxism," for what Engels was to christen "scientific socialism," and in general, for the orthodox Marxist, non-Leninist claimants to the heritage.

* * *

In retrospect Marx and Engels * * * attribute the uprisings of 1848–49 one-sidedly to an economic crisis, ignoring or greatly underestimating the national tensions and discontents, the growth of democratic movements and conspiracies, the various socialist currents in Paris that had played so large a formative role in the fashioning of the doctrines of Marx himself. This new emphasis on the state of the economy as crucial to the "real facts of the situation" which determine the appropriateness and timeliness of political actions, conspiracies, uprisings, expectations of proletarian rule or proletarian dictatorship. * * * The key passage on the relation of politics to economics is the following:

> In view of the general prosperity which now prevails and permits the productive forces of bourgeois society to develop as luxuriantly (*üppig*) as is possible within the limits of bourgeois relationships, there can be no question of a real revolution. Such a revolution is possible only in a period in which these *two factors*, the *modern productive forces* and the *bourgeois forms of production*, have come into *conflict* with each other. . . . A *new revolution* is only possible as a result of a new crisis. *But the former is also just as certain as the latter.*[1]

With this, the interests of Marx and Engels shifted to the scrutiny of the economy of England, "the demiurge of the bourgeois cosmos." The great expansion of the productive forces of society by the bourgeoisie which the *Communist Manifesto* had celebrated so eloquently had not reached its end then, as the *Manifesto* had assumed.

* * *

With this discovery that "bourgeois society is still in the ascendant,"[2] the rift in Marxism between the sense of fatality and the exaltation of the omnipotence of the revolutionary will to change the world, became complete—or as complete as the irreducible revolutionary passion in Marx's temperament could make it. As early as September 1850, when the two friends split with the Communist League, and November 1850, when they published their *Revue*, the isolation of Marx and Engels was complete.

Reluctantly, Engels left London for Manchester, where he joined his father's textile firm once more, this time sticking with it until he became its director. And with distaste and rage, Marx began the long mole's work of burrowing through the mounds of economic literature to find the nature and probabilities of crises, the conditions and "law of motion" which, in spite of everything, must one day put revolution once more on the order of the day, and, this time, make its triumph inevitable. In place of trying to run a revolution that

1. *Werke,* VII, p. 440.
2. Letter of Marx to Engels, Oct. 8, 1858. *MEGA* III/2, p. 342.

was no longer there, he began to dig a scientific tunnel—a tunnel through modern industrial or "capitalist" society, at the end of which he hoped to see the daylight of the social revolution. The task was still unfinished when death came.

* * *

As we read Marx's savage utterances in public documents, his strictures on bourgeoisie and petty bourgeoisie, on bourgeois democrats and petty bourgeois democrats, on republicans and socialists, all of them portrayed as lacking in revolutionary spirit, consistency, courage, understanding of their "tasks" and their "role in history"; as we add to the published discussion of the immaturity of the German workingmen the harsher and more contemptuous judgments of Marx and Engels on their own "communist élite" in letters to each other written during the '48 period—all this testimony adds up to an overwhelming proof

> that in Germany there was neither a bourgeoisie nor a proletariat in the ideal-typical form and full development of antagonisms such as the *Communist Manifesto* had assumed.[3]

Actually, the stormy year 1848 produced neither a bourgeois revolution nor a proletarian revolution nor a revolution in permanence. It proved to be a great and contagious explosion of nationalism and democracy (only in Paris did the workingmen give it a somewhat different character with their demand for a guaranteed right to work and national workshops), and it was followed by dynastic, absolutist and bureaucratic counterrevolution rather than "feudal" reaction.

Thus the *Communist Manifesto* was a stirring fantasy in the French manner, with little relationship to the actual events of 1848 or the subsequent history of Germany and Europe. Marx himself put it on ice when he went to Germany in 1848. By the autumn of 1850, he was excoriating (with Willich and Schapper as the targets) his theory of the imminent petit-bourgeois democratic revolution and the proletarian revolution in permanence. With that ended the first heroic, or romantic, period of Marxism, and the more patient and less dramatic heroism of "scientific investigation" engaged his powerful mind.

Yet, as a fantasy seductive in its inner coherence, strong in the impact of its aphorisms and slogans, memorable in its phrasing, and most memorable in its dream of a Utopia bedecked in the parti-colored raiments of science and prophecy, the *Communist Manifesto*

3. Werner Blumenberg, *Karl Marx: In Selbstzeugnissen und Bilddokumenten* (Hamburg, 1962), p. 87.

continued to possess the imagination of millions in coming generations. So, too, the *Circular* on extremist tactics and revolution in permanence more unreal than the *Manifesto*, issued in March of 1850
and recalled and condemned by its author that same summer, was
to provide the chief stock-in-trade of Trotsky and Lenin in the twentieth century. Nothing makes so manifest the ambiguities in the
heritage and the ambiguities in the heirs than the contrast in the
fate of those two documents in the hands of their progenitor, and in
the hands of the rival claimants to the legacy.

THE
COMMUNIST MANIFESTO
IN THE HISTORY OF
MARXISM

EDUARD BERNSTEIN

[Revising the *Communist Manifesto*]†

* * *

I set myself against the notion that we have to expect shortly a collapse of the bourgeois economy, and that social democracy should
be induced by the prospect of such an imminent, great, social
catastrophe to adapt its tactics to that assumption. That I maintain
most emphatically.

The adherents of this theory of a catastrophe, base it especially
on the conclusions of the *Communist Manifesto*. This is a mistake
in every respect.

The theory which the *Communist Manifesto* sets forth of the evolution of modern society was correct as far as it characterised the
general tendencies of that evolution. But it was mistaken in several
special deductions, above all in the estimate of the *time* the evolution would take. The last has been unreservedly acknowledged by
Friedrich Engels, the joint author with Marx of the *Manifesto*, in
his preface to the *Class War in France*. But it is evident that if social
evolution takes a much greater period of time than was assumed, it
must also take upon itself *forms* and lead to forms that were not
foreseen and could not be foreseen then.

Social conditions have not developed to such an acute opposition of
things and classes as is depicted in the *Manifesto*. It is not only useless, it is the greatest folly to attempt to conceal this from ourselves.
The number of members of the possessing classes is today not smaller
but larger. The enormous increase of social wealth is not accompanied by a decreasing number of large capitalists but by an increasing number of capitalists of all degrees. The middle classes change
their character but they do not disappear from the social scale.

* * *

In all advanced countries we see the privileges of the capitalist
bourgeoisie yielding step by step to democratic organisations.
Under the influence of this, and driven by the movement of the
working classes which is daily becoming stronger, a social reaction
has set in against the exploiting tendencies of capital, a counterac-
tion which, although it still proceeds timidly and feebly, yet does
exist, and is always drawing more departments of economic life
under its influence. Factory legislation, the democratising of local
government, and the extension of its area of work, the freeing of

† From *Evolutionary Socialism*, trans. Edith C. Harvey (1898; New York: B. W. Huebsch,
1909), pp. xxiv–ix.

trade unions and systems of co-operative trading from legal restrictions, the consideration of standard conditions of labour in the work undertaken by public authorities—all these characterise this phase of the evolution.

But the more the political organisations of modern nations are democratised the more the needs and opportunities of great political catastrophes are diminished. He who holds firmly to the catastrophic theory of evolution must, with all his power, withstand and hinder the evolution described above, which, indeed, the logical defenders of that theory formerly did. But is the conquest of political power by the proletariat simply to be by a political catastrophe? Is it to be the appropriation and utilisation of the power of the State by the proletariat exclusively against the whole non-proletarian world?

He who replies in the affirmative must be reminded of two things. In 1872 Marx and Engels announced in the preface to the new edition of the *Communist Manifesto* that the Paris Commune had exhibited a proof that "the working class cannot simply take possession of the ready-made State machine and set it in motion for their own aims." And in 1895 Friedrich Engels stated in detail in the preface to *War of the Classes*[1] that the time of political surprises, of the "revolutions of small conscious minorities at the head of unconscious masses" was today at an end, that a collision on a large scale with the military would be the means of checking the steady growth of social democracy and of even throwing it back for a time—in short, that social democracy would flourish far better by lawful than by unlawful means and by violent revolution. And he points out in conformity with this opinion that the next task of the party should be "to work for an uninterrupted increase of its votes" or to carry on a slow *propaganda of parliamentary activity.*

* * *

[I]f one subscribes to his conclusions, one cannot reasonably take any offence if it is declared that for a long time yet the task of social democracy is, instead of speculating on a great economic crash, "to organise the working classes politically and develop them as a democracy and to fight for all reforms in the State which are adapted to raise the working classes and transform the State in the direction of democracy."

* * *

No one has questioned the necessity for the working classes to gain the control of government. The point at issue is between the theory of a social cataclysm and the question whether with the given

1. Reference to Engels's preface to Marx's *The Class Struggles in France, 1848–1850* [*Editor*].

social development in Germany and the present advanced state of its working classes in the towns and the country, a sudden catastrophe would be desirable in the interest of the social democracy. I have denied it and deny it again, because in my judgment a greater security for lasting success lies in a steady advance than in the possibilities offered by a catastrophic crash.

*   *   *

In this sense I wrote the sentence that the movement means everything for me and that what is *usually* called "the final aim of socialism" is nothing; and in this sense I write it down again today.

*   *   *

V. I. LENIN

[The *Communist Manifesto* and the Revolutionary State][†]

The first works of mature Marxism—*The Poverty of Philosophy* and the *Communist Manifesto*—appeared just on the eve of the revolution of 1848. For this reason, in addition to presenting the general principles of Marxism, they reflect to a certain degree the concrete revolutionary situation of the time. It will, therefore, be more expedient, perhaps, to examine what the authors of these works said about the state immediately before they drew conclusions from the experience of the years 1848–51.

In *The Poverty of Philosophy*, Marx wrote:

> The working class, in the course of development, will substitute for the old bourgeois society an association which will preclude classes and their antagonism, and there will be no more political power proper, since political power is precisely the official expression of class antagonism in bourgeois society.[1]

It is instructive to compare this general exposition of the idea of the state disappearing after the abolition of classes with the exposition contained in the *Communist Manifesto*, written by Marx and Engels a few months later—in November 1847, to be exact:

> . . . In depicting the most general phases of the development of the proletariat, we traced the more or less veiled civil war, raging

[†] From *The State and Revolution, Collected Works* (Moscow: Progress Publishers, 1964) 25, pp. 401–6.
1. *Marx-Engels Collected Works* (New York: International Publishers, 1971–) 6, p. 212 [*Editor*].

> within existing society up to the point where that war breaks
> out into open revolution, and where the violent overthrow of
> the bourgeoisie lays the foundation for the sway of the
> proletariat . . .
>
>   . . . We have seen above that the first step in the revolution by
> the working class is to raise the proletariat to the position of
> ruling class, to win the battle of democracy.
>
>   The proletariat will use its political supremacy to wrest, by
> degrees, all capital from the bourgeoisie, to centralise all instru-
> ments of production in the hands of the state, i.e., of the prole-
> tariat organised as the ruling class; and to increase the total of
> productive forces as rapidly as possible.

Here we have a formulation of one of the most remarkable and
most important ideas of Marxism on the subject of the state, namely,
the idea of the "dictatorship of the proletariat" (as Marx and Engels
began to call it after the Paris Commune); and also, a highly interesting definition of the state, which is also one of the "forgotten words"
of Marxism: *the state, i.e., the proletariat organised as the ruling class.*

This definition of the state has never been explained in the prevailing propaganda and agitation literature of the official Social-
Democratic parties. More than that, it has been deliberately ignored,
for it is absolutely irreconcilable with reformism, and is a slap in the
face for the common opportunist prejudices and philistine illusions
about the "peaceful development of democracy."

The proletariat needs the state—this is repeated by all the oppor-
tunists, social-chauvinists and Kautskyites,[2] who assure us that this
is what Marx taught. But they "*forget*" to add that, in the first place,
according to Marx, the proletariat needs only a state which is withering away, i.e., a state so constituted that it begins to wither away
immediately, and cannot but wither away. And, secondly, the working
people need a "state, i.e., the proletariat organised as the ruling class."

The state is a special organisation of force: it is an organisation of
violence for the suppression of some class. What class must the proletariat suppress? Naturally, only the exploiting class, i.e., the bourgeoisie. The working people need the state only to suppress the
resistance of the exploiters, and only the proletariat can direct this
suppression, can carry it out. For the proletariat is the only class
that is consistently revolutionary, the only class that can unite all
the working and exploited people in the struggle against the bourgeoisie, in completely removing it.

The exploiting classes need political rule to maintain exploitation,
i.e., in the selfish interests of an insignificant minority against the
vast majority of the people. The exploited classes need political rule
in order to completely abolish all exploitation, i.e., in the interests of

2. Followers of the leader of German Social Democracy, Karl Kautsky (1854–1938).

the vast majority of the people, and against the insignificant minority consisting of the modern slave-owners—the landowners and capitalists.

The petty-bourgeois democrats, those sham socialists who replaced the class struggle by dreams of class harmony, even pictured the socialist transformation in a dreamy fashion—not as the overthrow of the rule of the exploiting class, but as the peaceful submission of the minority to the majority which has become aware of its aims. This petty-bourgeois utopia, which is inseparable from the idea of the state being above classes, led in practice to the betrayal of the interests of the working classes, as was shown, for example, by the history of the French revolutions of 1848 and 1871, and by the experience of "socialist" participation in bourgeois Cabinets in Britain, France, Italy and other countries at the turn of the century.

All his life Marx fought against this petty-bourgeois socialism, now revived in Russia by the Socialist-Revolutionary and Menshevik parties. He developed his theory of the class struggle consistently, down to the theory of political power, of the state.

The overthrow of bourgeois rule can be accomplished only by the proletariat, the particular class whose economic conditions of existence prepare it for this task and provide it with the possibility and the power to perform it. While the bourgeoisie break up and disintegrate the peasantry and all the petty-bourgeois groups, they weld together, unite and organise the proletariat. Only the proletariat—by virtue of the economic role it plays in large-scale production—is capable of being the leader of *all* the working and exploited people, whom the bourgeoisie exploit, oppress and crush, often not less but more than they do the proletarians, but who are incapable of waging an *independent* struggle for their emancipation.

The theory of the class struggle, applied by Marx to the question of the state and the socialist revolution, leads as a matter of course to the recognition of the *political rule* of the proletariat, of its dictatorship, i.e., of undivided power directly backed by the armed force of the people. The overthrow of the bourgeoisie can be achieved only by the proletariat becoming the *ruling class*, capable of crushing the inevitable and desperate resistance of the bourgeoisie, and of organising *all* the working and exploited people for the new economic system.

The proletariat needs state power, a centralised organisation of force, an organisation of violence, both to crush the resistance of the exploiters and to *lead* the enormous mass of the population—the peasants, the petty bourgeoisie, and semi-proletarians—in the work of organising a socialist economy.

By educating the workers' party, Marxism educates the vanguard of the proletariat, capable of assuming power and *leading the whole people* to socialism, of directing and organising the new system, of being the teacher, the guide, the leader of all the working and exploited people in organising their social life without the bourgeoisie and against the bourgeoisie. By contrast, the opportunism now prevailing trains the members of the workers' party to be the representatives of the better-paid workers, who lose touch with the masses, "get along" fairly well under capitalism, and sell their birthright for a mess of pottage, i.e., renounce their role as revolutionary leaders of the people against the bourgeoisie.

Marx's theory of "the state, i.e., the proletariat organised as the ruling class," is inseparably bound up with the whole of his doctrine of the revolutionary role of the proletariat in history. The culmination of this role is the proletarian dictatorship, the political rule of the proletariat.

But since the proletariat needs the state as a *special* form of organisation of violence *against* the bourgeoisie, the following conclusion suggests itself: is it conceivable that such an organisation can be created without first abolishing, destroying the state machine created by the bourgeoisie *for themselves?* The *Communist Manifesto* leads straight to this conclusion, and it is of this conclusion that Marx speaks when summing up the experience of the revolution of 1848–51.

*   *   *

MAX ADLER

Socialism and Communism†

"A spectre is haunting Europe—the spectre of Communism." With these words, the classic basic text of modern socialism, the *Communist Manifesto*, begins, thereby giving penetrating expression to how much the old powers of bourgeois society were struck dumb with anxiety and depression by the great historical fact of the awakening and strengthening in the proletariat of the ideas of class struggle and socialism. Since then, the *Communist Manifesto* has increasingly become the immovable foundation of the great proletarian emancipation struggle. Until quite recently, it would have been incomprehensible to any Social Democrat that it could occur to anyone to separate Social Democracy and Communism from one another, or even more to bring them into opposition. This was possible, to be sure, only through another monstrosity that completely violates the meaning of the *Communist Manifesto*; namely, that

† Forward to *Das kommunistische Manifest* (Vienna: Ignaz Brand, 1919), pp. 2–7. Translated from the German by Frederic L. Bender for this volume.

Communism has once again become not merely a spectre for the old exploiting and oppressing powers, but above all a spirit of confusion and dissension within the socialist proletariat itself. A special faction, which has broken off from the great mass of the social democratic proletariat, under the name of a "Communist Party," utilizes the consonance of this name with the title of the historically fundamental writing of modern socialism, to set up a barrier between itself and Social Democracy; as if the *Communist Manifesto* had not always been the authentic program of Social Democracy and Marx and Engels had not always been its great leaders.

The causes of this unnatural division in modern socialism can essentially be traced along three lines. It is chiefly a matter of the terrible disillusion that has been experienced by socialism through the failure of the [Second] International at the outbreak of the [First] World War. At that time, it became evident that this organism of Social Democracy, which appeared so powerful and revolutionary, did not have a matching spirit. The world-historical development of the last two decades, through which capitalism was translated into imperialism, has also not left the working class untouched. It is not possible to go into this process in detail here; let it suffice as an indication that in the wake of imperialistic development the resulting prosperity of production and sales created at first a situation favorable for the development of one kind of unionized struggle of the worker, through which the idea sprang up in many strata of the working class that its interests coincided with the furthering of the expansionary power politics of their national capitalist class. And this advocacy of a mere improvement of the working class within capitalist society was able to move all the more into the foreground, as it coincided with the idea that the economic strengthening of the working class is a necessary means to the realization of socialism. Only, this did not take into account that economic improvement could operate as such a means only *if it remained united with the revolutionary will to the overcoming of capitalist society*—and exactly this was endangered to the extreme through identification with imperialist economic policy. Thus, ways of thinking and feeling were cultivated in many layers of the proletariat, which were later designated during the World War as social patriotism and social imperialism. The failure of the International at the outbreak of the war, and the policy of carrying on to the end during the war—which was ultimately intensified to the ignominy of a policy of victory among the German majority party as well as by the majority parties of the countries of the *Entente*—was not a consequence of "betrayal by the leaders," but only an expression of the factual sentiment of the vast mass of the working class. The reaction to this fact was the rise of the Social Democratic Left in all the countries at war. This division was and is in reality a process of healing, in that it keeps alive the old revolutionary spirit of Marxist socialism, the idea of international class struggle, in the face of all nationalistic falsification and reformist superficialization. On the other hand, the pointed opposition between Communism and Social Democracy that resulted from that same need to combat social imperialist degeneration by no means brings about clarification; on the contrary, it can only create confusion. For since the Social Democratic Left is of course also communistic, the so-called Communist Party employs a completely unsuitable name to distinguish itself, a name behind which something quite different is concealed. They don't call themselves Communists, for example, because Social Democracy does not strive for communism, but because they wish to realize this by another path. This path, as we shall soon see, is the path of the Russian revolution, that is of Bolshevism. * * *

But it would not have been possible to promote the formation of a new party had it not been for the benefit of a great historical event. And this is the victory of the Bolshevik revolution in Russia. Because an entirely unique configuration of social relations coupled the overthrow of capitalism with the success of Bolshevik policies, and because these policies externally emerged as a pure workers' dictatorship, it henceforth appeared to the masses not only that the victory of socialism is possible in this way, but that it is attainable solely in this way. * * *

Thus, it is evident * * * that a so-called Communism whose essential program is to assume the dictatorship of the proletariat in the form of the Russian Soviet system of government is only a tactic, growing out of entirely unique local conditions, that passes itself off as the only revolutionary essence of socialism. Nothing in all this justifies the appropriation of the name of Communism for this special tactical direction. All the things that the so-called Communists put forward in their agitation—communism as the goal, class struggle as means, the destruction of the class state as the machine of capitalist oppression—are the old victorious ideas of revolutionary Social Democracy; only there they were not used as mere slogans, beyond space and time, but an account of their feasibility was also given. And the great delusion that is now being perpetrated on the working masses *is that two inseparable things, Communism and socialism, are being represented to them as separate: and two things which are very different, communism and Bolshevism, [are being represented] as one and the same.*

At bottom, the new style Communism is only an acute relapse into Utopian socialism. Only this is not the utopianism of the philosophers and moralists, but that of the ignorant mass man; and it is not the belief in the miracle of the counsel of reason and morality, but of the "counsel of councils."[1] It is a utopia that * * * breeds a dangerous self-deception in the masses about their strength and about the possibilities of their efforts. If the old utopianism was politically without power, but nevertheless progressive in its ideas, the new utopianism degenerates into a boundless cult of power through which it destroys the ideal recruiting ability of socialism. * * * Thus, it is not such stormy revolutionary demands and disputes that lead to socialism as a fact, but rather, and more than ever today with the influx of completely unripe masses, it is still the old Marxist way: *unceasing political and economic clarification, reform of consciousness*. This Marxist demand remains, as before, the genuine lever with which the old society will be overturned more radically than by machine guns and hand grenades, and by which communism will be built more securely than through terrorism. The *Communist Manifesto* has taken a determined step toward this reform of consciousness, and if its ideas and conceptions have become the common property of the working people, then a "Communist Party" may no longer be possible, but communism itself will be.

LEON TROTSKY

On the Ninetieth Anniversary of the *Communist Manifesto*†

* * * Already in the preface to the edition of 1872, Marx and Engels declare that, although certain parts of the *Manifesto* had become dated, they did not believe that they had the right to modify the original text, because in the course of the previous twenty-five years, the *Manifesto* had become a historical document. Since then, sixty-five more years have passed. Certain isolated parts of the *Manifesto* have slid still more into the past. We will strive * * * to present, in summary form * * * the ideas of the *Manifesto* that have conserved their force in full until today, and those that today have need of serious modification or complement.

1. The materialist conception of history discovered by Marx only shortly before the appearance of the *Manifesto*, and which is found applied in it with a perfect mastery, has completely resisted the trial of events and the blows of hostile criticism; it constitutes today one of the most precious instruments of human thought. All other interpretations of the historical process have lost [even] the least scientific

---

1. *I.e.*, of the *soviets* [*Editor*].
† From "90éme Anniversaire du *Manifeste communiste*," *Le Manifeste Communiste* (Brussels: Szatan, 1945), pp. 5–10. Trotsky wrote this piece in 1937. Translated from the French by Frederic L. Bender for this volume.

value. One can say, with assurance, that it is impossible today to be
not only a revolutionary militant, but even simply a politically literate
man, without adopting the materialist conception of history.

2. The first chapter of the *Manifesto* begins with the following
phrase: "the history of all hitherto existing society is the history of
class struggles."

This thesis, which constitutes the most important conclusion of
the materialist conception of history, has not delayed in itself becoming the object of the class struggle. The theory that replaced the
"common well-being," the "national unity," and the "eternal truths of
morality" by the struggle of material interests considered as the
motive force has sustained some particularly fierce attacks on the
part of reactionary hypocrites, doctrinaire liberals, and idealist
democrats. To these were added later, this time at the heart of the
workers' movement itself, the so-called revisionists,[1] i.e., the parti-
sans of the revision of Marxism in the spirit of the collaboration and
reconciliation of classes. Finally, in our era, the contemptible epig-
ones of the Communist International (the Stalinists) have taken the
same road: the politics of what is called the "popular fronts" follows
entirely from the negation of the laws of the class struggle. Nevertheless, it is the era of imperialism that, in pushing all the social contradictions to their extreme expression, constitutes the *theoretical*
triumph of the *Communist Manifesto*.

3. The anatomy of capitalism, as a definite stage of the economic
evolution of society, was explained by Marx in his *Capital* in complete form (1867). But already in the *Communist Manifesto* the
fundamental lines of the future analysis were traced firmly: recompense for socially necessary labor; the appropriation by the capitalists of surplus value; competition as the fundamental law of social
relations; the ruin of the middle classes, i.e., of the petty bourgeoisie
of the towns and the peasantry; the concentration of riches in the
hands of an ever smaller number of possessors, at one pole, and the
numerical growth of the proletariat at the other; the preparation of
the material and political conditions of the socialist regime.

4. The thesis of the *Manifesto* on the tendency of capitalism to
reduce the standard of living of the workers, and even to pauperize
them, has undergone a violent attack. The priests, professors, min-
isters, journalists, social-democratic theorists, and union chiefs
rise up against the theory of increasing "pauperization." They
invariably discover the growing well-being of the workers by passing off the workers' aristocracy as the proletariat, or by taking a
temporary tendency for the general tendency. In the meantime, the
most powerful evolution of capitalism, that of North America, has

1. An allusion to Edward Bernstein and his followers [*Editor*].

transformed millions of workers into paupers, provided for at the expense of government, municipal, or private charity.[2]

5. In opposition to the *Manifesto*, which described commercial-industrial crises as a series of growing catastrophes, the revisionists affirm that the national and international development of trusts guarantees the control of the market and leads gradually to the control of crises. It is true that the end of the past century and the beginning of the present one were distinguished by such an impetuous development that crises seemed to be only "accidental" lulls. But that epoch is irremediably gone. In the last analysis, the truth will be found on this question as well on the side of the *Manifesto*.

6. "The executive of the modern state is but a committee for managing the common affairs of the whole bourgeoisie." In this concentrated formulation, which appeared to the social-democratic leaders [to be] a journalistic paradox, is in reality contained the only scientific theory of the state. The democracy created by the bourgeoisie is not an empty shell that one may, as Bernstein and Kautsky once thought, fill peacefully with the desired class contents. Bourgeois democracy can serve only the bourgeoisie.

7. "Every class struggle is a political struggle." "This organization of the proletarians into a class, and consequently into a political party . . ." The trade unionists on the one side and the anarcho-syndicalists on the other have for a long time fled from the comprehension of these historical laws—and still try to escape them today. "Pure" trade unionism is receiving today a crushing blow in its principal refuge, the United States. Anarcho-syndicalism has sustained an irreparable defeat in its last citadel, Spain. On this question, the *Manifesto* has been equally correct.

8. The proletariat cannot conquer power within the legal framework enacted by the bourgeoisie. The Communists "openly declare that their ends can be attained only by the forcible overthrow of all existing social conditions." Reformism has tried to explain this thesis of the *Manifesto* by the immaturity of the movement then, and by an insufficient development of democracy. The fate of the Italian, German, and a long series of other "democracies" demonstrates that if anything was not ripe, it was the reformist ideas themselves.

9. In order to bring about the socialist transformation of society, the working class must concentrate in its hands power capable of smashing all the political obstacles on the way to the new order. The "proletariat organized as the ruling class" is the dictatorship [of the proletariat]. At the same time it is the only true proletarian democracy. Its extent and its depth depend on concrete historical conditions. The greater the number of states that take themselves upon

2. Written in the depths of America's Great Depression [*Editor*].

the path of the socialist revolution, the more the forms of the dictatorship will be free and flexible and the more the workers' democracy will be broad and deep.

10. The international development of capitalism implies the
international character of the proletarian revolution. "United action,
of the leading civilized countries at least, is one of the first conditions for the emancipation of the proletariat." The subsequent development of capitalism has so tightly bound to one another all the
parts of our planet, "civilized" and "uncivilized," that the problem of
the socialist revolution has completely and definitely assumed a
worldwide character. The Soviet bureaucracy has tried to liquidate
the *Manifesto* on this fundamental question. The Bonapartist degeneration of the Soviet state was a deadly illustration of the falsehood
of the theory of socialism in one country.[3]

11. "When, in the course of development, class distinctions have
disappeared, and all production has been concentrated in the hands
of a vast association of the whole nation, the public power will lose
its political character." Stated otherwise, the state withers away.
There remains society free from its straightjacket [*camisole*] of force.
This is socialism. The inverse theorem—the monstrous growth of
statist constraint in the USSR—demonstrates that society is moving away from socialism.

12. "The working men have no country." This phrase of the
Manifesto has often been taken by the Philistines to be a sally good
[only] for agitation. In reality it gives the proletariat the only rational directive on the problem of the capitalist "fatherland." The suppression of this directive by the Second [Socialist] International
(1889–1916) brought on not only the destruction, lasting four years,
of Europe,[4] but further the current stagnation of world culture.
Before the new war that approaches, for which the Third International ["Communist International" or "Comintern," 1919–43][5] has
cleared the road, the *Manifesto* still remains today the surest coun-
selor on the question of the capitalist "fatherland."

Thus we see that the little work of two young authors continues
to furnish irreplaceable indications on the most burning and fundamental questions of the liberation struggle. * * * However, that
hardly means that after ninety years of the unparalleled development of productive forces and great social struggles, the *Manifesto*
does not have need of adjustment and complement. Revolutionary
thought has nothing in common with idolatry. Programs and prog-
nostications verify and correct themselves in the light of experi-

3. "Socialism in one country": a Stalinist phrase of the 1930s subordinating the interests
of all Communist parties to the interests of the U.S.S.R. [*Editor*].
4. The Great War, 1914–18 [*Editor*].
5. The "Communist," or Stalinist, International [*Editor*].

ence, which is the supreme example for human thought. Corrections and complements, as historical experience itself testifies, can only be applied with success by starting out with the method that is found at the basis of the *Manifesto*. We will attempt to demonstrate this by attending to some important examples.

1. Marx taught that no social order leaves the scenes before having exhausted its creative possibilities. The *Manifesto* stigmatized capitalism because it fetters the productive forces. Yet, in its period, as in the following decades, this fetter had only a relative character; if, in the second half of the nineteenth century, the economy could have been organized on socialist foundations, the rhythm of its growth would have been incomparably more rapid. This thesis, incontestable in theory, does not change the fact that the productive forces continued to increase on the global scale without interruption until the world war. It is only within the last twenty years that, despite the most modern conquests of science and technology, the age of direct stagnation and even of the decadence of the world economy has begun. Humanity is beginning to live on accumulated capital, and the approaching war threatens to destroy for a long while the very bases of civilization. The authors of the *Manifesto* anticipated that capital would destroy itself a long time before transforming itself from a relatively reactionary regime into an absolutely reactionary one. This transformation didn't become clear except to the eyes of the current generation and has made our era one of wars, revolutions, and Fascism.

2. The error of Marx and Engels with regard to historical delays flowed in part from the underestimation of the subsequent possibilities inherent in capitalism, and in another part from the overestimation of the revolutionary maturity of the proletariat. The revolution of 1848 did not transform itself into a socialist revolution, as the *Manifesto* had anticipated, but later opened to Germany the possibility of a formidable [capitalist] expansion. The Paris Commune demonstrated that the proletariat cannot seize the bourgeoisie's power without having at its head a proven revolutionary party. However, the long period of capitalist impetus that followed brought about not the education of a revolutionary vanguard, but, on the contrary, the bourgeois degeneration of the workers' bureaucracy,[6] which became, in its turn, the principal restraint on the proletarian revolution. This "dialectic," the authors of the *Manifesto* could not themselves foresee.

3. Capitalism is for the *Manifesto* the reign of free competition. Speaking of the growing concentration of capital, the *Manifesto* does not yet draw the necessary conclusion on the subject of monopoly

6. An allusion to Social Democracy, especially Bernstein's Revisionism [*Editor*].

capitalism, which has become the dominant form of capital of our era, and the most important premise of the socialist economy. It is only much later that Marx proved, in his *Capital*, the tendency toward the transformation of free competition into monopoly. The scientific characterization of monopoly capitalism was given by Lenin in his *Imperialism*.[7]

4. By referring above all to the example of the English "industrial revolution," the authors of the *Manifesto* saw the process of liquidation of intermediate classes in too rectilinear a fashion, as a total proletarianization of the classes of artisans, of small commerce, and of the peasantry. In reality, the elemental forces of competition did not complete this progressive and barbarous work from afar. Capital ruined the petty bourgeoisie much faster than it proletarianized it. Further, the conscious policy of the bourgeois state has been aiming for a long time to artificially conserve the petty bourgeois strata. The growth of technology and the rationalization of large [scale] production, at the same time engendering forced unemployment, slowed down the proletarianization of the petty bourgeoisie from the opposite end. At the same time the development of capitalism has enlarged extraordinarily the army of technicians, administrators, and commercial employees, in a word, what is called the "new middle class." The result of this is that the middle classes, the disappearance of which the *Manifesto* forecasts so categorically, form, even in a country as highly industrialized as Germany, about half the population. However, the artificial conservation of petty bourgeois strata long outdated in no way lessens the social contradictions; on the contrary, it renders them particularly morbid. In adding itself to the permanent army of unemployed, it is the most malevolent expression of the *putrefaction* of capitalism.

5. The *Manifesto*, conceived for a revolutionary era, contains (at the end of the second section) ten demands that relate to the period of the immediate transition of capitalism to socialism. In the preface of 1872, Marx and Engels indicated that these demands were partially obsolete, and in any case retained only a secondary significance; they interpreted it to mean that these transitory revolutionary slogans definitively gave way to the "minimum program" of social democracy, which itself, as we know, did not go beyond the limits of bourgeois democracy.

In reality, the authors of the *Manifesto* indicated very precisely the principle correction to bring to their transition program; namely: "the working class cannot simply lay hold of the ready-made state machinery, and wield it for its own purposes." Stated otherwise,

---

7. Lenin. *Imperialism: The Highest Stage of Capitalism* (1916). "Characterization": *charactéristique* in the original [*Editor*].

the correction aimed at the fetishism of bourgeois democracy. To the capitalist state, Marx opposed much later the state of the Commune type. This "type" eventually took the more precise form of the *soviets*.[8] Today there can be no revolutionary program without *soviets* and without *workers' control*. As for all the rest, the ten demands of the *Manifesto*, which, in the period of peaceful parliamentary activity, seemed "archaic," have now resumed all their importance. On the other hand, what has aged beyond hope is the "minimum program" of social democracy.

6. To justify the hope that "the bourgeois revolution in Germany will be but the prelude to an immediately following proletarian revolution," the *Manifesto* invokes the much more advanced general conditions of European civilization, in comparison to the England of the seventeenth and the France of the eighteenth century, and the far superior development of the proletariat. The error of this prognosis consists not only in the delay. Some months later, the revolution of 1848 showed precisely that in the presence of a more advanced [political] evolution, none of the bourgeois classes is capable of leading the revolution to the end: the big and middle bourgeoisies are too tied to the landed proprietors and too united by the fear of the masses; the petty bourgeoisie is too dispersed and too dependent, by the intervention of its leaders, on the big bourgeoisie. As the subsequent evolution in Europe and Asia has demonstrated, the bourgeois revolution, taken in isolation, can no longer be realized at all. The purification of the society of the defrocked feudalists is only possible if the proletariat, freed from the influence of the bourgeois parties, is capable of placing itself at the head of the peasantry and of establishing its revolutionary dictatorship. Likewise, the bourgeois revolution is tied up with the first step of the socialist revolution into which it will afterward be dissolved. The national revolution thus becomes a link in the international revolution. The transformation of the economic foundations and of all the relations of society takes on a permanent character.

For the revolutionary parties of the backward countries of Asia, Latin America, and Africa, the clear comprehension of the organic relation between the democratic revolution and the dictatorship of the proletariat, and consequently with the international socialist revolution, is a question of life or death.

7. In showing how capitalism draws along in its wake the backward and barbaric countries, the *Manifesto* does not yet say anything about the struggle of the colonial and semicolonial peoples for their independence. To the extent that Marx and Engels thought that the socialist revolution, "in the civilized countries at least," was the affair

8. *Soviets*: workers', peasants' and soldiers' councils [*Editor*].

of the years near at hand, the question of the colonies was resolved
in their eyes not as [the] result of an autonomous movement of the
oppressed peoples, but as the result of the victory of the proletariat
in the metropolises of capitalism. This is why questions of revolutionary strategy in the colonial and semicolonial countries are not
even touched upon in the *Manifesto*. But these questions demand
special solutions. Thus, for example, it is quite evident that if the
"national fatherland" has become the worst historical check in the
developed capitalist countries, it still remains a relatively progressive factor in the backward countries that are obliged to struggle for
their independent national existence. "The Communists," the *Manifesto* declares, "everywhere support every revolutionary movement
against the existing social and political order of things." The movement of the colonial races against their imperialist oppressors is one
of the most powerful and important movements against the existing
social order, and this is why it requires the complete support, undis-
puted and without reticence, of the proletariat of the white race.
The credit for having developed the revolutionary strategy of the
oppressed peoples belongs principally to Lenin.

8. The most obsolete part of the *Manifesto*—with respect not to
method but to purpose—is the critique of the "socialist" literature
of the first half of the nineteenth century (chapter 3) and the definition of the opposition, parties (chapter 4). The tendencies and parties enumerated in the *Manifesto* were swept away so radically by
the revolution of 1848 or by the counterrevolution that followed that
history doesn't even mention them any more. Nevertheless, in this
part also, today the *Manifesto* is nearer to us than to the preceding
generation. In the period of prosperity of the Second International,
when Marxism seemed indisputably to prevail, the ideas of socialism before Marx could be considered as definitely finished. Today
this is no more the case. The decadence of social democracy and
of the C[ommunist] I[nternational] engenders at each step monstrous ideological crimes. Senile thought relapses, so to speak, into
infancy. In search of saving formulas, the prophets of the era of
decline rediscovered the doctrines buried a long time ago by scientific socialism. As for the question of the opposition parties, the
decades have brought about the most profound changes: not only
have the old parties been replaced long ago by the new ones, but
moreover the very character of the parties and of their mutual relations changed radically in the conditions of the imperialist era. The
Manifesto must therefore be completed by the documents of the
first four congresses of the Communist International, by the fundamental literature of Bolshevism, and by the decisions of the confer-
ences of the Fourth [Trotskyite] International.[9]

9. Founded by Trotsky in 1940. [*Editor*]

We have recalled already that, according to Marx, no social order leaves the scene before having exhausted the possibilities that are inherent in it. However, the social order, even outdated, does not give way to a new order without resistance. The succession of social regimes presupposes the sharpest class struggle, i.e., revolution. If the proletariat, for one reason or another, proves incapable of overthrowing the bourgeois order that outlives its day, it remains to finance capital, in the struggle to maintain its shaken domination, only to transform the petty bourgeoisie, led by it to despair and demoralization, into a pogrom army of Fascism. The bourgeois degeneration of social democracy and the fascist degeneration of the petit bourgeoisie are interwoven as cause and effect.

INTERPRETATION

Y. WAGNER AND M. STRAUSS

[The Theoretical Foundations of the *Communist Manifesto's* Economic Program]†

The *Communist Manifesto* contains a programme of action which, far from implying a frontal attack upon the whole of the bourgeoisie and the capitalist mode of production, regards cooperation with a section of the bourgeoisie and the continued cooperation of certain aspects of the capitalist system as compatible with the early stages of the transition to socialism.

* * *

This plan, which sketches in general lines the intermediate stage of the movement towards socialism, assumes that political power is already in the hands of the socialist proletariat. The plan is, therefore, the economic programme of the future socialist Government, a programme which will direct the socialist transformation of society throughout a whole period.

Nevertheless, the plan does not include several important socialist measures which were accepted—not least by the authors of the programme themselves—as essential to the completion of a socialist structure. The plan does not include the total socialization of the means of production. It does not demand or necessitate the abolition of hired labour or the elimination of the profit derived by the employer from its use. Finally, the plan does not include the nationalization of commerce.

* * *

The ten measures which have to be taken in a despotic way seem insufficient and untenable because they constitute a partial intervention by the State in the economic mechanism of capitalism. The question then arises whether there is any guarantee that, as a result, exploitation will be eliminated. The answer is that although it is true that in themselves they are insufficient, they will outstrip themselves, leading necessarily to further reforms, and it will be possible to use them in order to revolutionize the whole mode of production. Furthermore, they are unavoidable, in that normally there are no other means which can be substituted for them in the development towards socialism.

† From "The Programme of the Communist Manifesto and Its Theoretical Foundations," trans. Dr. Elena Lourie, *Political Studies* 17.4 (December 1969): 470–84. Reprinted by permission of Wiley Blackwell.

Clause 1: Abolition of property in land and the application of rents, etc. This means that the ownership of land and natural resources will be transferred to the State, but their use will be private. The employment of hired labour in general and on private farms in particular is not prohibited. The intention of the clause is not to abolish the class of farmers, of the capitalist employer of agricultural labour, but to eliminate the rentier. In addition, the intention is to put an end to speculation in land, to abolish the profits derived, not directly from the exploitation of labour, but indirectly as a result of rises in the price of land which are a byproduct of the work done on neighbouring land.

Clause 3: Abolition of the right of inheritance. Given the spirit of the plan as a whole, it appears that an absolute abolition was not intended, that, for example, small-holders' property was not to be included in this ruling. The practical implication of this clause would be a matter of degree. * * *

Clause 5: Nationalization of the banks and the creation of an exclusive monopoly for the State bank. This does not mean the confiscation of deposits either big or small, but the transfer of the management of banks and their profits to the State. The importance of this measure is threefold: first, it involves the transfer of a considerable portion of the national income to public ownership. In the second place it produces greater efficiency in the organization of money and banks. Finally, it transfers the control over production, over industry and agriculture, which banks possess, from private into public hands. This is particularly important when the question is not of a loose control but of a veritable domination by the banks over spheres of production.

Clause 6: Control of the railways confers an advantageous position in the whole economy and enables those who control them to interfere in the management of various spheres of production, by means of unequal transportation tariffs for competing firms. Control of the railways was particularly advantageous before the emergence of the motor-car.

Clause 7: National factories. The intention here is to create a productive sector under public ownership and constantly to widen it. The clause—and indeed the whole plan—does not imply the creation of a public sector by expropriating private factories, but rather by setting up new state factories. In *Principles of Communism*, a suggested draft for the manifesto of the Communist Party, drawn up by Engels in 1847, there appears a list of measures almost identical with those we are discussing. Yet under clause 2 he writes: "Gradual expropriation of landed proprietors, *factory owners*, railway magnates and shipping magnates, partly through competition on the part of the State industries and partly through payment of compensation in currency notes." It appears, therefore, that in their final draft Marx and Engels decided to exclude the industrialist from the general run of capitalists whose property is to be abolished, at that stage. It is worth noting, moreover, that the expropriation suggested by Engels is not necessarily a direct legal confiscation (cf. "competition on the part of the State industries") and, in so far as such confiscation is suggested it is accompanied by the payment of compensation.

Clause 8: The term "labour" is usually subject to several meanings. Let us first examine it in its narrowest sense: According to this interpretation labour is human activity which transforms nature in order to supply a need or to make it into a means for supplying a need. This meaning of the term includes the mental work done during production, or preceding and directing it.

Labour in this sense does not include social activity—activity which creates social relations in the field of economics, politics and culture. Thus the activity of the businessman, the politician and the artist, etc., is excluded from this notion of labour. Yet, if we abide by this narrow definition of labour, it is obvious that even in a socialist society not everyone is a worker and one cannot therefore talk of the "liability of all to labour." Hence the narrow definition is not suitable here. * * *

The question then arises: if the term "labour" is constantly broadened, against whom, after all, is this clause directed? It can be directed only against those capitalists who are not employed in any economic activity and, in general, are engaged permanently in nothing but consumption. These people will be asked to limit the time devoted to consumption and to engage in some activity which will be of use to the state-capitalist economy described in this plan. In the *Demands of the Communist Party in Germany* the following statement appears under clause 9: "The landed proprietor who is neither a peasant nor a farmer, has no share in production. Consumption on his part is, therefore, unwarrantable." The ruling on the liability of all to labour includes the right to work for all who seek it. The creation of national workshops is a means to ensure this right.

Taking now the programme as a whole, what was the guiding principle behind these clauses? A study of the plan shows that its authors did not think that during the first stage a socialist Government had to eliminate the exploitation of workers by employers, but only profits of these sections of the bourgeoisie who did not exploit workers directly. It is possible then to ask what made Marx and Engels think that direct exploitation should not at once be eliminated. Did they consider it possible to take steps to eliminate the anarchy of capitalist production without putting an end to exploitation? Does the Marxist analysis conceive of an effective difference, within the capitalist economy, between exploitation, or the employment of hired labour, and anarchy? And even if there is, why should the socialist movement postpone the abolition of exploitation until the second stage?

We must, therefore, examine to what extent Marx and Engels gave answers to these questions in their theoretical writings. It is necessary to see how the practical plan follows from their analysis of capitalism.

According to Marx and Engels[1] capital has two main spheres of activity:[2] production and circulation.

In the sphere of production capital is conceived of first and foremost as an accumulator of materialized, past labour, labour which has congealed into means of production, and which serves to subject living labour to the capitalist, to extract surplus values from living labour and to add them to original capital. In this process of absorbing surplus-value that is, in the process of labour, capital changes its physical form. Capital is the social form of physical process whereby factors of production are transformed into products. It is in this sphere that capital appears as an employer of labour.

In the sphere of circulation the activities of commerce, the banks and the Stock-Exchange, take place. Here capital changes its physical form, alters and transforms itself from one use-value to another without any work being done (in the narrow sense of the word), without any additional use-values being created and consequently without the creation of any additional exchange-values. This is the sphere *par excellence* of capital, its unadulterated field of action, one in which the movement of already-created surplus-values takes place.

What is the role of the sphere of circulation as a whole, in this view? It is conceived of as complementing the activity of capital in the sphere of production. The chief concern of circulation capital[3] is the distribution of produce. By "produce" is meant first of all consumption-goods, primarily wage-goods. From this point of view

---

1. The economic doctrine of *Capital* is taken to represent views shared by Marx and Engels.
2. We use the terminology employed by Marx in *Capital*, Vol. III (Moscow: Foreign Language Publishing House, 1959), pp. 274, 310–12, etc.
3. Not to be confused with *circulating* capital, which, like the fixed capital from which it is distinguished, is part of any one independent, functioning capital. Circulation is a macroeconomic category: the part of the social category engaged in activities within the sphere of circulation, and composed, like capital generally, of fixed and circulating portions (cf. ch. XIX, *Capital*, Vol. III).

circulation capital mediates between the sphere of production, producing necessities, and the production of labour-power for the productive network as a whole. In fact, circulation capital regulates the
proportions within the sphere of production. Secondly, the means of
production are also included in the product to be distributed. Here
too, circulation capital regulates the proportions between various
branches of production, between the sector producing means of
production and the sector producing necessities.

To sum up: Marx views the sphere of circulation as the mechanism which regulates, through the distribution of the social product, the division of social labour. The modern division of labour, to
which the industrial revolution gave rise, calls, even in its capitalist
form for some regulation in the sphere of production. All branches
of production being interdependent, regulation of their mutual
relations, which, under capitalism, takes the form of a flow of capital from branch to branch (in Marx's terms: a flow of materialized
labour which trails living labour after it), calls for a special activity.
This activity is undertaken by the "money-dealing capitalist," i.e.
bankers and the Stock Exchange operators, and is carried out by
the respective financial institutions.[4] It may be asked in what way
does this concept of circulation tally with the statement often met
with in Marx and Engels that production under capitalism is—on
the social scale—anarchic, i. e. unregulated?[5] In view of the foregoing, their meaning must not be taken as implying absolute anarchy. From the analysis in *Capital*, Vol. III, it becomes clear that
what is meant is this: the manner in which the division of labour is
regulated by capitalist circulation is not a unified social plan, based
on a scientific understanding of the sphere of production, and the
proportionate changes within it as it grows in quantity and quality.
This regulation, in fact, consists of a series of private plannings
of the social economy, the component parts of which are interdependent. The private character of this planning contradicts the
social character of the planned object, a contradiction which manifests itself in the cyclical crises from which the capitalist economy
suffers. Regulation of the division of labour by way of circulation is,
on this view, merely the capitalist substitute for social planning.

* * *

It becomes clear that the programme of the *Manifesto* is aimed
at reforming fundamentally the sphere of circulation, and only

4. *Capital*, Vol. III, p. 593 (banks); pp. 429–32 (trade in stock); see also Engels's note on
   the stock exchange, ibid, pp. 884–6.
5. E.g., *Selected Works* (London, 1942), Vol. I, pp. 140, 176, 261; Vol. II, pp. 232, 504;
   Selected Correspondence (London, 1941), p. 247; Engels, *Origin of the Family, etc.*
   (Moscow, 1948), p. 249.

indirectly the sphere of production. Its purpose is to transfer the sphere of circulation, in so far as it regulates the division of labour, from control of private capitalists to that of the State. This transfer enables it to become a tool with which social planning—albeit still only partial—can be imposed on the sphere of production, which at this stage remains largely in private ownership.

Although the sphere of circulation is one of which, by Marx's definition, no labour takes place, nevertheless it needs the investment of capital. This capital is called for because of the period of time during which the commodities (both the means of production and means of consumption) remain within the sphere of circulation.[6] Capital is also needed because production for the market demands money, so that a part of the social capital is permanently to be found in the form of money within the sphere of circulation.[7] And since capital within the sphere of circulation cannot at the same time function within the sphere of production, capital as a whole is divided into two parts.

Just as the development of labour productivity depends on an ever increasing division of labour into separate pursuits, so the development of capital depends on an ever increasing division of the functions of capital and their consolidation into separate enterprises.[8] An analogy may be drawn between Marx's description of the relation between money-dealing capital and productive capital in part V of Vol. III, and his analysis of relations between the two "departments" of production, in part iii of Vol. II,[9] where one "department" furnishes the means whereby the other produces. This analogy between Marx's conception of the division of labour among workers and the division of roles among capitalists has yet another aspect. Just as the first sphere of labour (department I) supplies the technical means for the activity of the second (department II), so the first sphere of capital, circulation, supplies the economic means for the activity of the second, production, or employment of labour. It is possible to regard the institutional mechanisms of the sphere of circulation (banks, the money-market), which regulate the distribution of the product and thereby the division of labour generally, as economic means or economic tools.

Just as in the capitalist economy the second productive department (necessities) buys the product of the first (means of production), so the sphere of production as a whole buys the services of the mechanisms of circulation. In other words, the sphere of pro-

---

6. *Capital*, Vol. II, pp. 121–33; also *Capital*, Vol. III, pp. 262–75, 310–11.
7. *Capital*, Vol. II, pp. 135–6; *Capital*, Vol. III, p. 311.
8. Cf. *Capital*, Vol. II. p. 267.
9. See *Capital*, Vol. II, p. 395.

duction pays for these services, for its use of the circulation mechanism, with part of the surplus value it extracts from the living
labour done within its own sphere. The splitting of capital into two
branches is, therefore, logically connected with the splitting of surplus value. Hence we find, as against the industrialist's profit, interest
and the profit of the merchant.[1]

Common to both branches of capital, and to all capital, is the
fact that, as such it does not create values, but only distributes values, appropriates values, organizes and regulates, for the purposes
of that distribution, the creation of values, i.e., labour. This is what
is peculiar to the capitalist or the activity of capital, in contrast to
the worker's activity or in contrast to labour.

What distinguishes the two branches one from another is that
only productive capital creates surplus value, that is to say, transforms values into surplus values, appropriates new values and adds
them to capital; whereas circulation capital arranges the distribution
of productive capital to the various branches of production and levies
in return, as a tax, part of the surplus value which productive capital
creates.[2] It is a matter, therefore, of two different kinds of appropriation; the object of the first is labour, whereas that of the second is
the result of the first's activity, its fruit.[3] As a result the subjects of the
two kinds of capital are also opposed to each other: "Whether the
industrial capitalist operates on his own or on borrowed capital, does
not alter the fact that the class of money-capitalists confronts him as
a special class of capitalists, money-capital as an independent kind of
capital and interest as the independent form of surplus-value peculiar of this specific capital."[4]

* * * Hence, subjectively, from the point of view of the capitalists
within the two branches, the difference entails a struggle between
conflicting interests.

The conflict is, first of all, a simple one between sellers and buy-
ers—a quantitative conflict over the price of the "commodity," the
cost of using the economic apparatus. * * *

* * * Consequently not only is the activity of capitalist circulation mechanisms not aimed at increasing the sum of use-values at
society's disposal, nor even the total production of values (exchange-
values), but it is not even directed at increasing the total profit of
social capital, for the portion of the profit which goes to the owners of
these mechanisms and their enterprises is not any fixed proportion of

---

1. Also, by the same token, as against the farmer's profit: rent, as against the dividend-
   bearing share, the profits that come from trading in shares. See *Capital*, Vol. III, pp.
   277, 284–5, 369–72.
2. *Capital* (Moscow, 1957), Vol. II, p. 55.
3. *Capital*, Vol. III, pp. 351, 363.
4. *Capital* (London, Moscow, 1962), Vol. III, p. 369.

the total. The activity of the organizers of these mechanisms is aimed at increasing their portions, and hence they construct the mechanisms not according to the requirements of the employers, not according to the needs of the capitalist process of production, but in accordance with their special mode of appropriation.[5] They cease to be, therefore, agents of the whole capitalist class and become instead a special class. It is, consequently, a logical corollary to make their expropriation a special task which can be carried out separately from the expropriation of capitalists generally; i.e., the very conclusion reached by the *Communist Manifesto*, before the theoretical premise had been fully worked out.

Second, whereas the employer regulates the division of labour in detail in his individual enterprise, the "circulator" deals with the general division of labour between branches of production without which the division of labour in detail would be useless.[6] For the owner of the enterprise could organize the division of labour within it as efficiently as he pleased, but without circulation he would find neither the elements of production (raw materials, for example) which he draws from the market as commodities, nor the purchasers for the product which he in turn throws onto the market.

This characteristic gives the owners of circulation capital an advantage.[7] They hold the commanding heights of the economy and, by the nature of their role, they are organized in a more concentrated way. On the other hand, their concentrated organization facilitates the transfer of their role into the hands of society's representatives. * * * The ten-clause programme in the *Manifesto* outlines a solution to the conflict between private appropriation and the general division of labour and does not concern itself with the division of labour within the framework of the individual enterprise: obviously this was considered a problem the social solution to which involved a lengthier process.

* * *

For Marx and Engels * * * the logic * * * expressed in the ten-clause programme, that the first step towards socialism does not necessitate the total abolition of bourgeois property and the capitalist mode of appropriation, led to the conclusion that one must try to fulfil the programme with the political cooperation of those sections of the bourgeoisie who would benefit by it. They thought that there was room for continuity and an evolving development of socialist revolutionary policies within the capitalist regime and

---

5. *Capital*, Vol. III, p. 532.
6. *Capital*, Vol. I (Moscow, n.d.), p. 351.
7. Marx dwells on this throughout chapters 29–34 of *Capital*, Vol. III.

during the process of transformation. They did not regard the transition from the ten-clause programme to full socialism, nor from a democratic Government which would carry out the plan, to a socialist Government, as a single step, but as a process.

*   *   *

[T]he authors of the 1848 programme did not define the realization of socialism as a single act and hence did not define it as an event taking place somewhere in the distant future, beyond the present day politics of the existing capitalist regime, at some date when politics within the capitalist regime will have somehow come to an end. For them the policy which would realize socialism was a continuation of socialist politics within capitalism, and "the revolutionary starting point" of the former was to be found in the latter. This meant that the splitting of the bourgeoisie into two camps had an immediate bearing on the struggle for socialism and it permitted a start to be made towards the full realization of socialism by fighting for the political destruction of the conservative camp within the bourgeoisie, in other words for the expropriation of the sphere of circulation.

According to this view the full realization of socialism involved a whole series of steps, spread out over a more or less lengthy historical period; each step constituted an essential structural change in its own right and only all of them together would add up to an absolute transformation of the old mode of production into that of "associated labour."

The 1848 programme * * * looked to changes in the direction of socialism, which were to be based upon the division of forces within capitalist society. The assumption on which th[is] programme rested was that [its] realization would not injure the industrialists and therefore it was not impossible to interest the latter, in some form or another, in their achievement.

MIHAILO MARKOVIĆ

[The State and Revolution in the *Communist Manifesto*]†

*   *   *

In the *Manifesto of the Communist Party* Marx maintains that a "more or less veiled civil war is raging within existing society, up to

† From *From Affluence to Praxis: Philosophy and Social Criticism* (Ann Arbor: U of Michigan P, 1974), pp. 180–83. Reprinted by permission.

the point where that war breaks out into open revolution, and where the violent overthrow of the bourgeoisie lays the foundation for the withering away of the proletariat."

In this militant text there is a strong emphasis on the cataclysmic character of the workers' revolution.[1] Contrary to his earlier views, he speaks here about "the conquest of political power by the proletariat" (not about the abolition of political power as an alienated *social* power). It is true, he says, "the Communist revolution is the most radical rupture with traditional property relations: no wonder that its development involves the most radical ruptures with traditional ideas" (about freedom, property, family, nationalism, religion and morality). But he also, for the first time, speaks about the formation of the workers' *state* as the result of the overthrow of the bourgeois political power:

> the first step in the revolution by the working class is to raise the proletariat to the position of ruling class, to win the battle of democracy. The proletariat will use its political supremacy to wrest, by degrees, all capital from the bourgeoisie, to centralize all instruments of production in the hands of the state, i.e. of the proletariat organized as the ruling class. . . .

Granted that this evolution of Marx's views toward the idea of "proletariat as a ruling class" and toward the idea of a workers' state (which, in a series of steps had to revolutionize the old mode of production and transform profoundly the old social order) was a practical necessity and a sign of Marx's growing sense of reality, the question remains: If political power is *alienated* power (presupposing a ruling elite which mediates among citizens) how is this new alienation to be overcome? How is this new state to "wither away," what is there in the state itself (even one of this new type, "organized, armed proletariat") to secure a process of gradual self-abolition?

Theoretically Marx has seen the way out and the solution is still valid:

> When in the course of development, class distinctions have disappeared, and all production has been concentrated in the hands of a vast association of the whole nation, the public power will lose its political character. Political power, properly so called, is merely the organized power of one class for oppressing another. If the proletariat during its contest with the bourgeoisie is compelled, by the force of circumstances, to organize itself as a class, if by means of a revolution, it makes

---

1. The *Manifesto* ends with these words: "The Communists disdain to conceal their views and aims. They openly declare that their ends can be attained only by forcible overthrow of all existing social conditions."

itself the ruling class, and as such, sweeps away by force the old conditions of production, then it will, along with these conditions, have swept away the conditions for the existence of class antagonisms and of classes generally, and will thereby have abolished its own supremacy as a class.

In place of the old bourgeois society, with its classes and class antagonisms, we shall have an association, in which the free development of each is the condition for the free development of all.

It is clear from this passage that for Marx the ultimate goal of a communist is a *radical economic and political democratization*: a full freedom of development for each *individual* (not class or party, or any other mediator among individuals). However, it is not at all clear how to dismantle organized political power once it has been established on a new ground. It is true, Marx never speaks about the power of the party, or of the *avant-garde* of any kind—he keeps speaking about the power of the whole workers' class. But experience has shown how easy it is for a small group within a class to monopolize the power of the whole class, and to manipulate the vast majority of the class. Marx could not have foreseen Stalinism. But Rousseau was aware of the inherent difficulties in the formation and expression of the general will. He strongly suspected that there was always a danger of people's representatives alienating themselves from the people. Unfortunately, Marx was not so suspicious and he did not realize that this problem, far from being specific for liberal bourgeois democracy, holds for any organized human society. Only much later in his analysis of the Paris Commune, did Marx learn from experience how the problem has to be dealt with.

> The Commune was formed of the municipal councillors, chosen by universal suffrage in the various wards of the town, responsible and revocable at short terms. The majority of its members were naturally working men, or acknowledged representatives of the working class. . . . From the members of the Commune, downwards, the public service had to be done at *workmen's wages*. The vested interests and the representation allowances of the high dignitaries of state disappeared along with the high dignitaries themselves. Public functions ceased to be the private property of the tools of the Central Government. Not only municipal administration but the whole initiative hitherto exercised by the state was laid into the hands of the Commune.[2]

2. Marx, *The Civil War in France*. Address to the General Council of the International Working Men's Association, in *Marx-Engels Selected Works* (New York: International Publishers, 1968) p. 291. Engels in his introduction to a new edition of the two *Addresses to the General Council of the International* (1891) sees the danger of postrevolutionary bureaucratization quite clearly. He praises the Commune: "Against this transformation

In the decades which followed, few people bothered to put all the pieces of Marx's theory of revolution together. His more sophisticated, philosophical ideas about human emancipation and politics as a sphere of alienation were forgotten, or even rejected (as immature, Hegelian, or youthful utopian visions); the later insights from his historic writings were overlooked. What survived vividly in the consciousness of many generations of Marxists were simple ideas from the militant, programatic, popular texts. Socialist revolution was widely accepted to mean a violent, political overthrow of the bourgeois rule and the establishment of the workers' state ("the dictatorship of the proletariat"), which is supposed to build up a new "socialist" society (whatever this term might mean).

Marx later allowed the possibility of a peaceful socialist revolution under certain conditions (in England and Holland during his time).[3] Engels even went as far in the revision of his and Marx's earlier views as to prefer legal, parliamentary means of struggle to "illegal and *revolutionary* tactics!"[4]

This new more flexible approach was received with considerable interest in the international social-democrat movement but it was ignored by the Third International. Nevertheless in both cases the revolution was construed as a sudden, catastrophic event which requires many years of preparation, organized resistance and political education—directed and controlled by the well-organized revolutionary *avant-garde—The Party*.

---

of the state and the organs of the state from servants of society into masters of society—an inevitable transformation in all previous states—the Commune made use of two infallible means. In the first place, it filled all posts—administrative, judicial, and educational—by election on the basis of universal suffrage of all concerned, subject to the right of recall at any time by the same electors. And, in the second place, all officials high or low, were paid only the wages received by other workers. The highest salary paid by the Commune to anyone was 6000 francs. In this way an effective barrier to place-hunting and careerism was set up, even from the binding mandates to delegates to representative bodies which were added besides" (Engels, in *Selected Works*, p. 261).

3. In his preface to the English edition of *Capital* in 1886, Engels noted that Marx allowed the possibility that in England "the inevitable social revolution might be effected entirely by peaceful and legal means."

   Marx himself said in an interview to *The World* on July 3, 1871 that in England "a rebellion would be a stupidity since the goal could be attained more quickly and more surely by peaceful agitation." In his speech at the London Congress of the International on September 21, 1871, Marx said that workers would rise against governments peacefully whenever possible, or with arms-in-hand should that become necessary. Then, in his speech after the Hague Congress of the International on September 15, 1872, Marx pointed out that the paths to a new organization of labor are not the same everywhere. The institutions, manners, and traditions in various countries should be taken into consideration. There are countries such as America, England, and perhaps the Netherlands, in which the members can attain their goals peacefully.

4. Engels, in his foreword to Marx's *Class Struggles in France*, written 1895 speaks of political revolution in terms of street fighting and the erection of barricades. Further, he opposes propaganda work and parliamentary activity to *revolutionary* [!] forms of struggle. "We revolutionaries," he said, referring to the conditions in Germany in the last decade of the nineteenth century, "can advance far more quickly by legal means than by illegal and revolutionary tactics."

HAL DRAPER

[The *Communist Manifesto* and the Myth of the Disappearing Middle Classes][†]

* * *

The myth about the "disappearance of the middle classes" is usually based on selected phrases from the *Communist Manifesto*. This is enough to give pause, since it is precisely in matters of basic economic theory that the *Manifesto* is most obviously an immature work of Marx's. However brilliantly the *Manifesto* fulfilled its task of simplifying many complex ideas and telescoping history into a compendium of lapidary formulations, for the sake of a sweeping view of social evolution and political perspectives and a maximum impact as a party programmatic statement—all in a few pages—it is not fair to expect it also to take the place of *Capital*.

Still, let us see what is, and what is not, in the *Manifesto* on this question.

It is well known that the *Manifesto*, striving to spotlight the struggle of the polar classes, enthusiastically depicted something like a duel situation: "Society as a whole is more and more splitting up into two great hostile camps, into two great classes directly facing each other: bourgeoisie and proletariat." This clearly puts it as a tendency, a direction of development. So also the glowing description of the triumph of the bourgeoisie as it "pushed into the background every class handed down from the Middle Ages." When a class is pushed into the background, it does not disappear.

The *Manifesto*'s glorification of bourgeois achievement becomes a little stickier when it proclaims that the bourgeoisie "has converted the physician, the lawyer, the priest, the poet, the man of science, into its paid wage-laborers." *Has* converted, mind you—this is not a prediction. This either proves that Marx thought his father (a lawyer), his poet friend Heine, Alexander Humboldt, Adam Smith, et al., were all working for proletarian wages—or else it proves we have to read the language of the *Manifesto* with some common sense. This swingeing statement has a point to make, but it hardly intends to proclaim a grandiose theory about the Disappearance of the Professional Classes. In fact, the *Manifesto* is crammed with global statements, beginning with "all . . . ," which no one would support under oath—like the good news for obese burghers that "All that is solid melts into air . . ."

---

† From *The Politics of Social Classes*, vol. 2 of *Karl Marx's Theory of Revolution* (New York: Monthly Review Press. 1978), pp. 615–19. Reprinted by permission of Monthly Review Press.

But the passage that refers specifically to the petty-bourgeoisie is not as far-reaching as the announcement about the converted lawyers, priests, poets, et al. Nor is it as expansive as it is sometimes made out to be, *if the original text is read, as published in 1848:*

> The previously existing small intermediate strata [*Mittelstände*]—the small industrials, merchants and rentiers, the artisans and peasants—all these classes sink down into the proletariat, partly because their small capital does not suffice for the carrying on of large-scale industry and succumbs in competition with the larger capitalists, partly because their skill is rendered worthless by new methods of production. Thus the proletariat is recruited from all classes of the population.[1]

Thus, through a qualifier, "previously existing"—*which was omitted from the English version*—this statement makes clear it is referring to the *old* class structure. And this is exactly what one would expect from the context, which has to do with what has been happening up to the present and not with predictions about the future.

But isn't there another passage, a couple of pages later, which explicitly predicts that "other classes" will "finally disappear"? No, there is not—*not in the original text of the Manifesto as published in 1848.* The "disappearance" is again shadowed forth by a translation which was worded in 1888 without clairvoyant anticipation of what clever exegetes can do. This passage uses much the same language as the one just discussed. A translation of the original shows that it too was concerned with tendencies going on in the

---

1. So goes the original text. Moore's standard translation of 1888, edited by Engels, sought to modernize the language, with the result that it is an uncertain guide to unanticipated controversies. It goes as follows, with some points of difference italicized:

> The *lower strata of the middle class*—the small *tradespeople*, shopkeepers, and *retired tradesmen* generally, the handicraftsmen and peasants—all these sink *gradually* into the proletariat, partly because their diminutive capital does not suffice for the scale on which Modern Industry is carried on, and is swamped in the competition with the *large* capitalists, partly because their *specialized* skill is rendered worthless by new methods of production. Thus the proletariat is recruited from all classes of the population.

The key change is in the first phrase, which states what the passage is about the small intermediate strata *that have existed up to now.* The italicized qualification is completely omitted, perhaps because the time reference was considered superannuated in 1888. Whatever the reason was in 1888, it is quite clear that the passage was concerned with the old intermediate strata, and was not a statement about middle classes in general or for the future. Moreover, the 1848 text clearly included both the old petty-bourgeoisie and small bourgeois employers and manufacturers: two phrases pointing to the latter were dropped in 1888. Thus, insofar as the subject was broader than the old petty-bourgeoisie, it extended not to other types of intermediate elements but to the lower ranks of the bourgeoisie itself.

present, and not with predictions of the class structure of the
future:

> Of all the classes that stand face to face with the bourgeoisie
> nowadays, the proletariat alone is a really revolutionary class.
> The other classes are decaying and being ruined in the face of
> large-scale industry; the proletariat is its most characteristic
> product.
>
> The intermediate strata, the small industrial, the small
> merchant, the artisan, the peasant, all these fight against the
> bourgeoisie, to safeguard their existence from ruin as inter-
> mediate strata. They are therefore not revolutionary, but
> conservative.[2]

Once we remove the changes introduced by the 1888 English version, the meaning is perfectly plain: it is a statement about present
tendencies. And it is about the same intermediate strata as the
previous passage.

But if the intermediate strata are "being ruined," doesn't this mean
they will eventually "disappear"? This would require a separate demonstration: but fortunately a passage in the *Manifesto* finally does get
explicit about the coming fate of the petty-bourgeois intermediates
and does look into the future. Even the word *disappear* occurs. But
the mythical theory does not.

> In the countries where modern civilization developed, a new
> petty-bourgeoisie was formed, which hovers between the pro-
> letariat and the bourgeoisie and continually renews itself as a
> supplementary part of bourgeois society. The members of
> this class, however, are being constantly hurled down into
> the proletariat by the action of competition; indeed, with the

---

2. The English version goes as follows, with some points of difference italicized:
   Of all the classes that stand face to face with the bourgeoisie today, the proletariat alone is a really revolutionary class. The other classes *decay and finally
   disappear* in the face of Modern Industry: the proletariat is its special and essential product.
   The lower middle class, the small manufacturer, the shopkeeper, the artisan, the
   peasant, all these fight against the bourgeoisie, *to save from extinction their existence as fractions of the middle class*. They are therefore not revolutionary, but
   conservative.
   Alas, Moore used *disappear* for *gehen unter* (go under), which is not what a rabbit
   does in the hands of a magician. Interpreting the present tense as future, he gratuitously inserted *finally*, even though the passage is tied to the present with the strong
   word *heutzutage* (nowadays, in the present day). And so the meaning of the English
   version is distorted by the two words *finally disappear*—and neither of these two words
   exists in the original! The new language about *fractions of the middle class* is an added
   flourish, which Moore perhaps thought very contemporary-sounding. The word *extinction* is of a piece with *disappear*: the German is *Untergang*, a going-under (noun
   equivalent of *gehen unter*). All these little modernizing changes would have seemed
   harmless in 1888—until the myth of the disappearing middle class was invented.

development of large-scale industry they can see a time
approaching when they will completely disappear as an independent part of modern society and will be replaced, in commerce, manufacturing and agriculture, by labor overseers
and stewards [*Domestiken*].[3]

Here we learn that not even the traditional petty-bourgeoisie is
actually disappearing. Just the reverse: it "continually renews itself."
True, individual members of this class are "constantly" being proletarianized, but the class limps on, in a more and more ruined state.
Furthermore, some day this class will completely disappear *as an
independent part of society*—which is not identical with simply disappearing like the rabbit in a magician's hat. But while these petty-
bourgeois elements (small-property-holding producers) move into
the background of society as more and more dependent hangers-
on of the real bourgeois powers, the *Manifesto* immediately indicates that their places in the foreground are taken by new elements
arising out of the needs of the bourgeoisie itself. They tend to be
replaced, as capital develops, by another kind of intermediate element, the various employees of capital hired to superintend the
labor process and to serve the new needs of the owners of commerce, factory and farm—"labor overseers and stewards." These
elements are certainly new in the mass, and they are certainly in the
middle of something, and so they are "new middle class" elements of
a sort.

If, then, one looks for Marx's theory of the disappearing middle
classes in the *Communist Manifesto*, which is supposed to be its
natural habitat, it hardly meets the eye. But even if it were much
clearer in the *Manifesto*, the conclusion to follow would not be
essentially affected.

✳   ✳   ✳

3. Again, this is the original text. The important difference from the standard English
version comes in the last phrase, where *durch Arbeitsaufseher und Domestiken* is
blurred into: "by overlookers, bailiffs and shopmen." The import of *Domestiken* is thus
lost. This word cannot here mean domestics in the sense of household servants, since
it refers to people "in commerce, manufacturing and agriculture." I translate it *stewards* (as did the first English version of the *Manifesto* in 1850), instead of *servitors*, since
stewards has a broader connotation; in fact, many elements of new clerical, white-
collar, salaried, managerial bureaucratic sectors of the so-called "new middle classes"
function as stewards of the capitalist controllers on a high or low level.

ERNEST MANDEL

[Marx's Theory of Wages in the *Communist Manifesto* and Subsequently]†

* * *

In *The Poverty of Philosophy*, in the "Arbeitslohn" manuscript, in *Wage Labor and Capital*, and in the *Communist Manifesto*, Marx and Engels remain wedded to the idea that the general tendency of wages under capitalism is to fall absolutely and to sink to the physiological subsistence minimum. * * * The two driving forces of this tendency for real wages to fall are, on the one hand, the replacement of workers by machines (that is, a form of capital accumulation that does away with more jobs than it creates), and, on the other, *the growing competition among workers*, as a result of this permanent and increasing unemployment.

When he wrote his "Arbeitslohn" notes in Brussels in 1847, Marx still believed that the objections to trade unions made by economists (claiming that the unions could not prevent wages from falling because their activity inevitably provoked new forms of division of labor, the shifting of capital from one sector to another, the introduction of new machines, and so on) were basically well founded. Marx nevertheless defended these "associations" of workers, taking the view that it was in them that the workers learned to prepare themselves for the overthrow of the "old society."[1] He was to revise and amplify this opinion, too, some years later.

In short, during the whole of this period Marx's fundamental idea on wages was that the "natural price" (the value) of labor (of labor power) is the minimum wage, this being conceived as a physiological notion.[2] When and how did he revise this conception? It is not easy to establish this with precision, but it was doubtless his study of the cyclical fluctuations of the economy and of trade-union activity in Britain that led him to form more correct views.

In the *Grundrisse*, written in 1857–1858, exactly ten years after the passages just quoted, Marx already held a more dialectical, more finished, and more mature view of the wage problem, a view that

---

† From *The Formation of the Economic Thought of Karl Marx*, trans. Brian Pearce (New York: Monthly Review Press, 1971), pp. 143–52. Reprinted by permission of Monthly Review Press.
1. *Kleine ökonomische Schriften* (Berlin: Dietz Verlag, 1955) pp. 246–47.
2. See the well-known passage in the *Communist Manifesto*: "The cost of production of a workman is restricted, almost entirely, to the means of subsistence that he requires for his maintenance, and for the propagation of his race. But the price of a commodity, and therefore also of labor, is equal to its cost of production. In proportion, therefore, as the repulsiveness of the work increases, the wage decreases."

was to remain practically unchanged down to the writing of *Capital*. Thus in the *Grundrisse* Marx observes that the only thing that distinguishes the worker from the slave is that he can *expand* the range of his enjoyment during a period of economic prosperity, that he can "take part in higher forms of enjoyment, even spiritual forms, can agitate for his own interests, buy newspapers, listen to lectures, educate his children, develop his tastes," in short, "participate in civilization" in the only way that remains open to him, *by increasing his needs*.[3] Now here Marx is saying by implication that this increase in consumption, this expansion of needs, is possible for the worker, at least in periods of high conjuncture, and that the value of labor power thus includes *two* elements: a more or less stable physiological element, and a variable element, regarded as necessary for the reproduction of labor power *in accordance with the increasing needs acquired by the worker*.

A few pages farther on in the *Grundrisse* Marx points out that capital has a tendency to drive the worker to replace his "natural [i.e., physiological] needs" with "historically created" needs.[4] This idea had already been dealt with in an earlier passage, where Marx emphasized that the worker is also regarded as a *consumer* by the capitalist, who therefore tends to seek to stimulate consumption, except on the part of his own workers.[5]

* * *

But it was in his address to the General Council of the First International, on June 20 and 27, 1865, that Marx fully set out his theory of wages.

* * *

Marx here deduces that while the minimum limit of wages can be more or less exactly defined, there is no maximum limit. Or, more precisely: the maximum wage is whatever permits the maintenance of a sufficient level of profit, below which capital will no longer be interested in hiring workers. Between this minimum and this maximum the concrete determination of the level of wages depends on "the respective powers of the combatants," that is, upon the vicissitudes of the class struggle. This was, indeed, what Marx was striving to show, since his address was above all aimed at refuting the view that trade-union activity was useless and even harmful to the workers.[6]

3. Karl Marx, *Grundrisse der Kritik der politischen Ökonomie* (Berlin: Dietz Verlag, 1953) pp. 192–98.
4. Ibid., p. 211.
5. Ibid., pp. 194, 198.
6. See his letter to Engels of May 20, 1865, in *Selected Correspondence: 1846–1895* (New York: International Publishers, 1942) p. 202.

But these "respective powers of the combatants" are in their turn determined, at least in part, by objective factors. Among these Marx mentions first and foremost the fluctuation in the supply and demand of labor, which gives him occasion to explain that, in relatively underpopulated overseas countries like the United States where the labor market is "being continuously emptied by the continuous conversion of wage laborers into independent, self-sustaining peasants,"[7] the law of supply and demand favors the worker and enables him to obtain higher wages than in Europe. * * *

How do the supply and demand of labor evolve in countries that are already largely industrialized? By the constant replacement of workers by machines, the constant increase in the organic composition of capital. Marx believed that the long-term tendency is thus one of imbalance between supply and demand in favor of the capitalists and to the disadvantage of the workers: ". . . the general tendency of capitalist production is not to raise, but to sink the average standard of wages. . . ."[8]

* * *

In any case, the conclusion regarding the tendency of average wages to fall needs to be qualified by two observations. It applies only to capitalist society taken as a whole, that is, on the *world* scale; and it may well find concrete expression in a tendency for average wages in the industrialized countries to rise, since there the accumulation of capital takes place on such a scale that employment constantly expands, in comparison with the growth of population, *because the abolition of jobs implied by this movement takes place not so much inside these countries as outside them, in the countries of the "Third World."* It may be tempered, too, by the fact that alongside the increasing use of machinery there is also an increase in the number of jobs in the service sector, and a "new middle class" develops which prevents continual growth in the industrial reserve army—phenomena which Marx had foreseen long before they occurred, in two passages in *Theories of Surplus Value.*[9] And large-scale migratory movements, such as the emigration of some 70 million Europeans to America and other overseas regions during the nineteenth century, may eventually profoundly alter the tendencies in the evolution of supply and demand of labor.

7. *Wages, Price and Profit*, in *Selected Works in Three Volumes* (Moscow: Progress Publishers, 1969, 1970), Vol. II, p. 73.
8. Ibid., p. 74.
9. Karl Marx, *Theories of Surplus Value* (Moscow: Progress Publishers, 1963–1971), Vol. II, pp. 571, 572, 573.

At the same time, the useful effect of trade-union activity is that it abolishes, to a large extent at least, that famous competition among the workers that had seemed to the young Marx to be the reason for the inevitable decline of wages to the minimum level.[1] In *Wages, Price and Profit*, Marx expresses himself more scientifically when he says that when there is abundant supply on the "labor market," especially in a period of economic crisis and large-scale unemployment, labor power may actually be sold *below its value*. The workers' coalition, the abolition of competition among workers, collective bargaining on wages, trade-union activity—all these in the last analysis are meant to insure that, on the average, labor power is sold at its value and not below it. And Marx thus considers these forms of action absolutely indispensable, since without them the working class "would be degraded to one level mass of broken wretches past salvation."[2] But the *objective possibilities* of successful trade-union activity depend in turn on the *relative* size of the industrial reserve army which, as Marx was to say later on, in *Capital*, is the regulator of wages. It is only when unemployment tends to remain stable or even decline over a long period that a long-term rise in real wages can be achieved.

Marx's essential concern was to bring out the *relative* impoverishment of the proletariat, the fact that even when wages rise they rise much less than the wealth of capital. As early as *Wage Labor and Capital* we find, in this connection, the metaphor of the house, which "may be large or small," beside which a palace rises. Twenty years later Marx was to write in *Capital*: "The lot of the laborer, be his payment high or low, must grow worse." * * * All the evidence we have presented shows clearly that in his mature works Marx never expounded any "law" of the *absolute* impoverishment of the workers, though he regarded their relative impoverishment as inevitable.

Eliane Mossé[3] quotes the well-known passage from Volume I, Chapter XXV, of *Capital* in which Marx speaks of the "accumulation of wealth at one pole" being "at the same time accumulation of misery, agony of toil, slavery, ignorance, brutality, mental degradation, at the opposite pole, i.e., on the side of the class that produces its own product in the form of capital."[4] But she does not seem to notice that, if one takes into account the context—the sentences that lead up to this passage—Marx's formulation is intended not to apply to the employed workers but to "the lazarus-layers of the

1. See in particular *Wage Labor and Capital* in *Selected Works*, Vol. I, pp. 171–73.
2. *Wages, Price and Profit*, in *Selected Works*, Vol. II, p. 75.
3. Eliane Mossé, *Karl Marx et le problème de la croissance dans une économie capitaliste* (Paris: Armand Colin, 1956), p. 60.
4. *Capital*, Vol. I, p. 645.

working class," that is, to the mass of unemployed who make up the industrial reserve army. This is further emphasized by the preceding passage in which Marx explains "the absolute general law of capitalist accumulation": "The relative mass of the industrial reserve army increases therefore with the potential energy of wealth. But the greater this reserve army in proportion to the active labor army, the greater is the mass of a consolidated surplus population, whose misery is in inverse ratio to its torment of labor. The more extensive, finally, the lazarus-layers of the working class, and the industrial reserve army, the greater is official pauperism.[5] *This is the absolute general law of capitalist accumulation.* Like all other laws it is modified in its working by many circumstances, the analysis of which does not concern us here."[6] There is therefore nothing to be deduced from this passage as far as the evolution of *wages* is concerned, especially as almost immediately afterward comes the observation already referred to: "It follows therefore that in proportion as capital accumulates, the lot of the laborer, be his payment high or low, must grow worse."

Many studies confirm the existence of these "lazarus-layers of the working class" in all the capitalist countries. The most striking example is provided by the country with the highest wage level, the United States, where the "absolute general law of capitalist accumulation" has been verified in dramatic fashion. Since the publication of Michael Harrington's book *The Other America*, it is generally accepted in the United States that a quarter of the nation, 50 million Americans, are poor and bear the stigmata of poverty.[7] And if this figure is not higher, it is due in part to the fact that between 1940 and 1957 the percentage of married women employed, or in receipt of wages, increased from 15 to 30 percent, which implies, in a country whose social services are notoriously underdeveloped, "the impoverishment of home life, of children who receive less care, love and supervision."[8]

* * *

5. In the *Communist Manifesto*, Marx and Engels had already made use in an unclear and ambiguous way of the well-known formula "the laborer . . . becomes a pauper" (*der Arbeiter wird zum Pauper*) since this formula could be taken to refer no less to the decline in the wages of the workers still in employment (which the *Manifesto* declares to be inevitable) than to the workers ousted from the production process. In *Capital*, the term "pauperism" is used only in relation to this "lazarus-layer" of the proletariat.
6. *Capital*, Vol. I, p. 644.
7. Michael Harrington, *The Other America: Poverty in the United States* (Baltimore: Penguin Books, 1962), pp. 177–78.
8. Ibid., p. 174.

HOWARD SELSAM

The Ethics of the *Communist Manifesto*[†]

It is often said today that Marxists repudiate all morality, that they deny the validity of ethical judgments, that they eliminate the "moral factor" from history, whether past or in the making. As absurd and untrue as such pronouncements are, they have this much justification—Marx and Engels early became weary of the *mere* "ethical" examination of capitalist society, or *mere* moral assaults on it. The utopians had done enough of that. Besides, capitalism had neither come into being because of moral considerations nor would it pass away because of them. Scientific analysis is required to understand it and a mighty organized physical force is required to overthrow it.

Nevertheless, the reading of the *Manifesto* reveals that Marx and Engels had the "highest" moral reasons for abhorring capitalism and seeking to achieve socialism. But such moral reasons, they believed, were rooted in the historic process itself as scientific study reveals it to us; not imposed upon it by any whim or fancy of this or that individual or class. * * *

It is our purpose, on the basis of these few introductory considerations, to elucidate the ethical principles that are employed in the *Manifesto* and that are revealed by it. * * *

Much more attention is conventionally paid to relatively incidental moral issues raised in the *Manifesto* than to the basic ethical philosophy it employs. A few of these should be noted, if only to show their essentially incidental character. The bourgeoisie, it stated for example, "has left no other nexus between man and man than naked self-interest, than callous 'cash payment.' It has drowned the most heavenly ecstasies of religious fervour, of chivalrous enthusiasm, of philistine sentimentalism, in the icy water of egotistical calculation. It has resolved personal worth into exchange value, and in place of the numberless indefeasible chartered freedoms, has set up that single, unconscionable freedom—Free Trade. In a word, for exploitation, veiled by religious and political illusions, it has substituted naked, shameless, direct, brutal exploitation." In other writers of the period such a statement would constitute an absolute indictment of capitalism. Not so for Marx and Engels. Here it has a dual character, depending on the use to be made of it. On one side it points to a progressive feature of capitalism, its tearing asunder

† From *Science and Society* 12.1 (Winter 1948): 23–32. Excerpts reprinted by permission of the board of Editors of *Science and Society*.

"the motley feudal ties that bound man to his 'natural superiors',"
and thus enabling the working class to see their oppression without
illusions. On the other side, it presents the essential inhumanity of
capitalist relations.

Similarly, in Section II of the document many ethical questions
are raised in the discussion of such charges as: the communists seek
to abolish private property, they threaten the destruction of culture;
they seek abolition of the family, of countries and nationality. The
first and obvious answer given to these questions is that the bourgeoisie has done these things far beyond the communists' power to add or
to detract, and the authors sometimes with biting wit and sometimes
with passionate seriousness discuss the charges. But the real answer
occurs at the end of the discussion and is often missed. * * * The
answer is: "The charges against communism made from a religious,
a philosophical and, generally, from an ideological standpoint, are
not deserving of serious examination." This is because all such
arguments are from the standpoint of the bourgeoisie, for they are
expressions of the ruling ideas of the age which are inevitably "the
ideas of its ruling class." Marx and Engels believe, in short, that the
proletarian condemnation of the bourgeois order is so profound
and so devastating, its justification for revolution *so* overwhelming,
that the bourgeoisie has lost all right to question the proletariat in
this manner. Bourgeois moral principles are but the ideological
expression of its class rule, and once the latter is under sentence
the former cannot be invoked in its behalf.

The central feature of the *Manifesto* from an ethical viewpoint is
that it passes judgment on a whole order of society and finds it wanting. It pronounces the death sentence on capitalism and demands
that the sentence be carried out. But even while passing sentence, it
reads a eulogy of its victim. It *was* a great system, "it has accomplished wonders"; it "has created more massive and colossal productive forces than have all preceding generations together." A paean of
praise is sung to the achievements of the bourgeois system. Its world,
however, is not good enough, and its greatest achievement is that it
makes possible and necessary the transition to socialism. Thus it is
the reasoned judgment of the *Manifesto* that capitalism will be
remembered in history as that system of *class* society which prepared the way for the abolition of classes.

But when we look for the grounds upon which such sweeping
condemnation is passed we find none of the conventional ethical
ideas of the philosophers. Neither "right" nor "justice" is anywhere
invoked. There is no appeal to a "golden mean" or a "moral law."
Men are neither told that they do nor that they should follow their
self-interest or pursue their happiness. Sympathy, benevolence,
charity are sarcastically scorned. None of the traditional moral

appeals are made; no accepted standards invoked. Why? The clue is to be found in this simple statement: "The communist revolution is the most radical rupture with traditional property relations; no wonder that its development involves the most radical rupture with traditional ideas." Professor E. H. Carr, in writing of Marxism, correctly said: "A true revolution is never content merely to expose the abuses of the existing order, the cases in which its practice falls short of its precept, but attacks at their root the values on which the moral authority of the existing order is based."[1] Since in this case the attack is not only on the existing order, but on the very form of all previous historic society as well, its attack on their moral authority cannot be made by means of the moral idea or precepts derived from them. If "the history of all hitherto existing society is the history of class struggles," then all previous ethics, too, is at least suspect, for it "moves within certain common forms or general ideas which cannot completely vanish except with the total disappearance of class antagonisms."

* * *

This brings us to the root of the problem, which is found only in the conception of the historic process itself. But this, too, can be viewed only from the standpoint of one or another class in society—in this case, obviously, that of the proletariat. The concepts of class and history are here so interwoven that neither can be taken without the other. The basis of the moral judgments of the *Manifesto* is to be found only in the historical position of the proletariat. Hegel quoted from Schiller that the "history of the world is the world's court of judgment."[2] This is equally true for Marx and Engels, except that for them such judgment is pronounced not by a world spirit but by the historical process itself, and the instrument of the historical process has been the struggle of classes. Under capitalism it is the proletariat which necessarily pushes this struggle to its logical conclusion and is therefore the leading class and the best representative, today, of history's judgment.

In this approach there is no need for an eternal moral law. Capitalism is bad because the proletariat finds it so from the standpoint of its own class needs and interests. It became bad at the point when the proletariat, having become conscious of itself as a class, could also project a plan for the reorganization of society without classes and give birth to communist theory and practice. These arose precisely because "the bourgeoisie is unfit any longer to be the ruling class in society and to impose its conditions of existence

1. Edward Hallett Carr, *The Soviet Impact on the Western World* (New York, 1947), p. 94.
2. *Hegel's Philosophy of Right*, transl. by T. M. Knox (Oxford, 1942), sect. 340.

on society as an overriding law. It is unfit to rule because it is incompetent to assure an existence to its slave within his slavery, because it cannot help letting him sink into such a state, that it has to feed him, instead of being fed by him." (If this seems an exaggeration or appears to the reader not to describe existing conditions, let him only think of capitalism today on a world scale.)

* * *

The struggle of the working class for the overthrow of capitalism is justified and right not only because it expresses their needs and interests, hence their ethics, but because their ethics is the highest or best possible at this stage of history. This is so because, in the nature of things, moral judgments reflect reality, and the judgments of the workers today reflect the contradictions in this reality. As Engels eloquently expressed it: "When the moral consciousness of the masses declares this, that, or the other economic phenomenon to be wrong, as happened at one time in the case of slavery and at another in the case of serfdom, this means that the phenomenon in question has already outlived its time, that new economic conditions have arisen, thanks to which the old ones have become intolerable, and must be swept away."[3]

There is a direction of history, Marx and Engels believe, which the struggle of the working class is carrying forward. This is expressed in many places in the *Manifesto*. They call reactionary, for example, the fight of the lower middle class against the bourgeoisie: "for they try to roll back the wheel of history." They say again, "In bourgeois society, . . . the past dominates the present; in communist society, the present dominates the past." There is a "march of modern history" the feudal socialists are unable to comprehend, and they forget further "that the modern bourgeoisie is the necessary offspring of their own form of society." But this conception of the direction of history from a lower to a higher form appears most clearly of all in the very analysis of the achievements of capitalism. What are some of these "achievements" which merit the praise of capitalism's foremost enemies? It has established the world market, "the universal interdependence of nations." "It has been the first to show what man's activity can bring about" by accomplishing wonders of production. It "draws all, even the most barbarian, nations into civilization." By creating great cities it "has thus rescued a considerable part of the population from the idiocy of rural life." Unlike all previous industrial classes, the bourgeoisie "cannot exist without constantly revolutionizing the instrument[s] of production, and thereby

3. Quoted by D. Riazanov in his edition of *The Communist Manifesto* (London: Martin Lawrence, 1930), p. 172.

the relations of production, and with them the whole relations of society." But the heart of it all is the fact that the bourgeoisie "during its rule of scarce one hundred years, has created more massive and more colossal productive forces than have all preceding generations together." It has developed fabulous instruments of production and communication, cleared continents, changed the course of rivers. It has in a word subjected "nature's forces to man." And they ask, "what earlier century had even a presentiment that such productive forces slumbered in the lap of social labour?"

The greatness of the bourgeois world lies in its development of productive forces, in its increase of man's mastery over nature. But this was an inevitable development out of feudalism; such is the direction of social evolution. Right here is found the fatal weakness of capitalist relations. For capitalism "is like the sorcerer who is no longer able to control the powers of the nether world whom he has called up by his spells." The capitalist forces of production come into conflict with capitalist relations, are fettered by them. Only the proletariat can take the next step, can free the forces of production from capitalist fetters, can create such social relations as can carry ever further mankind's ability to produce, man's mastery over nature. History is therefore on the side of the working class, or to put it better, the working class in its revolutionary struggle is on the side of history. * * *

The objection can be raised at once that this proves nothing, that it is a circular argument, that there is already a moral judgment implicit in such an interpretation of history. Why is increasing productivity good? Why should it be taken as an index of progress? Why is man's increasing mastery of nature desirable? * * * Marx and Engels, neither in the *Manifesto* nor elsewhere argue this point. Perhaps, because they consider it irrelevant. They are social scientists, not "moralizers." * * * [T]hey know, first, that history moves that way; second, that the proletariat becoming class conscious under the conditions created by capitalism will struggle to free the productive forces from private property relations. Finally, they know that the members of the classless society of the future will recognize the prevailing ideological attacks on communism for what they are: the moral cynicism or nihilism of those who would hold back the wheel of history.

There is no other way. Either ethics and morality are derived from the concrete changing conditions of human life or they are not. Materialism must insist that they have no other basis. Under the conditions of class struggle Marx and Engels are discussing, therefore, the inevitable tendency is for two positions to crystallize, that of the bourgeoisie and that of the proletariat. But when the struggle is seen in its broadest historical terms, they can say that the position of the proletariat conforms to the needs and interests of the human race as a whole.

On one side, recurrent crises, war, famine, mass misery, reversion to barbarism. On the other side, free men freely developing their relations with one another and with nature in the interests of all. On one side, each for himself, "dog eat dog," men as means to profits and as appendages to the machine; on the other side, men as the end and goal of production, guided by the principle that "the free development of each [is] the condition for the free development of all." The proletariat works for the interests of all men in furthering its own interests; that is why it has the allies without which, as Lenin said, it could never win. Marx and Engels, taking their stand only on the concrete and ever changing nature of men in society in constant development are led by all their studies to believe that the ethics of the proletariat is a higher ethics than is that of the bourgeoisie, higher in the sense that it represents a movement in a direction which mankind, in its subsequent historical development, will pronounce good. And here history's judgment means, of course, nothing but the collective opinions of men in historical development. In reference to any particular form of society at any particular time, such a judgment is relative. From the standpoint of the historical process as a whole it is absolute. But it is absolute only in the sense of direction, not as a state or stage conceived as eternally existing or as realized at any one time.

* * *

KARL LÖWITH

[Marx's Prophetic Messianism]†

* * *

[T]he secret history of the *Communist Manifesto* is not its conscious materialism and Marx's own opinion of it, but the religious spirit of prophetism. The *Communist Manifesto* is, first of all, a prophetic document, a judgment, and a call to action and not at all a purely scientific statement based on the empirical evidence of tangible facts. The fact that "the history of all hitherto existing society" shows various forms of antagonisms between a dominant minority and a dominated majority does not warrant the interpretation and evaluation of this fact as an "exploitation" and even less the expectation that what has

† From *Meaning in History* (Chicago: University of Chicago Press, 1964), pp. 43–45. Excerpts reprinted by permission of the publisher.

been hitherto a universal fact will necessarily in the future cease to be what it was. Marx may explain the fact of exploitation "scientifically" by his theory of surplus-value; exploitation, nevertheless, remains an ethical judgment, something which is what it is by being unjust. In Marx's outline of universal history it is no less than the radical evil of "prehistory" or, in biblical terms, original sin. And, like original sin, exploitation, too, affects not only the moral but also the intellectual faculty of man. The exploiting class cannot comprehend its own system of living except through a deceptive consciousness, while the proletariat, free from the sin of exploitation, understands the capitalistic illusion together with its own truth. As a supreme and all-pervading evil, exploitation is far more than an economic fact.

Even if we assume that all history is a history of class struggles, no scientific analysis could ever infer from this that class struggle is *the* essential factor that "determines" all the rest. To Aristotle as well as to Augustine the institution of slavery was one fact among many others. To the first it was a most natural fact, far from being repulsive; to the second a social fact, which should be alleviated by charity but which was not at all decisive for eternal salvation or condemnation. Only with the rise of an emancipated bourgeois society did the relation between rulers and ruled become felt and identified as exploitation, out of the desire for emancipation. It is a strange misinterpretation of Marx by himself when he insists on his being unprejudiced by moral judgments and evaluations and yet sums up his enumeration of various forms of social antagonisms in the challenging words: "oppressors and oppressed." The fundamental premise of the *Communist Manifesto* is not the antagonism between bourgeoisie and proletariat as two opposite facts; for what makes them antagonistic is that the one class is the children of darkness and the other the children of light. Likewise, the final crisis of the bourgeois capitalist world which Marx prophesies in terms of a scientific prediction is a last judgment, though pronounced by the inexorable law of the historical process. Neither the concepts of bourgeoisie and proletariat, nor the general view of history as an ever intensified struggle between two hostile camps, nor, least of all, the anticipation of its dramatic climax, can be verified "in a purely empirical way." It is only in Marx's "ideological" consciousness that all history is a history of class struggles, while the real driving force behind this conception is a transparent messianism which has its unconscious root in Marx's own being, even in his race. He was a Jew of Old Testament stature, though an emancipated Jew of the nineteenth century who felt strongly antireligious and even anti-Semitic. It is the old Jewish messianism and prophetism—unaltered by two thousand years of economic history from handicraft to large-scale industry—and Jewish insistence on absolute righteousness which explain the idealistic basis of Marx's materialism. Though perverted into secular prognostication, the *Communist Manifesto* still retains the basic features of a messianic faith: "the assurance of things to be hoped for."

It is therefore not by chance that the "last" antagonism between the two hostile camps of bourgeoisie and proletariat corresponds to the Jewish-Christian belief in a final fight between Christ and Antichrist in the last epoch of history, that the task of the proletariat corresponds to the world-historical mission of the chosen people, that the redemptive and universal function of the most degraded class is conceived on the religious pattern of Cross and Resurrection, that the ultimate transformation of the realm of necessity into a realm of freedom corresponds to the transformation of the *civitas Terrena* into a *civitas Dei*, and that the whole process of history as outlined in the *Communist Manifesto* corresponds to the general scheme of the Jewish-Christian interpretation of history as a providential advance toward a final goal which is meaningful. Historical materialism is essentially, though secretly, a history of fulfillment and salvation in terms of social economy. What seems to be a scientific discovery from which one might deduce, after the fashion of Marxist "revisionists," the philosophical garb and the relic of a religious attitude is, on the contrary, from the first to the last sentence inspired by an eschatological faith, which, in its turn, "determines" the whole sweep and range of all particular statements. It would have been quite impossible to elaborate the vision of the proletariat's messianic vocation on a purely scientific basis and to inspire millions of followers by a bare statement of facts.

* * *

HAIG A. BOSMAJIAN

A Rhetorical Approach to the *Communist Manifesto*†

Late in February, 1848, an octavo pamphlet of thirty pages published by a German printer in London at 46 Liverpool Street, Bishopsgate, appeared for the first time with a title page which read, in part: "Manifest der Kommunistischen Partei. . . . Prolertarier aller Länder vereinigt Euch." The ideas expressed in this *Manifest* had been presented, for the most part, previously in speeches, books, and pamphlets by predecessors and contemporaries of Karl Marx

† From *Dalhousie Review* 43.4 (Winter 1963–64): 457–68. Excerpts reprinted by permission of *The Dalhousie Review*.

and Friedrich Engels. In fact, Marx and Engels, in their own writings, had previously presented the ideas that finally made up the *Communist Manifesto*. However, of the many "socialist-communist" tracts written during the eighteenth and nineteenth centuries, it was the *Communist Manifesto* which survived to be translated into almost one hundred different languages.

Why has it been the *Manifesto* which has survived to influence so many people in so many lands during the past one hundred years when other "socialist-communist" works stand undisturbed on dusty library shelves? Certainly a major factor is Marx's ability to present his content in such a form as to make the arguments appear forceful and valid, to arouse the emotions of his audience, and to make the author of the tract worthy of belief. If he were going to influence and move people, Marx realized that he would have to use all available means of persuasion, including what Aristotle called the "good style" in the *Rhetoric*, parts of which Marx had translated in his university days.[1]

There is no doubt that Marx was aware of and thoroughly conscious of various rhetoric devices. He was an avid reader of plays, speeches, poetry, and novels. He did various translations and wrote verse, the latter of questionable literary value. In a letter to his father, Marx wrote in November, 1837, that he had translated Tacitus's *Germania*, Ovid's *Tristium libri*, and parts of Aristotle's *Rhetoric*. Paul Lafargue, who married Marx's second daughter, Laura, wrote that Marx "had a preference for eighteenth century novels, and was especially fond of Fielding's *Tom Jones*. The modern novelists who pleased him best were Paul de Kock, Charles Lever, the elder Dumas, and Sir Walter Scott, whose *Old Mortality* he considered a masterpiece. Marx looked upon Cervantes and Balzac as "the greatest masters of romance," and *Don Quixote* was for him "the epic of the decay of chivalry."[2]

Two orators of whom Marx thought highly were John P. Curran and William Cobbett. Of Curran, Marx said in a letter to Engels: "I consider Curran the only great advocate—people's advocate—of the eighteenth century and the noblest nature. . . ."[3] Lafargue tells us that Marx sought out and classified the characteristic expressions in some of the polemical writing of William Cobbett, "for whom he had great esteem."[4] Many of the characteristics of Cobbett's pamphleteering and oratorical style, especially the lucidity, sarcasm, and invective, seemed to appear later in the *Manifesto*.

1. Karl Marx, *Selected Works* (New York, 1933), 1. p. 85.
2. Ibid.
3. Karl Marx and Friedrich Engels, *Selected Correspondence*, trans. Dona Torr (New York, 1934), p. 281.
4. Marx, *Selected Works*, p. 84.

Upon Cobbett's death in June, 1835, *The Times* commented on his style: "The first general characteristic of his style is perspicuity, unequalled and inimitable. A second is homely masculine vigor. A third is purity, always simple, and raciness often elegant. His argument is an example of acute, yet apparently natural, nay, involuntary logic, smoothed in its progress and cemented in its parts, by a mingled storm of torturing sarcasm, contemptuous jocularity, and slaughtering invective. . . ."[5]

Wilhelm Liebknecht, one of Marx's "pupils" who was for a time a daily visitor to Marx's home in London, writes in his reminiscences that "Marx attached extraordinary value to pure correct expression and in Goethe, Lessing, Shakespeare, Dante, and Cervantes, whom he read every day, he had chosen the greatest masters. He showed the most painstaking conscientiousness in regard to purity and correctness of speech."[6] Marx's attitude towards words and language is displayed in his efforts to achieve clarity in his own works. Lafargue wrote that Marx "would not publish anything until he had worked over it again and again, until what he had written obtained a satisfactory form."[7] It may well have been this thoroughness which delayed Marx's completion of the *Manifesto*, much to the displeasure of the Communist League.

* * *

From the beginning of the *Manifesto*, Marx establishes that communism is a powerful force to be reckoned with; in so doing, he establishes at the same time a part of his *ethos* by identifying himself with a movement opposed by great powers, a movement which is itself powerful and which openly publishes its aims and views for all to see. He does this in the *exordium* by pointing out that "all the powers of old Europe have entered a holy alliance to exorcise" the spectre of communism and by asserting that "communism is already acknowledged by all European powers to be itself a power."

The *Manifesto's* short *exordium* is followed by a *narration* which follows Aristotle's advice: ". . . if there is narration at all [in deliberative speaking], it must be of the past, and its object to remind your audience of what happened in the past, with a view to better plans for the future. It may be used in condemning people. . . ."[8] After stating in his *exordium* that it is about time that the communists openly publish their views, aims, and tendencies "to meet this nursery tale of the spectre of communism with a manifesto of the party itself,"

5. G. D. H. Cole, *The Life of William Cobbett* (London, 1947), p. 431.
6. Marx, *Selected Works*, p. 111.
7. Ibid., p. 91.
8. All the quotations from Aristotle are taken from Aristotle, *The Rhetoric of Aristotle*, trans. Lane Cooper (New York, 1932).

he follows, in the *narration*, not with elaborations of these aims and views, but with a historical description of the growth of the bourgeois with all its evils: new forms of oppression, "naked, shameless, direct, brutal exploitations," breakdown of the family relationship, enslavement and pauperization of the labourer. In this process of discrediting his opponents by identifying them with all that is evil, Marx has again added to his *ethos*; he has branded his adversaries as selfish, oppressive, unjust, intemperate, and dishonorable, and in the process of linking his opponents with that which is not virtuous he has focused attention upon the probity of his own character. From the very beginning, he attempts to establish character and good will, not by elaborating on his own cause and its virtues (this will come later), but by condemning his opponents, their cause, and their actions: it is the bourgeois that has "reduced the family relation to a mere money relation," it is the bourgeois that has forced labourers to sell themselves piecemeal, it is the bourgeois that has reduced poets, priests, and doctors to its paid wage-labourers. It is this bourgeois against which Marx and the communists stand.

Not only does Marx establish his *ethos* by calling his adversaries selfish, oppressive, and dishonorable; he also arouses, in the *narration*, the emotions of anger, hate, and fear. Aristotle, in his *Rhetoric*, has defined anger as "an impulse attended by pain, to a revenge that shall be evident, and caused by an obvious, unjustified, slight with respect to the individual or his friends." By portraying the bourgeois as contemptuous of and insolent to the proletariat, Marx arouses the worker's anger towards the bourgeois. Has not the bourgeois, after taking all that it can from the labourer, handed him over to "other portions of the bourgeois, the landlord, the shopkeeper, the pawnbroker?" Has not bourgeois industry benefited only the ruling class and sent the labourer "deeper and deeper below the conditions of existence of his own class?" Has not the bourgeois transformed the proletarian children "into simple articles of commerce and instruments of labor?" Has not the bourgeois taken for its own pleasures the wives and daughters of the workers? The bourgeois has shown only indifference and insolence to the plight of the labourer and his family, and as Aristotle explained, just as a sick man is angered by indifference to his illness, so too is the poor man angered by indifference to his poverty.

Marx not only attempts to arouse anger, which is always attended by a certain pleasure arising from the expectation of revenge against a particular person or persons, but he also attempts to arouse hatred which is directed not only against an individual, but also against a class. Marx obviously was interested in more than arousing his audience to anger which would induce them to wish the object of their anger to suffer; his goal was to arouse his listeners to that state in which they would wish the bourgeois eradicated. As Aristotle put it, "the angry man wishes the object of his anger to suffer in return; hatred wishes its object not to exist."

In his *narration*, Marx also seems to be trying to arouse fear, which is caused by whatever seems to have a great power of destroying us or of working injuries that are likely to bring us great pain. One way of arousing fear is to argue that others greater than the listener have suffered. "Have not men of science, lawyers, doctors become the paid wage-labourers of the bourgeois?" asks Marx. Another way of arousing fear is to portray injustice coupled with power. "Has not the bourgeois organized the workers like soldiers and placed them under the command of a perfect hierarchy of officers and sergeants?" asks Marx. However, at the same time, he is careful not to arouse so much fear as to create in his listeners the feeling that there is no hope of deliverance. The proletariat may be ruled, enslaved, and oppressed by the bourgeois, but still there is hope that things will change for the better, in fact, it is inevitable that things will get better. "Fear sets men deliberating," said Aristotle, ". . . but no one deliberates about things that are hopeless." And things are not hopeless, Marx tells the proletariat in his *narration*, which he ends with the logical conclusion to all the historical evidence he has compiled up to that point: the bourgeois is unfit to rule; society no longer can live under the bourgeois; the fall of the bourgeois and the victory of the proletariat are equally inevitable. It is on this note that the *narration* ends, a *narration* in which the word *communism* never once appears.

If the evils of the bourgeois predominate in Part I of the *Manifesto*, the virtues of communism pervade Part II. This is not to say that Marx ceases his attacks against the bourgeois; the attacks continue, but the perspective is different. The evils of the bourgeois, as they appear in Part II, are juxtaposed with the virtues of communism: In bourgeois society, living labor is but a means to increase accumulated labor. In Communist society, accumulated labor is but a means to widen, to enrich, to promote the existence of the laborers. In bourgeois society, "the past dominates the present; in communist society, the present dominates the past."

Section II takes on the characteristics of a debate in which logic and rhetoric are blended. Marx's character, the character of his adversaries, argument, and the arousing of emotion are all fused, thus making the whole more forceful and more moving. By using the refutative process to present his case for communism, Marx places side by side the evils of the bourgeois and the virtues of communism; he places side by side the weak objections of the bourgeois and the sensible answers of the communists: "You are horrified at our intending to do away with private property. But in your existing society, private property is already done away with for nine-tenths of the population. . . ." "Do you charge us with wanting to stop the exploitation of children by their parents? To this crime we plead guilty." This type of presentation is effective, for as Aristotle has explained, "The refutative process always makes the conclusion more striking, for setting opposites side by side renders their opposition more distinct." Marx seems to further take Aristotle's advice when the latter suggests: "You should . . . make room in the minds of the audience for the argument you are going to offer; and this will be done if you demolish the one that pleased them. So combat it—every point of it, or the chief, or the successful, or the vulnerable points, and thus establish credit for your own arguments." Through this process Marx builds his case for the acceptance of the various measures the communists will put into effect once they gain control; the presentation of the positive measures comes late in Section II.

In answering bourgeois objections, Marx often takes the line that the communists cannot take from the masses that which they never had in the first place while living under bourgeois rule. The communists, he asserts, cannot take from the masses private property they never possessed; they cannot take from the masses a happy family relationship never possessed by the masses while living under bourgeois rule; they cannot abolish nationality, for "the workingmen have no country. We cannot take from them what they have not got." After answering bourgeois questions and objections with communist answers, Marx says, "let us have done with the bourgeois objections to communism," and it is only then that he presents, for the first time, the specific measures which the communists advocate.

Whereas Marx focused attention upon the probity of his character in Part I by linking his opponents and their cause with what is not virtuous, in Part II he establishes his *ethos* by associating his message with what is virtuous and desirable to his audience. Further, he minimizes unfavorable impressions of his cause previously presented by his opponents. It is his cause which wants to create a world in which children will be educated and women will be respected; it is his cause which wants to see the workers given their just rewards for their labour; it is his cause which wants a world where there will be no exploitation of one individual by another, no hostility of one nation to another. It is his cause which will be inevitably successful. Just as he added to his *ethos* early in the *Manifesto* by attributing injustice coupled with power to his adversaries, so too has he added to his *ethos* by joining justice and the inevitability of its success to his own cause.

Marx concludes Section II with a sentence which sets side by side "the old bourgeois society, with its classes and class antagonism," and the communist society which will be "an association, in which the free development of each is the condition for the free development of all." But he cannot conclude the *Manifesto* on this note.

During the eighteenth and nineteenth centuries, there were too many other "socialists" and "communists" who asserted that their movements and their philosophies were the ones that would bring to the labourers what they deserved. Marx could not ignore these other movements. He may have persuasively argued early in the *Manifesto* that the bourgeois was not fit to rule, but there were others who had said or were saying the same thing. He may have shown that the private property of the bourgeois should be abolished, but there were others preaching much the same doctrine. So Marx had to go on in his *Manifesto* to tell the world that these other "socialists" and "communists" were false prophets. In Section III, he proceeds to point out the absurdities and falsities of Feudal Socialism, Petty Bourgeois Socialism, "True" Socialism, Conservative Socialism, and Critical-Utopian Socialism. The representatives of these movements, said Marx, only *appeared* to have the answers; in some cases their analyses were incorrect; in others, their tactics were inappropriate. Some of these false prophets, Marx contended, want only to restore the old means of production and the old society; others reject the class struggle; still others, "the philanthropists, humanitarians, improvers of the condition of the working class, organizers of charity, members of societies for the prevention of cruelty to animals, temperance fanatics," want the proletariat to remain within the bounds of existing society and "cast away all its hateful ideas concerning the bourgeois." The representatives of these other movements, Marx attempted to demonstrate, were either deceitful, self-deceived, impractical pedants, innocent reformers, or starry-eyed experimenters.

Marx's *peroration* is as trenchant as is his *exordium*. After stating that the communists "everywhere support every revolutionary movement against the existing social and political order of things" and that they "labor everywhere for the union and agreement of the democratic parties of all countries," he reaches the climax toward which he has been building. "Let the ruling classes tremble at a Communist revolution. The proletarians have nothing to lose but their chains. They have a world to win. Workingmen of all countries, unite!"

From "A specter is hauting Europe—the specter of communism" to "Working men of all countries, unite!" Marx has clothed his message in a rhetorical style permeated with tropes and figures of speech. Through the use of numerous different rhetorical tropes and figures, the author of the *Manifesto* has emphasized, clarified, and elaborated through sheer repetition, through exaggeration and comparison. Marx's style is that of controversial speaking, not that of written prose. Aristotle has pointed out in his *Rhetoric* that "such devices as *asyndeta* and repetition of the same word, which are rightly enough censured in the literary style, have their place in the controversial style when a speaker uses them for their dramatic effect." To a very great extent Marx uses rhetorical stylistic devices which rely for their effectiveness not so much on silent reading as on oral presentation.

Marx was very conscious of style; in his evaluations of various personages whom he admired and some he did not admire, he would comment on their style. For instance, concerning Pierre-Joseph Proudhon's *What is Property?*, Marx wrote: "This book of Proudhon's has also, if I may be allowed, a strong muscular style. And its style is in my opinion its chief merit. . . . The provocative defiance, laying the ordinary bourgeois mind, the withering criticism, the bitter irony, and, revealed hands on the economic 'holy of holies,' the brilliant paradox which made a mock of here and there behind these, a deep and genuine feeling of indignation at the infamy of the existing order, a revolutionary earnestness—all these electrified the readers of *What is Property?* and produced a great sensation on its first appearance."[9] Again his concern for style is reflected in his criticism of Proudhon's *The Philosophy of Poverty*: "The style is often what the French call *ampoulé* [bombastic]. High-sounding speculative jargon, supposed to be German-philosophical, appears regularly on the scene when his Gallic acuteness of understanding fails him. A self-advertising, self-glorifying, boastful tone and especially the twaddle about 'science' and sham display of it which are always *so* unedifying, are constantly screaming in one's ears. Instead of the genuine warmth which glowed in his first attempt [*What is Property?*], here certain passages are systematically worked up into a momentary heat by rhetoric."[1] From these comments, and comments on the style of Cobbett and others, it appears that Marx favored the style which avoids the abstract and displays the concrete, which is lucid, ironic, and trenchant. His appreciation for this kind of style is reflected in the *Manifesto*.

Marx did not hesitate to pile trope and figure one upon another in succession. Perhaps he had read Longinus, who wrote: "Nothing so effectively moves, as a heap of figures combined together."[2] In the following four-sentence paragraph Marx has combined his rhe-

9. Marx and Engels, *Selected Correspondence*, pp. 169–70.
1. Ibid., p. 173.
2. Longinus, *On the Sublime*, trans. William Smith (London, 1752), p. 97.

torical questions with metaphor, irony, personification, antithesis, and anaphora (beginning a series of clauses with the same word):

> Nothing is easier than to give Christian asceticism a socialist tinge. Has not Christianity declaimed against private property, against marriage, against the state? Has it not preached in the place of these charity and poverty, celibacy and mortification of the flesh, monastic life and Mother Church? Christian socialism is but the holy water with which the priest consecrates the heart-burnings of the aristocrat.

Into the two sentences preceding this paragraph, Marx incorporates balance, metonymy (use of the name of one thing for that of another associated with or suggested by it), metaphor, synecdoche (a trope which heightens meaning by substituting the part for the whole or the whole for the part), and antithesis: "In political practice, therefore, they join in all coercive measures against the working class; and in ordinary life, despite their high-falutin phrases, they stoop to pick up the golden apples dropped from the tree of industry, and to barter truth, love, and honor for traffic in wool, beetroot-sugar, and potato spirits. As the parson has ever gone hand in hand with the landlord, so has Clerical Socialism with Feudal Socialism." It is important to note that the foregoing translated lines do not have the same overall flavor and effect that the original German text has; the sentence beginning "In political practice, therefore, they join," for instance, has lost much of its impact in translation. An underlying irony in the entire sentence is lost. That particular sentence reads, in Marx's German, *"In der politischen Praxis nehmen sie daher an allen Gewaltmassregeln gegen die Arbeiterklasse teil, und im gewöhnlichen Leben bequemen sie sich, allen ihren aufgeblähten Redensarten zum Trotz, die goldenen Äpfel aufzulesen und Treue, Liebe, Ehre mit dem Schacher in Schafswolle, Runkelreuben und Schnaps zu vertauschen."* Obviously, the "golden apples" referred to in the English translation are not the same "golden apples" of the original German text. However, it is the English version of the *Manifesto* with which I am concerned here, and my purpose is not to examine the discrepancies between the German and English versions of the *Communist Manifesto*; but it must be remembered that some of Marx's impact and irony is lost in the translation.

To give his presentation force and clarity, Marx has made extensive use of various figures which rely for their effect on repetition of one type or another; hence we find him using accumulation, anaphora, epistrophe (ending a series of clauses or sentences with the same word), and anadiplosis (repetition of the word ending one clause or sentence at the beginning of the next). He precedes an anadiplosis with a rhetorical question: "What does this accusation reduce itself to? The history of all past society has consisted in the development of class antagonisms, antagonisms that assumed different forms at different epochs." Of the many figures, Marx is particularly fond of using anaphora and asyndeton (omission of conjunctions); he uses them singly, he uses them combined with other tropes and figures. In the following sentence he combines anaphora and asyndeton with personification and antithesis: "In this way arose feudal socialism: half lamentation, half lampoon; half echo of the past, half menace of the future; at times, by its bitter, witty, and incisive criticism, striking the bourgeoisie to the very heart's core, but always ludicrous in its effect through total incapacity to comprehend the march of modern history."

Another figure which adds to the speech-like quality of the *Manifesto* is Marx's use of *correctio*. In the first instance below *correctio* is used alone; in the second instance it is combined with the periodic sentence; in the third, it appears with antithesis and metaphor: (1) "Hence, they habitually appeal to society at large, without distinction of class; nay, by preference, to the ruling class." (2) "Capital is a collective product, and only by the united action of many members, nay, in the last resort, only by the united action of all members of society, can it be set in motion." (3) "They are therefore not revolutionary, but conservative. Nay more, they are reactionary, for they try to roll back the wheel of history."

As one would expect of a person who thought in terms of class conflict and thesis-antithesis-synthesis, Marx incorporated into the *Manifesto* many phrases, sentences, and paragraphs which rely heavily for their effectiveness on balance and antithesis. "This kind of style [antithesis] is pleasing," said Aristotle, "because things are best known by opposition, and are all the better known when the opposites are put side by side; and is pleasing also because of its resemblances to logic—for the method of refutation is the juxtaposition of contrary conclusions." One simply cannot escape the antithesis in the following sentence, which appears at the beginning of Section I to support Marx's contention that the "history of all hitherto existing society is the history of class struggles": "Freeman and slave, patrician and plebian, lord and serf, guildmaster and journeyman, in a word, oppressor and oppressed, stood in constant opposition to one another, carried on an uninterrupted, now hidden, now open fight, a fight that each time ended, either in revolutionary reconstruction of society at large, or in the common ruin of the contending classes." Then, at other times, the antitheses appear sentence after sentence, paragraph after paragraph:

> In bourgeois society, living labor is but a means to increase accumulated labor. In Communist society, accumulated labor

is but a means to widen, to enrich, to promote the existence of the laborer.

In bourgeois society, therefore, the past dominates the present; in Communist society, the present dominates the past. In bourgeois society capital is independent and has individuality, while the living person is dependent and has no individuality.

To emphasize and clarify, Marx not only uses antithesis, but he also sets similarities side by side; sometimes the balance and antithesis are combined: "Just as it has made the country dependent on the towns, so it has made barbarian and semibarbarian countries dependent on the civilized ones, nations of peasants on nations of bourgeois, the East on the West."

Marx uses the device of disputation to display the thoughts of his opponents, to anticipate objections, and to answer those objections. He uses the figure synchoresis, whereby the speaker, trusting strongly in his own cause, freely gives his questioner leave to judge him. This particular device reappears often in Section II of the *Manifesto* combined with irony. His procedure here is to present the adversary's contentions and then to answer them; for the first time he begins to refer to his opponents as "you." Edmund Wilson has pointed out that Marx's opinions seem always to have been arrived at through a close criticism of the opinions of others, as if the sharpness and force of his mind could only really exert themselves in attacks on the minds of others, as if he could only find out what he thought by making distinctions that excluded the thoughts of others."[3] By using this procedure in Section II, Marx cuts into his adversary's contentions with a savage irony, discrediting them and at the same time pointing out the positive features of communism:

> You are horrified at our intending to do away with private property. But in your existing society, private property is already done away with for nine-tenths of the population. . . . You reproach us, therefore with intending. . . .
>
> In a word, you reproach us with intending to do away with your property. Precisely so; that is just what we intend.

> "Undoubtedly," it will be said, "religion, moral, philosophical and judicial ideas have been modified in the course of historical development. But religion, morality, philosophy, political science, and law, constantly survived this change."
>
> "There are, besides, eternal truths, such as Freedom, Justice, etc., that are common to all states of society. But communism abolishes eternal truths, it abolishes. . . ."

3. Edmund Wilson, *To the Finland Station* (New York, 1940), pp. 152–53.

What does this accusation reduce itself to? The history of all past society has consisted in the development of class antagonisms, antagonisms that assumed different forms at different epochs.

Just as the *Manifesto* begins with "the spectre of communism" and "this nursery tale of the spectre of communism," so too does it end with the proletarians having nothing to lose but "their chains" and with "a world to win." Excellence of style, wrote the author of *On the Sublime*, comes from five sources, the third of which consists "in a skilful application of figures, which are twofold, of sentiment and language."[4] These figures, continued Longinus, "when judiciously used, conduce not a little to Greatness."[5] The proof that Marx has "judiciously used" his rhetorical tropes and figures is in his ability to disguise the means he has employed, so that he seems to be speaking "not with artifice, but naturally."

LUCIEN LAURAT

If One Were to Rewrite the *Communist Manifesto* Today[†]

* * *

The reality of that time is no more and the Marxist doctrine has degenerated for many of its adepts into a collection of tatters, of slogans congealed into dogmas and foreign to reality. Paleomarxism[1] thus appeared as the main utopian socialism of the twentieth century, to which it is important to oppose a new synthesis embodying the scientific socialism of our times. It is a matter of making an inventory of the vast experience acquired in all domains and of stripping, in the light of this experience, the currently recognized doctrines of social transformation of their utopian and dogmatic elements, to synthesize them into a new empirical socialism. * * *

The *Manifesto* of Marx–Engels begins with the balance sheet of historical evolution at the threshhold of the crucial year 1848. A new balance sheet is called for today.

In the course of a century, capital has conquered the world and has fashioned a vast part of it in its image. It has brought forth pro-

---

4. Longinus, op. cit., p. 24.
5. Ibid., p. 85.
† From *Le Manifeste communiste de 1848 et le monde d'adjourd'hui* (Paris: Éditions Self, 1948), pp. 181–89. Translated from the French by Frederic L. Bender for this volume. All notes are the editor's.
1. Denotes rigid, Soviet-style Marxism.

ductive (and destructive) forces to an unsuspected degree. It has multiplied the proletariat, erecting it against the existing order and obliging it to organize itself. At the same time that capitalism has organized itself at the interior of national frontiers, liberalism has given way to the directed economy (however badly and fragmentarily directed), thus creating the economic premises of the socialist order. In the course of this evolution, the system still characterized as capitalist more and more loses the principal specific characteristics of capitalism. The only thing still capitalist about the regime of property is the name; the automatic functioning of economic laws has been paralyzed for about twenty years; the market has lost its role as exclusive regulator. Planning [*planification*], sometimes intelligent (the United States), sometimes stupid (France), has everywhere replaced the free play of economic forces.

From the social angle, capitalism has reduced the immense majority of the people to direct or indirect hirelings, thrown the old middle classes into the proletariat, made of the new middle classes a fraction of the wage-earning class, transformed the majority of those bosses who are still active (active capitalists) into wage-earners and tax collectors of the large trusts: it has made of a fraction of the wage-earning class and of a fraction of the managerial class a social category (the technostructure [*techniciens*]) capable from now on of directing the economy. The same evolution has dislocated the capitalist *class* by reducing the majority of bosses to simple hired managers and reserved the surplus value for a small minority "without function"; plutocrats increasing the private trusts and bureautechnocrats increasing the state trusts. The interpenetration of the state and the economy, the formation of levers of economic control, has favored and accelerated this process.

But in conquering the globe and in transforming its old clients into competitors, classical capitalism entangled itself in an impasse. The chronic stagnation following the mortal crisis of 1929 dislocated the world market and pushed the industrial nations toward autarchy. It stirred up the indignation of the popular masses tired of suffering, revolutionary explosions, and warlike conflagrations. In the countries hit most by the crisis, notably Germany, capitalism believed it could assure its survival by throwing itself into a totalitarian adventure and by liquidating the juridical, political, etc. institutions that it had formerly created.

However, these apparently political convulsions are only the exterior signs of a more profound transformation. A new social category is getting ready to take the place of the dislocated bourgeoisie. The revolutionary period of 1789–1848 had cleared the terrain so that the bourgeoisie, already in the saddle economically, could become the ruling class politically by definitively driving back the aristocracy, which, no longer exercising any active function in the economy, had become a parasitic class. To the degree that some aristocrats continued to play a role, they secured it not at all as members of their class, but by individual claim, having been integrated into the bourgeois class. In the present revolutionary period, the new social category that is establishing its candidature for power, the technostructure, will find itself from now on at the head of the economic process; it is in control of the whole economy by virtue of its installation at the levers of command of the state and of the principle organisms of the private economy. It opposes "percentage feudalism" (*féodaux du tantième*),[2] which has become a useless and parasitic category in imitation of the aristocracy of olden times. Even in the United States, where plutocratic capitalism still seems intact and in full vigor, the effective direction of economic processes belongs at present to the technostructure.

In contrast to the situation of a century ago, the technostructure, master of economic power and candidate for political power, is not a social class as opposed to the majority of workers, as the bourgeoisie *as a class* opposed the proletariat. Whereas the *antagonism* "bourgeois-proletariat" of the last century rested on a *social polarity*, the *difference* between the current directors of the economic process and the majority of workers [today] reflects a simple *functional hierarchy*, that of the work of administration and the work of execution.

The present situation resembles that of 1848 in that the immense majority, in the modern nations, aspires to a profound transformation of the existing relations, and in that at the head of this revolutionary push is found, today as then, the social category invested from then on with real economic power. In 1848, the push of the masses aspiring to Liberty, Equality, and Fraternity, led to the political consolidation of the bourgeoisie, already in possession of economic sovereignty. Doesn't the current revolution risk simply bringing to political power a technostructure already invested with economic power and ending itself once more through the substitution of a new form of exploitation of man by man for the one preceding?

A simple conclusion by analogy would seem to justify such a hypothesis. But the essential difference between the situation of 1789–1848 and that of today resides in that the technostructure is not, at least for the moment, a special class, polarized, facing the mass of the people. They represent the work of administration as opposed to the work of execution, and not at all a class of exploiters opposite a class of exploited workers. The bourgeoisie was already an exploiting class before acceding to undivided political power.

2. Roughly equivalent to "coupon clipping."

The technocrats are not, but they could become so and *become a technocracy* by means of certain particularly unpleasant and ominous circumstances.

Two perils are to be avoided in order to ward off this menace, which should not be underestimated: violent revolution and statism.

A violent revolution, which would put legality fatally in abeyance, would permit the directors of the economy, once politically all-powerful, to transform their monopoly of competence, purely cultural and subject to an incessant verification by competition, into a political monopoly, profiting by the dictatorship in order to rid themselves of all public control and to set their remuneration at their fancy—what is happening in Russia and what happened in Germany are quite conclusive in this regard.

It follows from this that socialism (we are not thinking of such or such a party, but of the collection of groups making use of a socialist ideology of a communitarian objective) should, in a democratic regime, categorically repudiate violent methods and dictatorship. Liberty, democracy, and public control alone are capable of preventing the holders of the levers of economic command from becoming a new class of exploiters.

The other enemy is statism. By overburdening the state with economic powers for which it is neither suited nor prepared, one hands over the key positions of the economy to a voracious bureaucracy, mischief-making and above the incompetent market. This statist bureaucracy, fusing with the technocracy from now on in place, can become (and is becoming already in France!) a semi-exploitative, semi-parasitic class. If the remedy for the crystallization of the technostructure into technocracy is political democracy, the remedy for exuberant statism is economic democracy. The economy will not be able to reject the suffocating tutelage of a state become omnivorous except by organizing itself by its own means. Organized economy is the order of the day: if the directors of the economy do not satisfy this historical necessity, the state will impose it on them by constraint, with easily foreseeable results.

Only the autonomous organization of the world of work will be able to effectually oppose this menace. And by "world of work" we mean today the immense majority of the population, since the old antagonism of 1848, "proletariat against bourgeoisie," belongs to the past. This autonomous organization is a process of continuous and spontaneous creation, in which the state only has to intervene in order to orient, to coordinate, and to legislate to give force of law and legal life to the new forms created by those [directly] concerned themselves.

The experience of the last years has demonstrated that the *mechanical* process of automatic centralization, of arbitrary collectivization,

of political and partisan statization, advances more rapidly than the
development of consciousness, of competence, of aptitude, and of
morality, whether it is a matter of the masses or the "élite." If this
clash should worsen, the world would move toward totalitarianism or
devour the last vestiges of our civilization. It is thus a matter far less
of putting one's shoulder to the wheel in order to "socialize," "nation-
alize," and "statize" with all one's might, than of instilling into this
"collectivist" construction that is working itself out—here under the
aegis of a statist bureaucracy, there under the impetus of a plutocratic
capitalism, elsewhere under the pressure of the technostructure
itself—a really collective and communal spirit, a spirit that abandons
this bureaucratic cement, a truly human motivation.

WAL SUCHTING

What Is Living and What Is Dead in the *Communist Manifesto*?[†]

In a primarily theoretical context (rather than, say, an aesthetic one)
there are, broadly speaking, two ways of considering a work like the
Communist Manifesto. They may be called the "historical" and the
"systematic" approaches. The first asks questions about the conditions of its production (for example, in what concrete problem-
situation, theoretical and/or practical, was it an intervention? what
discursive materials went into bringing it about?), and about the
effects which it had, once produced, about its 'consumption', as it
were (for example, how has it affected various currents of thought and
people's actions?). The second asks questions about its logical structure, its assumptions and premises, explicit and perhaps also implicit,
its conclusions, and about the value, from the point of view of current
thinking, for tackling current problems to which it may be considered relevant. * * * These two general approaches are distinct and,
up to a point, separable, though always ultimately complementary.

What follows takes primarily the second path. So, in a nutshell, it
poses the question: what, if anything, in the *Manifesto* is relevant
today to the search for solutions to the sorts of problems it addresses,
and hence, by implication, what in it is, on the contrary, of "merely
historical" significance? * * *

Among the central claims of the *Manifesto* are the following.

(1) Theoretical claim (1.1): Capitalism, after a period of development which had as one of its contradictory aspects a hitherto

† From Mark Cowling, ed., *The Communist Manifesto: New Interpretations* (New York:
NYU Press, 1998), pp. 157–65. Reprinted by permission of Edinburgh University Press.

unimaginable progress for humanity, as regards its productive powers and level of civilisation in general, is, in 1848, in terminal crisis,
as a result of a contradiction between the very growth of those powers and the social relations within which this has occurred. Capitalism cannot develop any further; indeed the bourgeoisie 'is incapable
of assuring its slave any kind of existence within his slavery . . .
because it is forced to let him sink into a condition, where it must
feed him, instead of being fed by him'. Hence "the class struggle
comes to a head."

(2) Practical-political claims: (2.1) In the past, class struggles
have "finished each time with a revolutionary transformation of
society as a whole, or in the common ruin of the contending
classes." In the case of capitalism there has been an overreaching
tendency for the "contending classes" to be reduced to two, capitalists and proletariat. The alternative of a "revolutionary transformation of society" can only be realized if the proletariat takes over the
existing state, the power of which "is merely a device for administer-
ing the common affairs of the whole bourgeois class." The central
aim in doing so is to be the abolition of private property, this making
possible the institution of a communist order of society, "an association, in which the free development of each is the condition for the
free development of all" (2.2). In this movement communists must
naturally play a vanguard role, for, "they have an advantage over the
general mass of the proletariat in terms of a theoretical insight into
the conditions, progress and general result of the movement."

(3) Theoretical claim (2): (2.1) is not only a fundamental practical-
political aim, but also what indeed will certainly happen: "Above all
[the bourgeoisie] produces its own gravediggers. Its downfall and the
victory of the proletariat are equally unavoidable." In fact, the imminent "bourgeois revolution in Germany can be merely the immediate
prelude to a proletarian revolution."

Claim (1) and at least the second part of (3) were hardly made
before they were shown by events to be completely false. What
the *Manifesto* diagnosed as its death throes quickly proved to be, on
the contrary, the travail attending the birth of a capitalism not only
economically dominant, as, broadly speaking, it was before, but
now politically so as well; in particular, the prediction concerning
Germany was quite off the mark. (However, it must be added that
Marx and Engels almost immediately saw their errors.) Every subsequent announcement of the imminent death of capitalism has
proved to be no less premature.

All this by itself does not rule out the more general claim in (3)
about the inevitability of the fall of the bourgeoisie and the victory
of the proletariat. However, this is so only because it is essentially
vacuous empirically. * * *

It is, of course, obvious now that, at the time anyway, neither of the authors had theoretical equipment at all adequate to the problems of analysis and prediction addressed in the *Manifesto*, in particular, nothing like an adequate political economy of the capitalist mode of production, an attempt to construct which would prove to be the major task of the rest of Marx's life. * * *

What can explain (in theoretical terms that is, rather than, say, psychological ones) the seemingly apodictic character of claims (1) and (3) in the *Manifesto*? One such explanation is as follows.

It is arguable that the *Manifesto* makes at least two assumptions: one implicit, the other reasonably explicit.

Assumption 1: the development of capitalism is governed by certain necessary economic laws which flow from its very nature. Such an assumption is not explicit in the *Manifesto*, but Marx expressed a view of this sort from time to time at least as late as the first volume of *Capital*. Thus in the preface to the first edition (1867) he writes of "the natural laws of capitalist production . . . working and enforcing themselves with iron necessity," and in the "Afterword" to the second edition (1873) he quotes with approval a long passage from a Russian review of the earlier edition, which says, among other things: "Marx treats the social movement as a process of natural history, governed by laws which are . . . independent of the will, consciousness and intentions of human beings." One consequence of these laws are that capitalism as such is subject, at a certain point, to chronic economic crises.

Now this by itself does not entail that the demise of capitalism is inevitable, fated, that it will happen no matter what people do, in particular, no matter what the proletariat does. It only becomes something like this when it is conjoined with at least one further assumption.

Assumption 2: to complete the quotation from the Russian reviewer referred to above: not only is it Marx's view that there are laws of the sort described but these "determine [*bestimmen*] their [human beings'] will, consciousness and intentions." Applied to present concerns this means that the economic laws which lead to crises and generally adverse effects on the proletariat work to give the latter a consciousness of their situation, of their objective interest in overthrowing capitalism, and, moreover, a will to do so. This assumption emerges in the *Manifesto* in passages like the following:

> The theoretical propositions of the communists . . . merely express in general terms the factual relations of an existing class struggle, a historical movement that is proceeding under our own eyes . . . man's presumptions, views and conceptions

alter according to their economic circumstances, their social relations, their social existence.

What else does the history of ideas demonstrate than that the products of the intellect are refashioned along with material ones? . . .

In speaking of ideas that revolutionise the whole of society, we merely express the fact, that within the old society the elements of a new one have formed, that the dissolution of the old ideas stays in step with the dissolution of the old conditions of life.

On these assumptions capitalism is seen as producing, parthenogenetically as it were, the necessary and sufficient conditions for its own dissolution. * * *

However, there are no empirical reasons for believing either of these assumptions. A simple argument for this is just a challenge to someone who thinks there are such: produce them! * * * They are of extra-scientific provenance.

If this is so, then what is this provenance? The overwhelmingly most likely answer is: Hegel.

On this diagnosis, the first assumption is related to Hegel's view that reality is ultimately Absolute Spirit, which is a necessarily articulated system. The atemporal structure of the latter (its structure *sub specie aeternitatis*) is revealed by logic (in the Hegelian sense of the word). This presents itself in a series of stages in which each attempt to grasp reality as anything short of Absolute Spirit ultimately exhibits contradictions—the process is thus 'dialectical'—which lead to more inclusive attempts until the category of the Absolute is attained. The structure of Absolute Spirit in its temporal projection, as it were, is manifested in the necessary movement of history and revealed by the philosophy of history. Here the timeless succession of categories exhibited in logic becomes a series of historical epochs, each one embodying an overriding category, each exhibiting internal contradictions and giving rise to the next, until the advent of one where there is a recognition of the true character of Absolute Spirit as an all-encompassing unity of finite selves.

Along similar lines, the second assumption may be related to Hegel's view that the true character of each phase, which to start with is implicit (*an sich*), eventually, after the phase has been completed, * * * becomes explicit and open to consciousness (*für sich*). The Owl of Minerva takes wing only at night: theory only formulates the character of what has already happened. * * * It is necessary that there should be ultimately this strict correlation between the real character of what is and its reflection in thought, since, after all,

finite thinkers are just the aspect of difference within the overarch-
ing identity in difference of Absolute Spirit.

Both assumptions 1 and 2 can then be seen to result from the
famous operation of standing Hegel on his head. Instead of matter's
being a way in which Absolute Spirit manifests itself, however inad-
equately, human consciousness is a way in which matter manifests
itself, matter including here the processes of history. Furthermore,
just as history as the temporal projection of Absolute Spirit has a
necessary structure, so history as a material process has one also,
specifically a necessary economic structure. Finally, just as the real
character of each phase of the historical self-revelation of Spirit
eventually becomes known to historical agents, so the character of
the material historical process necessarily reflects itself in the consciousness of human beings, even if only *post festum*.

*   *   *

So far, the discussion has focused on some central aspects of the
theoretical claims set out above and has, in effect, sought to identify what is arguably "dead" here. What is "living" in this area may
be located in at least two places.

One is at the point of various observations and explanatory glosses
about the development of capitalism, like its tendency towards periodic crises, the concentration and centralization of capital, the formation of a world market, and the dehumanisation of work, all
themes worked out in more sophisticated and detailed ways by Marx
and later by others following at least the general lines of his thought.

The other includes elements which may be described as raw
materials for the production of a conceptual framework for socio-
historical explanations, for modest predictions, and for the formulation and prosecution of certain political programmes. In this
regard it may be suggested that such a "materialist conception of
history" or "historical materialism" should be conceived as a reper-
tory of concepts and heuristic principles for inquiry rather than as
the repository of the sort of "laws of history," either in general or as
regards particular modes of production, which occur in the pages
of the *Manifesto*. * * *

The expression "raw materials" is used advisedly, for it cannot be
said that they exist in a satisfactory state in the *Manifesto*. Take, for
example, one of the fundamental principles of that work: "The history of all society up to now is the history of class struggles." To start
with, the concept of "class" appears in the *Manifesto* in a very inadequate form. Thus at the place where it is first introduced, at the
beginning of Section I, it seems to serve to identify, very generally,
"oppressor and oppressed," the heretofore pervasive "comprehensive
division of society into different orders, a multifarious gradation of
social rank." The existence of classes seems to be identified with

"the exploitation of one part of society by the other." All this is very vague, though it seems to limn a notion of "class" much broader than what Marx later meant by the term. It also tends to blur the fact that "the history of class struggles" has often been, basically and crucially, struggles, antagonisms, within the exploiting classes as a whole rather than between the latter and the exploited as a whole. (This is well illustrated by the history of the rise to dominance of the bourgeoisie in Europe, the most recent phases of which were incomparably analyzed by Marx himself in *The Eighteenth Brumaire, The Class Struggles in France* and elsewhere.) * * *

Turning now from the theoretical to the practical-political component of the *Manifesto*, set out above, it is, to start with, obvious enough that (2.2)—the idea of the vanguard role of communists— is dead. But what of the general goal of communism presented in (2.1)?

It is clear that this is also dead in the sense that there exists no social force with any claim to be taken seriously as a historical agent which has that goal on its political agenda, and that it is completely unlikely that one will exist within the however remotely foreseeable future. To the extent that, in the opening words of the *Manifesto*, "A spectre haunts the land of Europe—the spectre of communism," that spectre is not a premonition, terrifying to capitalists, of what is to come, but a ghost of the dead, and the following claim that "Communism is already recognized as a force by all the European powers" at best a report about the past.

The reasons for this are complex. On the one hand, they include capitalism's success so far in surviving its colossal internal economic and general social problems. On the other, they include the failure of all attempts so far to realize anything even distantly like the sort of communist programme which Marx envisaged: every "actually existing socialism" has been, or become more or less rapidly, economically dysfunctional and/or inegalitarian, and also politically repressive.

Of course, it is true that many different explanations, in terms of specific historical factors, have been given for such failures. However, even if there is some adequate explanation for each, this would provide no positive ground whatsoever for thinking that some future and reasonably lasting communist mode of organization of society is achievable, that future ventures will not fail, even if, each time, for explicable reasons.

If history so far furnishes no actual examples of successful socialist/communist projects then it furnishes no rational grounds for believing that they are really possible in the future.

However, if we discount crudely inductivist arguments from past failures, neither does it afford rational grounds for believing that such projects are really impossible.

Indeed the historical facts are consistent with a rational gamble
on a socialist/communist political programme. To start with, it
needs to be established, as far as anything of the sort can be, that
the ultimate goal of such a programme offers the best available
theoretical alternative to capitalism, in, as Brecht put it, "these dark
times," present and future. Then it can be further argued in the following way that it is rational to pursue such a programme without
any prior knowledge of the possibility of its success. If the programme is in fact achievable (though we cannot know this to be so),
and if pursuing it is a necessary condition for achieving it, then it is
rational to pursue it. If the programme is not in fact achievable
(though again we cannot know this to be so) then pursuing it is,
hopefully, merely futile. (In this regard the argument is not unlike
"Pascal's Wager" about belief in God.)

This sort of consideration may well be pretty thin gruel to offer to
an understandably desperate appetite for hope. But there is no point
in denying that, at the present time, we can see humanity's historical prospects, even in the fairly short term, through a glass at best
only very darkly. The fact is that, in general, there is an irreducible
element of contingency in history and therefore in politics (Lenin
for one never tired of stressing this)[1] which should bate too immod-
erate a desire for programmatic certainties of any sort.

*   *   *

The spectre of communism has ceased to haunt Europe, but the
Manifesto has not ceased to haunt revolutionaries. The preceding
remarks have only indicated a few broad lines for a discussion with
"that affable familiar ghost." Innumerable others remain. One,
chosen partly because it has very seldom been discussed, rather
than taken by most Marxists as virtually axiomatic, is the view,
classically set out in it,[2] of the overall progressive character of capitalism as a historical epoch, a discussion which would eventually
have to consider the issue of what it means to call an epoch "progressive" at all.[3] Perhaps what is truly living in the *Manifesto* resides
more in the questions it raises than in the answers it gives to them.

*   *   *

1. For example: 'History as a whole, and the history of revolutions in particular, is always
   richer in content, more varied, more multiform, more lively and ingenious than is
   imagined by even the best parties, the most class-conscious vanguards of the most
   advanced classes.' ('*Left-Wing*' *Communism—an Infantile Disorder* in Lenin, *Collected
   Works* (Moscow, Progress Publishers, 1966) Vol. 31, p. 95).
2. *Manifesto*, p. 16.
3. See I. Wallenstein, *Historical Capitalism with Capitalist Civilization* (London/New
   York, Verso, 1995), especially pp. 97ff. J. Vogel raised some related issues in his 'The
   Tragedy of History' in *New Left Review*, No. 220, November/December 1996, pp. 36–
   61, but not, I think, as radically as Wallerstein.

WENDY LYNNE LEE

Socialist Feminist Critique and the
Communist Manifesto†

In her groundbreaking 1983 work *Feminist Politics and Human Nature* (FPHN), Alison Jaggar argues that Karl Marx's biting critique of capitalism can illuminate the economic oppression not only of workers, but of women theorized in terms of their role in the reproduction of the capacity to labor (as unpaid domestic labor) as well as in the (sexual) reproduction of laborers. She argues that while Marx pays scant attention to women's role in the labor market, central Marxist concepts such as alienation, commodification, and the historical materialist method can shed substantial light on the economic and social conditions affecting women specifically, many of which are at least as oppressive as those confronted by male workers. No doubt Marx understood that the social and economic oppression of women was distinctive in a number of ways. In *The Communist Manifesto*, for example, he traces the oppressive effects of the rise of the bourgeoisie—the property owning class—on the family through its *commodification* of family relations. He writes, for example, that "[t]he bourgeoisie has torn away from the family its sentimental veil, and has reduced the family relation to a mere money relation," that in "modern industry, all family ties among the proletarians (working class people) are torn asunder, and their children transformed into simple articles of commerce and instruments of labor." In short, with the advent of capitalism,

> the family undergoes a radical if incremental transformation whose effects subordinate its basic social relationships to that of a single other, namely, the relationship between capitalist and laborer . . . [w]hereas a family member might otherwise have owed her or his primary fidelity and identity to the maintenance of kin relationships, allegiance is now owed only to the wage. Necessities once collectively produced and distributed must now be purchased . . . children once conceived as future projections of self are reducible to either asset or liability depending upon the dispatch with which they enter the labor force . . . the family now exists as a unit in support of the economy.[1]

---

† Written for this Norton Critical Edition.
1. Lee, Wendy Lynne, *On Marx*, (Wadsworth Philosophers Series. Belmont, CA: Wadsworth/Thompson Learning, 2002), p. 35.

Affection or familial bonds are replaced, Marx argues, by a valuation determined by the capacity to contribute to the family's survival as a "unit" of labor and exchange; family members are thus no longer (or merely nominally) fathers, mothers, or children, but rather owner/managers and labor force. Wage labor effectively converts mothers into instruments for the reproduction of labor and laborers and children into "articles of commerce."

It is thus *as* wives and mothers that Marx seems most cognizant of capitalism's negative consequences for women. Reference, however, to the oppression of women *as workers outside the domestic sphere* or even as *individual human actors* remains at best indirect throughout his critique. As Daniel Little puts it, "Marx's writings are most closely associated with the economic and social domination associated with class, with little attention to the inequalities associated with gender. Marx had little to say directly about the system of gender domination prevalent in his own time, and he was not publicly associated with the contemporary movement for the emancipation of women," even though a number of others such as John Stewart Mill, were "agitating for women's economic and political rights."[2]

Nonetheless, Little argues, "the fundamental themes of social criticism that Marx puts forward—alienation, domination, inequality, and exploitation, and a critique of the social relations that give rise to these conditions—have clear implications for a theory of gender equality and emancipation." Indeed, but Marx himself offers little direct help at this point, arguing (though not consistently) that the emergent bourgeoisie effectively *replaces* all other social relations, including patriarchal ones:

> The bourgeoisie, wherever it has got the upper hand, has put an end to all feudal, patriarchal, idyllic relations. It has pitilessly torn asunder the motley feudal ties that bound man to his "natural superiors," and has left no other nexus between man and man than naked self-interest, than callous "cash payment." It has drowned the most heavenly ecstasies of religious fervor, of chivalrous enthusiasm, of philistine sentimentalism, in the icy water of egotistical calculation.

What Marx fails to recognize is the extent to which patriarchal institutions are not replaced by capitalism but instead appropriated by it, supplying capitalist enterprise with a ready-made infrastructure for both the exploitation of labor and for the *reproduction* of laborers. As a number of feminist theorists have shown, the bourgeoisie transforms and retools the family taking advantage of a struc-

2. Little, Daniel, "Marxism, Communism, and Women," www-personal. umd.umich .edu/~delittl//Enrry%20communism%20and%20marxism%20on%20gender%20v2.htm.

ture already outfitted for the commodifying of women's sexuality and unpaid domestic labor. What is needed, as Zillah Eisenstein argues, is a critique of capitalism that takes into account the relationship between patriarchal institutions like the family and the church in light of their appropriation by capitalist enterprise. Eisenstein makes the connection clear: "[i]f women's existence is defined by capitalism and patriarchy through their ruling ideologies and institutions, then an understanding of either capitalism alone or patriarchy in isolation will not deal with the problem of women's oppression."[3]

Given, then, the absence of such a critique until well into the 20th century, it's not surprising that even in a manifesto designed to unify and empower workers to unite against their common oppressor, Marx's only specific reference to the status of women *as* women comes in the context of his refutation of bourgeois complaints against the Communists:

> But you Communists would introduce community of women, screams the whole bourgeoisie in chorus. The bourgeois sees in his wife a mere instrument of production. He hears that the instruments of production are to be exploited in common, and naturally can come to no other conclusion than that the lot of being common to all will likewise fall to the women.

On the one hand, Marx recognizes in the bourgeoisie the exploitation of women as "instruments of production" within the family. He sees too that the "community of women" characterizing both marriage and prostitution as long-standing institutions (or really the same institution) function to commodify women's sexuality:

> The Communists have no need to introduce community of women; it has existed almost from time immemorial. Our bourgeois, not content with having wives and daughters of their proletarians at their disposal, not to speak of common prostitutes, take greatest pleasure in seducing each other's wives. Bourgeois marriage is in reality a system of wives in common and thus, at the most, what the Communists might possibly be reproached with is that they desire to introduce, in substitution for a hypocritically concealed, an openly legalized community of women.

Marx's solution, however, for the concealed prostitution of which he accuses the bourgeoisie offers little more than cold comfort toward redressing women's commodified status since avoiding

---

3. Eisenstein, Zillah. "Constructing a Theory of Capitalist Patriarchy and Socialist Feminism." *Women, Class, and the Feminist Imagination: A Socialist-Feminist Reader*, Ed. Karen V. Hansen and Ilene J. Phillipson (Philadelphia: Temple University Press, 1990), p. 131.

hypocrisy through "an openly legalized community of women" is no call at all for women to unite against their common oppressor in the patriarchal family—bourgeois or Communist. On the other hand, then, it's difficult to come away from these passages without the sense that Marx was far less concerned with the welfare of women *per se* than he was with deploying the sexualized notion of a "community of women" as a strategy to undermine the moral legitimacy of the bourgeoisie. One thing is clear: the substitution of a legalized commodification of women's sexuality for its thinly concealed cousin in either marriage or backstreet prostitution offers little incentive to women to include themselves in Marx's call for workers to unite.

In fairness to Marx, he does point out that "[f]or the rest, it is self-evident, that the abolition of the present system of production must bring with it the abolition of the community of women springing from that system, i.e., prostitution both public and private." This aspiration, however, is not likely to be realized in that it seriously underestimates both the sheer durability of patriarchal institutions like marriage and—though consistent with Marx's earlier claim that the bourgeoisie will replace all earlier forms of oppression—fails to account for the advantage to the capitalist in retaining marriage and the family as an efficient unit of production and reproduction:

> At least three features identify the relationship of wife to husband as one of prostitution: First, the relationship itself is premised on an exchange value assigned to the wife *qua* women, e.g., *qua* her value as an instrument of production through whom her husband carries out various transactions. . . . Second, the nature of this exchange is specifically material in the sense that its instruments are women's bodies whose value or *currency* is assessed in terms of the performance of sexual and/ or reproductive service. She is commodifiable as production and as leisure. Lastly, the idea that women are commodities to be exploited *in common* attests to the substitutability of material bodies for sexual and reproductive labor.[4]

Capitalism *capitalizes* on existing social relations within marriage— and can only do so *because* women are already defined in terms of patriarchal dependence, obligation to sexual and reproductive service, and duty to domestic labor. To expose these facts about the status of women, to exchange an open for a hidden "community of women," does go some way towards an analysis of the relationship of capitalism and patriarchy, but not far enough. My argument,

4. Lee, pp. 37–38.

then, is that the *Communist Manifesto* must be read not only through socialist feminist criticism like Eisenstein's and Jaggar's, but through other of Marx's works such as *The Economic and Philosophic Manuscripts of 1844* (EPM) and *The German Ideology* where his conception of a material and embodied human being provides a compelling way to ground the socialist feminist critique of not only capitalism, but its economic bedfellows in marriage and the church.

Re-reading the Communist Manifesto *in Light of the Feminist Appropriation of Historical Materialism*

Like Eisenstein, Jaggar argues for a socialist feminism capable of articulating the mutually advantageous "marriage" of patriarchy and capitalist enterprise:

> On the socialist feminist analysis, capitalism, male dominance, racism, and imperialism are intertwined so inextricably that they are inseparable; consequently, the abolition of any of these systems of domination requires the end of all of them. Socialist feminists claim that a full understanding of the capitalist system requires a recognition of the way in which it is structured by male dominance and, conversely, that a full understanding of male dominance requires a recognition of the way it is organized by the capitalist division of labor. Socialist feminists believe that an adequate account of "capitalist patriarchy" requires the use of the historical materialist method developed originally by Marx and [Frederick] Engels.[5]

Although, as historian Isaiah Berlin points out, "[n]o formal exposition of historical materialism was ever published by Marx himself," Marx regarded it as "a practical method of social and historical analysis, and as a basis of political strategy."[6] It is this method that may best characterize Marx's approach in *The Communist Manifesto* whose first full section, "Bourgeois and Proletarians," opens with the claim that "[t]he history of all hitherto existing society is the history of class struggle." Socialist feminists don't disagree with this claim, but rather seek to utilize the historical materialist method to gain a clearer understanding of how the division of labor organizes both economic class *and* labor relations within the home. The feminist appropriation of the historical materialist method can, in other words, not only illuminate the patriarchal dimension of class struggle, it can show that the roots of this struggle lay in an older and more fundamental division of labor within the family.

5. Jaggar, Alison. *Feminist Politics and Human Nature* (Totowa, NJ: Rowman and Little-field Publishers, 1983), pp. 124–25.
6. Berlin, Isaiah. *Karl Marx.* (New York: Times, Inc., Book Division, 1963).

What Jaggar makes clear is that any analysis directed to class struggle alone—that fails to address unpaid domestic labor, the labor of sexual reproduction, and/or slave labor—cannot provide more than a distorted picture of what it would mean to unite workers. Marx goes on, for example, in *The Communist Manifesto* to argue that "[f]reeman and slave, patrician and plebian, lord and serf, guild-master and journeyman, in a word, oppressor and oppressed, stood in constant opposition to one another, carried on an uninterrupted, now hidden, now open fight, either in a revolutionary reconstitution of society at large, or in the common ruin of the contending classes." Such, however, is by no means an exhaustive list of the opposition responsible for structuring the conditions of class struggle. Indeed, were it not for the unpaid domestic labor provided by wives and mothers the struggle among these *recognized* classes of men would not have been possible. Hence, when Marx continues that "[i]n the earlier epochs of history, we find almost everywhere a complicated arrangement of society into various orders, a manifold gradation of social rank," he's surely right—but not for exactly the reasons he thinks, for this "complicated arrangement of society" depends on an even more complicated arrangement largely absent from his account, namely, that of the patriarchal order in collusion with its supporting hierarchy in the church. Contrary, then, to Marx's claim that "[o]ur epoch, the epoch of the bourgeoisie, possesses, however, this distinctive feature: it has simplified the class antagonisms" it has, in fact, reinforced and transformed an existing social order of oppressor and oppressed—making invisible the patriarchal conditions of the existence of class.

A socialist feminist appropriation of the historical materialist method takes as its conceptual point of departure what Marx calls "species being," namely, the notion that "human beings, are a species of animal who, like other sentient creatures, have real physical needs, are capable of suffering, live for a finite time, and eventually die."[7] Grounded in the material, embodied, and historical conditions of human existence and experience, the aim of the method is to evaluate human institutions including family structure, the organization of labor, the drafting of civil law, and the system of economic exchange in light of the success or failure with which each contributes to meeting human need. It is precisely because capitalism not only fails to meet human need, but does so in the process of empowering the few at the expense of the many, that the method offers something more than analysis, namely, the impetus to

---

7. Marx, Karl. *The Economic and Philosophic Manuscripts of 1844* (EPM). Trans. Martin Milligan. Ed. Dirk J. Struik (New York: International Publishers, 1964), pp. 112–14; Jaggar, 1983, pp. 52–60; Lee, p. 1.

revolution. As Marx puts the point in the *Communist Manifesto*: "But not only has the bourgeoisie forged the weapons that bring death to itself; it has also called into existence the men who are to wield those weapons—the modern working class—the proletarians."

What socialist feminism contributes to the historical materialist account, then, are answers to key questions concerning *who* is empowered by a form of exchange that otherwise so fails to meet human need, *whose* labor is responsible for creating wealth, how the division of labor is organized, to whose benefit, and what conditions define the relationship between workers and capitalists.[8] Consider, for example, Marx's discussion of the role played by machines in the division of labor:

> Owing to the extensive use of machinery and to division of labor, the work of the proletarians has lost all individual character, and, consequently, all charm for the workman. He becomes an appendage of the machine, and it is only the most simple, most monotonous, and most easily acquired knack, that is required of him. Hence the cost of production of a workman is restricted . . . to the means of subsistence that he requires for his maintenance and for the propagation of his race. . . . Modern industry has converted the little workshop of the patriarchal master into the great factory of the industrial capitalist.

Insofar as the labors of men are superseded by machinery, insofar as labor is degraded and deskilled by technology, so too is the status of the worker; so degraded in fact that the worker's wages reflect only subsistence and the "propagation of his race." The division of labor in the factory, in other words, is organized according to whatever is required to insure the worker's continuing capacity to work, namely, the production of his subsistence and the reproduction of his kind. But this latter labor—however invisibly—is not that of the worker who is displaced by the machine; it is that of his wife, that is, she who produces the conditions of his subsistence and bears his children. The language of this passage, moreover, suggests that "propagation of race" isn't real labor at all, but rather merely a pastime activity of men; the contribution women make to such propagation is entirely effaced.

The veiled implication of such a passage, then, is that however disempowered at the factory, the worker remains the "patriarchal master" of *his* home, a "complication" that defies Marx's claim that class antagonisms have become simplified. The extent to which Marx

---

8. For additional elaboration of this theme, see Barbara Ehrenreich's "What Is Socialist Feminism?" in *Materialist Feminism: A Reader in Class, Difference and Women's Lives* (New York: Routledge, 1997), p. 65–70.

disregards women's unpaid domestic labor is reinforced in the same passage when he argues that "[t]he less the skill and exertion of strength implied in manual labor . . . the more modern industry becomes developed, the more is the labor of men superseded by that of women. Differences of age and sex have no longer any distinctive social value for the working class." The assumption that underlies the claim that modern industry's machinery can be operated "even by a women" is precisely the same as that which allows Marx to ignore the essential role that women play in the home, namely, that there *are* "differences of age and sex." But far from being effaced by the development of industry, such differences are in fact necessary to it insofar as it is this domestic labor that provides workers to the factory—male or female.

That many of the workers occupying the lowest status, earning the lowest of wages, are women is a fact brought into stark relief by the socialist feminist analysis of labor. As Jaggar argues, capitalism's primary beneficiaries are *some* men, namely, white, Western (or Westernized) men whose dependence on the labor of a working class itself depends on the "private" or unpaid domestic labor of women. Among the substantial negative effects accruing to the invisibility of women's domestic labor must be included the exclusion of women from public life (other than as workers) and women's disempowerment as political actors. As Jaggar argues, "[o]n the traditional Marxist view, the organization of work under capitalism subjects housewives to a form of oppression that is even deeper than the direct oppression that they may suffer from their husbands. No matter how gentle and respectful their husbands may happen to be, housewives are oppressed by their exclusion from public life."[9] It would seem, as Marx advocates,[1] that the solution to this form of oppression would be found in the introduction of women into the active labor force.[2] Indeed, that Marx "applauds changes in the organization of labor that bring women into the work force as an opportunity for gainful activity implies that what counts as real labor for him occurs only outside the home, in the public but not the private sphere."[3]

As recent U.S. Census Bureau statistics show, however, hundreds of years of women's contribution to wage labor offers only cold comfort to pay equity despite the persistent drumbeat of arguments that competition is the remedy for economic inequality.[4] We can, of course, point to examples of union organizing (especially in

9. Jaggar, 1983, p. 220.
1. Ibid., p. 221.
2. Ibid., pp. 200–201.
3. Lee, p. 65.
4. http://en.wikipedia.org/wiki/Image:Income_inequity_US.png.

the textile industry) or the creation of regulatory agencies like the Equal Employment Opportunity Commission (EEOC) whose charge it is to address claims of sex (and race) based inequality. It is nonetheless telling, however, that "[a]t the time of the EPA's [1963's Equal Pay Act's] passage, women earned just 58 cents for every dollar earned by men. By 2005, that rate had only increased to 77 cents, an improvement of less than half a penny a year. Unsurprisingly, minority women fare the worst. African-American women earn just 69 cents to every dollar earned by white men, and for Hispanic women that figure drops to merely 59 cents per dollar."[5] These facts both support and conflict with Marx's assessment of the introduction of women into the labor force in the *Communist Manifesto*. On the one hand, that women would be likely to earn less is hardly surprising given a conception of labor mechanized in such a fashion that "even a women can perform it." Mechanization, in other words, feminizes the labor process converting it from one that requires "manly" strength and intelligence to one that requires only as much as a woman is presumed to be able to provide. On the other hand, that union organizing took place in a number of female-dominated industries like textiles, and that this gave impetus to the rise of government agencies like the EEOC, testifies to the political power that at least some women began to be able to exercise in the defense of their own public positions as workers.

What the endurance of wage disparity also implies, however, is that efforts to reform patriarchal capitalism internally can never be fully adequate, and the key, once again, lay in the concept of species being. Species being "cannot be defined as an unchanging given attendant on species membership, but rather must be conceived *dialectically*, that is, as an evolving work or project whose relationship to nature is both material and rational, physical and psychological."[6] A dialectical process "is one in which progress or change

5. www.infoplease.com/ipa/A0763170.html. For an alternative but complimentary feminist argument whose aim is to analyze reasons given for the wage gap, see Vicki Schultz's "Women 'Before' the Law: Judicial Stories about Women, Work, and Sex Segregation on the Job," in *Feminists Theorize the Political*, ed. Judith Butler and Joan W. Scott (New York: Routledge, 1992), pp. 297–338. Schultz argues that among the most common reasons given for the wage gap is that women prefer "women's work" even though it pays less than "men's work" because it allows women to do more of what they really want—to be wives and mothers. She then goes on to demonstrate the ways in which we define and inculcate gender actually reinforces the patriarchal and heterosexist attitudes that influence women's and men's "choices" of occupation. Despite critiques like Schultz's, this view is reiterated in a number of contemporary conservative critiques of feminism, for example, Warren Farrell's *Why Men Earn More: The Startling Truth Behind the Pay Gap*. Ironically, it's at least arguable that Marx's own conception of the division of labor actually reinforces a very similar conception of the division of labor. For an analysis in support of this claim, please see Wendy Lynne Lee's *On Marx*, pp. 12–17, p. 63–68, and pp. 74–79, and Jaggar's *Feminist Politics and Human Nature*, pp. 69–72.
6. Lee, p. 1, Marx: EPM, p. 112.

occurs through the overcoming of some initial set of conditions
itself the product of some earlier set overcome, and so on. To claim
that species being is dialectical, then, is to claim it as a product of
a continuous progress of overcoming those material conditions
through which change for it is made possible."[7] Institutions that
encourage dialectical progress through what Marx calls *praxis* or
creative labor are those which meet human need and support
human flourishing; institutions that hinder or stifle human creativity in the interest of creating wealth for a few regardless of cost to
the many (environmental, human, time) are, as Marx puts it, *alienating*, that is they result in the estrangement of the individual from
her or his own creative potential.[8]

It's no wonder then that, given the alienating conditions of mass
production, the bourgeoisie come to regard the proletariat as the
"dangerous class, the social scum, that passively rotting mass
thrown off by the lowest layers of old society." Such is precisely
what we would expect to transpire when the prospect of progress,
of overcoming, is made seemingly impossible. "The proletarian,"
writes Marx,

> is without property; his relation to his wife and children has no
> longer anything in common with the bourgeois family rela-
> tions; modern industrial labor . . . has stripped him of every
> trace of national character. Law, morality, religion, are to him
> so many bourgeois prejudices, behind which lurk in ambush
> just as many bourgeois interests.

What the bourgeoisie count on is that alienation at the level of individual workers will insure against the formation of class consciousness, that this "dangerous class" whose workers are remanded to
constant competition with each other for jobs and thus survival,
will never come to recognize itself as such. The dialectic, however,
operates not merely at the level of individual praxis and alienation,
but also at the level of class consciousness. The historical materialist method of the *Communist Manifesto* once again offers a clue:

> But whatever form they may have taken, one fact is common to
> all past ages, viz., the exploitation of one part of society by
> another. No wonder, then, that the social consciousness of past
> ages, despite all the multiplicity and variety it displays, moves
> within certain common forms, or general ideas, which cannot
> completely vanish except with the total disappearance of
> class antagonisms. The Communist revolution is the most

---

7. Lee, p. 2, Marx, Karl. *The German Ideology*, Ed. C. J. Arthur, (New York: International
   Publishers, 1981), p. 47.
8. Marx, EPM, pp. 107–09; Jaggar, 1983, 208–15.

radical rupture with traditional relations; no wonder that its development involves the most radical rupture with traditional ideas.

The emergence, in other words, of the revolutionary working class *as* a class can only be fully understood in light of past ruptures with "traditional relations," for example "[w]hen the ancient world was in its last throes, the ancient religions were overcome by Christianity," but later "Christian ideas succumbed in the 18th century to rationalist ideas."

Each of these struggles, argues Marx, can be "reduced" to class antagonisms: "[t]he history of all past society has consisted in the development of class antagonisms, antagonisms that assumed different forms at different epochs." These, then, will come finally to an end in the revolution by doing away with distinctions of class altogether:

> When, in the course of development, class distinctions have disappeared, and all production has been concentrated in the hands of a vast association of the whole nation, the public power will lose its political character. Political power, properly so called, is merely the organized power of one class for oppressing the other. If the proletariat . . . is compelled by the force of circumstances to organize itself as a class; if by means of a revolution, it makes itself the ruling class, and, as such, sweeps away by force the old conditions of production, then it will, along with these conditions, have swept away the conditions for the existence of class antagonisms, and of classes generally, and will thereby have abolished its own supremacy as a class.

The difficulty, from a socialist feminist point of view, is that while Marx is right that political power is the organized power of one class for oppressing another, he is nonetheless mistaken in thinking that the end of the relationship of the proletariat and the bourgeoisie is the end of oppressive relationships. That patriarchy continues to characterize the relation of men to women, husbands to wives, insures the continuation of oppression within the family, and thereby effectively excludes women from the revolution in the same way women are excluded from participating fully in public life.

Global Capitalism and the Place of Women in the Communist Revolution

In the *Communist Manifesto* Marx predicts that "[t]he need of a constantly expanding market for its products chases the bourgeoisie over the whole surface of the globe." "It must nestle everywhere," he continues, "settle everywhere, establish connections everywhere."

Foreseeing the emergence of the corporation without national affili-
ation or restriction of border, he writes that

> [t]he bourgeoisie has through its exploitation of the world mar-
> ket given a cosmopolitan character to production and consump-
> tion in every country . . . it has drawn from under the feet of
> industry the national ground on which it stood. All old-
> established national industries have been destroyed or are daily
> being destroyed. They are dislodged by new industries, whose
> introduction becomes a life and death question for all civilized
> nations, by industries that no longer work up indigenous raw
> material, but raw material drawn from the remotest zones;
> industries whose products are consumed not only at home, but
> in every quarter of the globe.

However prescient, there nonetheless remains a sense in which
the *Communist Manifesto* reaches both its zenith and its end in
this remarkable passage. Marx could not have foreseen the toll this
expansion would take on workers or on the domestic and subsistence farming labor traditionally performed by women, or on the
environmental resources polluted if not wholly exhausted by
mass production.[9] Indeed, what Marx fails to foresee is that the
very institutions that make capitalism possible—patriarchal marriage and the family—are precisely the institutions responsible for
the capacity of capitalist enterprise to attain global proportion.

In a recent essay, "A Feminist Critique of the Southern Debt,"
Jaggar points out that

> [l]arge-scale cash crop development has displaced women's
> subsistence farming and thereby contributed to famines, espe-
> cially in Africa. In India, the destruction of forests for large-
> scale agriculture has resulted in an increase in the time women
> must spend collecting firewood and fodder, which in turn
> means they have less time available for crop production; their
> income is reduced and their nutrition suffers. . . . [1]

Moreover, while Marx had high aspirations that technology would
replace at least the most arduous of labor, he did not foresee what
feminist writers like Swasti Mitter describe as its *casualization*:

> A significant yet grossly underemphasized aspect of the cur-
> rent global restructuring is . . . the emergence of an acutely
> polarized labor market. In such a market . . . a small number
> of core workers is going to exist with a vast array of peripheral
> workers. There are many names for these peripheral workers:

9. Lee, pp. 89–91.
1. Jaggar, Alison, "A Feminist Critique of the Alleged Southern Debt," *Hypatia* 17.4 (Fall
   2002), p. 126.

flexible workers, casual workers, or . . . temporary or part-time proletariat. All these terms have the same or similar connotations, and conjure up invariably the image of a worker who is a woman, and whose status as a wage-earner does not necessarily carry with it an automatic prospect of career progression. Nor does the image imply job security or other employment-related benefits such as a core worker enjoys. . . . [These workers] provide the base of a growing "shoe-shine" economy even in the affluent West.[2]

Writing in 1986, Mitter goes on to note the distinctively sexed and raced character of this expansion as well as the technologically mediated reality of its factories and assembly lines. The "casualized" working class, writes Mitter, is "not only ignored by the mainstream labor movement, but by most writers on economic and political issues" in virtue of the fact that it is composed primarily of women, persons of color, indigenous peoples, and children.[3] "Whereas literally thousands of articles have been written on the labor-replacing aspect of new technology," she concludes, "only a handful have been written on the casualization of work, and these mostly by committed women scholars."[4]

As the trend towards casualized labor continues into the 21st century its hallmark characteristic, as Jaggar shows, is the extent to which it has become *feminized* both nationally and globally:

> In the global North, women, especially women of color, are disproportionately impoverished by the economic inequality resulting from "free" trade, which has resulted in many hitherto well-paid jobs being moved from the North to low-wage areas in the global South. These jobs have been replaced in the North by so-called "McJobs," "*casual*," contingency, or part-time positions, often in the service sector, which are typically low-paid and lack health or retirement benefits. . . . The feminization of poverty was a term coined originally to describe the situation of women in the United States, but the United Nations reports that [it] has now become a global and growing phenomenon, with women comprising 70 percent of the world's 1.3 billion poor.[5]

For Jaggar, like Mitter, globalization represents less the economic development with which it is typically associated than, as Vandana Shiva puts it, the *maldevelopment* that leads, on the one hand, to

---

2. Mitter, Swasti. "Women Working Worldwide." *Materialist Feminism: A Reader in Class, Difference, and Women's Lives.* Ed. Rosemary Hennesy and Chrys Ingraham (New York: Routledge, 1997), pp. 163–74.
3. Ibid., p. 164.
4. Ibid., p. 164.
5. Jaggar, 2002, p. 124, author's emphasis.

tremendous wealth for a lucky—mostly Northern (Western)—
few, and on the other to an ever-deepening poverty for the many,
particularly women, nonwhites, indigenous peoples, and children.
Contrary, then, to Marx's pronouncement in the *Communist Manifesto* of its abolition, the status of women as it has been defined in
the patriarchal family remains a key determinant in the organization of labor. "The bourgeois family," writes Marx, "will vanish as
a matter of course when its compliment [the proletariat] vanishes, and both will vanish with the vanishing of capital."

Such a "vanishing," however, has not only failed to transpire,
but, instead, women and children have become the "raw materials"
of mass production in the now corporate quest for ever-expanding
markets. Marx is certainly right that the reach of capital is a "life
or death question" for national development. Insofar as the development of the global marketplace jeopardizes the relationship
between human agents, subsistence labor, and the natural resources
upon which these depend, development, argues Shiva, is at least
for some (especially women), maldevelopmental if not simply toxic.
The "cosmopolitan character of production and consumption" is
harmful for those whose lives are imperiled by consequences for
the environment, consequences that Marx did not foresee. While
it's no wonder, moreover, that women bear the brunt of the destruction of resources in terms of the destruction of their own opportunities to engage in productive (and reproductive) labor, what Shiva
highlights is that casualization begins in the displacement of those
forms of productivity more directly associated with soil, water, and
vegetation. It begins, in other words, not only with the destruction
of a variety of labor performed primarily by women, subsistence
farming, but with the alienation of a primary element of women's
cultural, gendered, and even personal identity, *the provision of
food*, from those whose work—once valued as essential to family
and community—is now displaced by casualized labor itself characterized as "women's work," that is, as feminized (Lee, p. 89).
Because, moreover, the conditions for food production are themselves jeopardized through the destruction of soil and water, the
pressure to enter the paid labor force increases as a way to secure
food—however grown and packaged elsewhere, or as Marx fore-
shadows in the *Communist Manifesto*, "industries whose products
are consumed not only at home, but in every quarter of the globe."

In short, what a socialist feminist reading of *The Communist
Manifesto* can show is the extent to which Marxist ideas remain
relevant and useful to the critique of capitalism. What such a reading can also demonstrate, however, is the extent to which fundamentally patriarchal institutions like marriage and the traditional
family are essential to capitalism's vitality and global expansion—

despite Marx's own significant underestimation of their role and power. There is deep irony in the socialist feminist analysis: it's not that Marx failed to see the importance of the role of the family as a key unit of production and consumption; he clearly struggles with this role and its consequences for the emergent revolutionary proletariat throughout *The Communist Manifesto*. However, in identifying marriage and family too narrowly with the bourgeoisie, and thus with its eventual vanquishing, Marx failed to see that patriarchal relationships provide the very model through which capitalist relations are empowered. Without this crucial understanding of the commodification of the sexuality of women, Marx's vision of the revolution—much less the utopia to follow—is destined to remain not merely closed to women but "revolutionary" in name only.

MICHAEL HARDT AND ANTONIO NEGRI

Marx's Mole Is Dead!†

"Every tool is a weapon if you hold it right."

—Ani DiFranco

"Men fight and lose the battle, and the thing that they fought for comes about in spite of their defeat, and then it turns out not to be what they meant, and other men have to fight for what they meant under another name."

—William Morris

In our book,[1] we propose a single concept, Empire, which is meant to name the political form of globalisation. Our primary question is, what is the political constitution of global order?

We use Empire to name the new form of sovereignty, a new form of political rule. Many argue that the globalisation of capitalist production and exchange means that economic relations have become more autonomous from political controls, and consequently that political sovereignty has declined. Some celebrate this new era as the liberation of the capitalist economy from the restrictions and distortions that political forces have imposed on it; others lament it as the closing of the institutional channels through which workers and citizens can influence or contest the cold logic of capitalist profit. It is certainly true that in step with the processes of globalisation the

---

† [www.eurozine.com/articles/2002-02-13-hardtnegri-en.html#] This text is based on a paper that Michael Hardt presented at SUNY, Buffalo in February 1999. The point of departure is a chapter in Hardt's and Negri's book *Empire* (Harvard UP, 2000). Reprinted by permission.
1. Michael Hardt and Antonio Negri (Harvard UP, 2000).

sovereignty of nation states, while still important, has progressively declined. The primary factors of production and exchange—money, technology, people and goods—move with increasing ease across national boundaries; hence the nation state has less and less power to regulate these flows and impose its authority over the economy. Even the most dominant nation states should no longer be thought of as supreme and sovereign authorities, neither outside nor even within their own borders. *The declining sovereignty of nation states, however, does not mean that sovereignty as such has declined!* Throughout the contemporary transformations, political controls, state functions and regulatory mechanisms continue to rule the realm of economic and social production and exchange. Our basic hypothesis, then, is that sovereignty has taken a new form, composed of a series of national and supranational organisms united under a single logic of rule. This new global form of sovereignty is what we call Empire.

We reject two hypotheses:

1. that there is a single, locatable source that dictates global order, that rules the globe: Washington, New York, Geneva, Tokyo (conspiracy theory);
2. that global order arises spontaneously from the anarchic interplay of global exchanges, from market forces (invisible hand)—in effect that there is not global order, only an economic dynamic that has finally freed itself from the regulation of the nation states and all other political fetters.

Between these two extremes we try to read the contemporary global political order as a mixed constitution. Mixed constitution is the term that Polybius uses to describe (and celebrate) the ancient Roman Empire.

The ancient Roman Empire was a mixed constitution, according to Polybius, in that it brought together in a single constitution all three primary forms of government: monarchy, aristocracy and democracy. In other words, in Empire monarchic, aristocratic and democratic powers all function together. Today, it sometimes appears that there is a single monarchic power that rules the world: during the Gulf War, for example, it seemed that the Pentagon was a monarchic global power; at other times the IMF might appear that way; at others Hollywood? On the other hand, sometimes it appears that aristocratic forces rule the world. Not the rule of the one but the rule of the few. Transnational corporations are aristocratic in this sense, as are often the nation states. Finally, there are those "democratic" powers, those that at least claim to represent the people. Nation states often fill this role too on the global scene, but the most interesting and complex democratic forces in Empire are the NGOs. In any case, a theory of mixed constitution allows us to recognise all of these powers within one coherent global constitution, but does not force us to claim that these forces are uniform or univocal. A theory of mixed constitution is a theory of difference within the constitution that allows for various separations of powers within the framework of a single order. The challenge then for our notion of the contemporary Empire as a mixed constitution is to discover what the various powers are and how they interact and negotiate with or dominate each other, in concert and in conflict. That's the difficult part. Mixed constitution only names the problematic; it doesn't really describe the dynamics of rule. But I hope it gives you a first approach to the framework in which we conceive Empire.

The declining sovereignty of nation states and their increasing inability to regulate economic and cultural changes is in fact one of the primary symptoms of the coming of Empire. The sovereignty of the nation state was the cornerstone of the imperialisms that European powers constructed throughout the modern era. By "Empire," however, we understand something altogether different from "imperialism." The boundaries defined by the modern system of nation states were fundamental to European colonialism and economic expansion: the territorial boundaries of the nation delimited the centre of power from which rule was exerted over external, foreign territories through a system of channels and barriers that alternately facilitated and obstructed the flows of production and circulation. Imperialism was really an extension of the sovereignty of the European nation states beyond their own boundaries. Eventually nearly all the world's territories could be parcelled out and the entire world map could be coded in European colours: red for British territory, blue for French, green for Portuguese and so forth. Whatever modern sovereignty took root, it constructed a transcendent Leviathan that overarched its social domain and imposed hierarchical territorial boundaries, both to police the purity of its own identity and to exclude all that was other.

No Limits

The passage to Empire emerges from the twilight of modern sovereignty. In contrast to imperialism, Empire establishes no territorial centre of power and does not rely on fixed boundaries or barriers. It is a *decentered* and *deterritorialising* apparatus of rule that progressively incorporates the entire global realm within its open, expanding frontiers. Empire manages hybrid identities, flexible hierarchies and plural exchanges through modulating networks of command. The distinct national colours of the imperialist map of the world have merged and blended in the imperial global rainbow.

We should emphasise that we use Empire here not as a *metaphor*, which would require demonstration of the resemblances between today's world order and the Empires of Rome, China, the Americas and so forth, but rather as a *concept*, which calls primarily for a theoretical approach. The concept of Empire is characterised fundamentally by a lack of boundaries: Empire's rule has no limits.

First and foremost, then, the concept of Empire poses a regime that effectively encompasses the spatial totality, or really that rules over the entire "civilised" world. No territorial boundaries limit its reign. Second, the concept of Empire presents itself not as a historical regime originating in conquest, but rather as an order that effectively suspends history and thereby fixes the existing state of affairs for eternity. From the perspective of Empire, this is the way things will always be and the way they were always meant to be. In other words, Empire presents its rule not as a transitory moment in the movement of history, but as a regime with no temporal boundaries and in this sense outside of history or at the end of history. Third, the rule of Empire operates on all registers of the social order extending down to the depths of the social world. Empire not only manages a territory and a population, but also creates the very world it inhabits. It not only regulates human interactions, but also seeks directly to rule over human nature. The object of its rule is social life in its entirety, and thus Empire presents the paradigmatic form of biopower. Finally, although the practice of Empire [is] continually bathed in blood, the concept of Empire is always dedicated to peace—a perpetual and universal peace outside of history.

A Methodological Point

The relationship between Italian politics and French philosophy is an interesting one, specifically the relationship between the Italian tradition of *operaismo* and *autonomia* on one hand and the philosophy of Gilles Deleuze on the other. There is a central point of commonality here and that is a methodological point, or really an axiom of research. On Deleuze's side, this axiom is that desire is active and power is reactive. Or rather, with respect to power, "*La résistance est première.*" Resistance is temporally and ontologically prior to power.

- *Operaismo* builds on Marx's claim that capital reacts to the struggles of the working class; the working class is active and capital reactive.
- Technological development: Where there are strikes, machines will follow. "It would be possible to write a whole history of the inventions made since 1830 for the sole purpose of providing capital with weapons against working-class revolt." (*Capital*, Vol. 1, Chapter 15, Section 5)

- Political development: The factory legislation in England was a response to the working class struggle over the length of the working day. "Their formulation, official recognition and proclamation by the State were the result of a long class struggle." (*Capital*, Vol. 1, Chapter 10, Section 6)
- *Operaismo* takes this as its fundamental axiom: the struggles of the working class *precede* and *prefigure* the successive restructurations of capital.

We will present an example of this methodology or this axiom in the relationship between social struggles and globalisation, or rather, the relationship between international cycles of struggles and capitalist globalisation.

Call to Globality

Flirting with Hegel, one could say that the construction of Empire is good *in itself* but not *for itself*. One of the most powerful operations of the modern imperialist power structures was to drive wedges among the masses of the globe, dividing them into opposing camps, or really a myriad of conflicting parties. Segments of the proletariat in the dominant countries were even led to believe that their interests were tied exclusively to their national identity and imperialist destiny. The most significant instance of revolt and revolution against these modern power structures therefore were those that posed the struggle against exploitation together with the struggle against nationalism, colonialism and imperialism. Through these events, humanity appeared for a magical moment to be united by a common desire for liberation and we seemed to catch a glimpse of a future when the modern mechanisms of domination would once and for all be destroyed. The revolting masses, their desire for liberation, their experiments to construct alternatives and their instances of constituent power have all at their best moments pointed toward the internationalisation and globalisation of relationships, beyond the divisions of national, colonial and imperialist rule. In our time this desire that was set in motion by the multitude has been addressed (in a strange and perverted but nonetheless real way) by the construction of Empire. One might even say that the construction of Empire and its global networks is a *response* to the various struggles against the modern machines of power and specifically to class struggle driven by the multitude's desire for liberation. The multitude called Empire into being.

Saying that Empire is good *in itself*, however, does not mean that it is good *for itself*. Although Empire may have played a role in putting an end to colonialism and imperialism, it nonetheless constructs its own relationships of power based on exploitation that are

in many respects more brutal than those it destroyed. The end of
the dialectic of modernity has not resulted in the end of the dialectic
of exploitation. Today nearly all of humanity is to some degree
absorbed within or subordinated to the networks of capitalist exploitation. We see now an ever more extreme condition of radical separation of a small minority that controls enormous wealth from
multitudes that live in poverty at the limit of powerlessness. The
geographical and racial lines of oppression and exploitation that were
established during the era of colonialism and imperialism have in
many respects not declined but instead increased exponentially.

Despite recognising all this, we insist on asserting that the construction of Empire is a step forward [in] order to do away with any
nostalgia for the power structures that preceded it and refuse any
political strategy that involves returning to that old arrangement,
such as trying to resurrect the nation state to protect us against
global capital. We claim that Empire is better in the same way that
Marx insists that capitalism is better than the forms of society and
modes of production that came before it. Marx's view is grounded
on a healthy and lucid disgust for the parochial and rigid hierarchies
that preceded capitalist society as well as on a recognition that the
potential for liberation is increased in the new situation. In the same
way today we can see that Empire does away with the cruel regimes
of modern power and also increases the potential for liberation.

We are well aware that in affirming this thesis we are swimming
against the current of our friends and comrades on the Left. In the
long decades of the crisis of the communist, socialist and liberal
Left that has followed the 1960s, a large portion of critical thought,
both in the dominant countries of capitalist development and in the
subordinated ones, has sought to recompense sites of resistance that
are founded on the identities of social subjects or national and
regional groups, often grounding political analysis on the *localisation of struggles*. Such arguments are sometimes constructed in
terms of "place-based" movements or politics, in which the boundaries of place (conceived either as identity or territory) are posed
against the undifferentiated and homogeneous space of global networks. Other times such political arguments draw on the long tradition of Leftist nationalism in which (in the best cases) the nation is
conceived as the primary mechanism of defence against the domination of foreign and/or global capital. Today the operative syllogism
at the heart of the precarious forms of "local" Leftist strategy seems
to be entirely reactive: If capitalist domination is becoming ever
more global, then our resistances to it must defend the local and
construct barriers to capital's accelerating flows. From this perspective, the real globalisation of capital and the constitution of Empire
must be considered signs of dispossession and defeat.

We maintain, however, that today this localist position, although we admire and respect the spirit of some of its proponents, is both false and damaging. It is false first of all because the problem is poorly posed. In many characterisations the problem rests on a false dichotomy between the global and the local, assuming that the global entails homogenisation and undifferentiated identity whereas the local preserves heterogeneity and difference. Often implicit in such arguments is the assumption that the differences of the local are in some sense natural or at least that their origin remains beyond question. Local differences pre-exist the present scene and must be defended or protected against the intrusion of globalisation. It should come as no surprise given such assumptions that many defences of the local adopt the terminology of traditional ecology or even identify this "local" political project with the defence of nature and biodiversity. This view can easily devolve into a kind of primordialism that fixes and romanticises social relations and identities. What needs to be addressed, instead, is precisely the *production of locality*, that is, the social machines that create and recreate the identities and differences that are understood as the local. The differences of locality are not pre-existing nor natural but rather effects of a regime of production. Globality similarly should not be understood in terms of cultural, political, or economic *homogeneisation*. Globalisation, like localisation, should be understood instead as a *regime* of the production of identity and difference, or really of homogenisation and heterogenisation. The better framework, then, to designate the distinction between the global and the local might refer to different networks of flows and obstacles in which the local moment or perspective gives priority to the reterritorialising barriers and the global moment privileges the mobility of deterritorialising flows. It is false, in any case, to claim that we can (re)establish local identities that are in some sense *outside* and protected against the global flows of capital and Empire.

The Leftist strategy of resistance to globalisation and defence of locality is also damaging because in many cases what appear as local identities are not autonomous nor self-determining but actually feed into and support the development of the capitalist imperial machine. The globalisation or deterritorialisation operated by the imperial machine is not in fact opposed to the localisation or reterritorialisation, but rather sets in play mobile and modulating circuits of differentiation and identification. The strategy of local resistance misidentifies and thus masks the enemy. We are by no means opposed to the globalisation of relationships as such—in fact, as we said, the strongest forces of Leftist internationalism have effectively led this process. The enemy, rather, is a specific regime of global relations that we call Empire. More importantly, this strategy of defending the local is damaging because it obscures and even negates the real alternatives and the potentials for liberation that exist *within* Empire. We should all be done once and for all with the search for an outside, a standpoint that imagines a purity for our politics. It is better both theoretically and practically to enter the terrain of Empire and confront its homogenising and heterogenising flows in all their complexity, grounding our analysis in the power of the global multitude.

Refrains of the Internationale

There was a time, not so long ago, when internationalism was a key component of proletarian struggles and progressive politics in general. "The proletariat has no country," or better, "the country of the proletariat is the entire world." The *Internationale* was the hymn of revolutionaries, the song of utopian futures. We should note that the utopia expressed in these slogans is in fact not really internationalist, if by internationalist we understand a kind of consensus among the various national identities that preserves their differences but negotiates some limited agreement. Rather, proletarian internationalism was antinationalist, and hence supranational and global. Workers of the world unite!—not on the basis of national identities but directly through common needs and desires, without regard to borders and boundaries.

Internationalism was the will of an active mass subject that recognized that the nation states were the key agents of capitalist exploitation and that the multitude was continually drafted to fight their senseless wars—in short, that the nation state was a political form whose contradictions could not be subsumed and sublimated but only destroyed. International solidarity was really a project for the destruction of the nation state and the construction of a new global community. This proletarian program stood behind the often ambiguous tactical definitions that socialist and communist parties produced during the century of their hegemony over the proletariat. If the nation state was a central link in the chain of domination and thus had to be destroyed, then the *national* proletariat had as a primary task destroying itself insofar as it was defined by the nation and thus bringing international solidarity out of the prison in which it had been trapped. International solidarity had to be recognized not as an act of charity or altruism for the good of others, a noble sacrifice for another national working class, but rather as proper to and inseparable from each national proletariat's own desire and struggle for liberation. Proletarian internationalism constructed a paradoxical and powerful political machine that pushed continually beyond the boundaries and hierarchies of the nation states and posed utopian futures only on the global terrain.

Today we should all clearly recognize that the time of such proletarian internationalism is over. That does not negate the fact, however, that the concept of internationalism really lived among the masses and deposited a kind of geological stratum of suffering and desire, a memory of victories and defeats, a residue of ideological tensions and needs. Furthermore the proletariat does in fact find itself today not just international but (at least tendentially) global. One might be tempted to say that proletarian internationalism actually "won" in the light of the facts that the powers of nation states have declined in the recent passage toward globalisation and Empire, but that would be a strange and ironic notion of victory. It is more accurate to say, following the William Morris quote that serves as one of the epigraphs for this book, that what they fought for came about despite their defeat. . . .

The practice of proletarian internationalism was expressed most clearly in the international cycles of struggles. In this framework the (national) general strike and insurrection against the (nation-)state were only really conceivable as elements of communication among struggles and processes of liberation on the internationalist terrain. From Berlin to Moscow, from Paris to New Delhi, from Algiers to Hanoi, from Shanghai to Jakarta, from Havana to New York, struggles resonated with one another throughout the nineteenth and twentieth centuries. A cycle constructed as news of a revolt was communicated and applied in each new context, just as in an earlier era merchant ships carried the news of slave revolt from island to island around the Caribbean, igniting a stubborn string of fires that could not be quenched. For a cycle to form the recipients of the news must be able to "translate" the events into their own language, recognize the struggles as their own and thus add a link to the chain. In some cases this "translation" is rather elaborate: the way in which Chinese intellectuals at the turn of the twentieth century, for example, heard of the anticolonial struggles in the Philippines and Cuba and translated them into the terms of their own revolutionary projects. In other cases it is much more direct: how the factory council movement in Turin, Italy, was immediately inspired by the news of the Bolshevik victory in Russia. Rather than thinking of the struggles as relating to each other like links in a chain, it might be better to conceive of them as communicating like a virus that modulates its form to find in each context an adequate host.

It would not be hard to map the periods of extreme intensity of these cycles. A first wave might be seen as beginning after 1848 with the political agitation of the First International, continuing in the

1880s and 1890s with the formation of socialist political and trade union organisations, and then rising to a peak after the Russian revolution of 1905 and the first international cycle of anti-imperialist struggles. A second wave arose after the Soviet revolution of 1917, which was followed by an international progression of struggles that could only be contained by fascisms on one side and reabsorbed by the New Deal and antifascist fronts on the other. And finally there was the wave of struggles that began with the Chinese revolution and proceeded through the African and Latin American liberation struggles to the explosions of the 1960s throughout the world.

These international cycles of struggles were the real motor that determined the development of the institutions of capital and that drove it in a process of reform and restructuring. Proletarian, anti-colonial and anti-imperialist internationalism, the struggle for communism, which lived in all the most powerful insurrectional events of the nineteenth and twentieth centuries, anticipated and prefigured the processes of the globalisation of capital and the formation of Empire. In this way the formation of Empire is a *response* to proletarian internationalism. There is nothing dialectical nor teleological about this anticipation and prefiguration of capitalist development by the mass struggles. On the contrary, the struggles themselves are demonstrations of the creativity of desire, utopias of lived experience, the workings of historicity as potentiality—in short, the struggles are the naked reality of the *res gestae*. A teleology of sorts is constructed only after the fact, *post festum*.

The struggles that preceded and prefigured globalisation were expressions of the force of living labour, which sought to liberate itself from the rigid territorialising regimes imposed on it. As it contests the dead labour accumulated against it, living labour always seeks to break the fixed territorialising structures, the national organizations and the political figure[s] that keep it prisoner. With the force of living labour, its restless activity and its deterritorialising desire, this process of rupture throws open all the windows of history. When one adopts the perspective of the activity of the multitude, its production of subjectivity and desire, one can recognize how globalisation, insofar as it operates a real deterritorialisation of the previous structures of exploitation and control, is really a condition of the liberation of the multitude. But how can this potential for liberation be realised today? Does that same uncontainable desire for freedom that broke and buried the nation state and that determined the transition toward Empire still live beneath the ashes of the present, the ashes of the fire that consumed the internationalist proletarian subject that was centred around the industrial working class? What has come to stand in the place of the subject? In what sense can we say that the ontological rooting of a new multitude has come to be a positive [or] alternative actor in the articulation of globalisation?

The Mole and the Snake

We need to recognize that the very subject of labour and revolt has changed profoundly. The composition of the proletariat has transformed and thus our understanding [of] it must too. In conceptual terms we understand *proletariat* as a broad category that includes all those whose labour is directly or indirectly exploited by and subjected to capitalist norms of production and reproduction. In a previous era the category of the proletarian centred around and was at times effectively subsumed under *industrial working class*, whose paradigmatic figure was the male mass factory worker. That industrial working class was often accorded the leading role over other figures of labour (such as peasant labour and reproductive labour) in both economic analyses and political movements. Today that working class has all but disappeared from view. It has not ceased to exist, but it has been displaced from its privileged position in the capitalist economy and its hegemonic position in the class composition of the proletariat. The proletariat is not what it used to be, but that does not mean it has vanished. It means, rather, that we are faced once again with the analytical task of understanding the new composition of the proletariat as a class.

The fact that under the category of proletariat we understand *all* those exploited by and subject to capitalist domination should not indicate that the proletariat is a homogeneous or undifferentiated unit—it is indeed cut through in various directions by differences and stratifications. Some labour is waged, some is not; some labour is limited to eight hours a day and forty hours a week, some expands to fill the entire time of life; some labour is accorded a minimal value, some is exalted to the pinnacle of the capitalist economy. We argue in our book that among the various figures of production active today the figure of immaterial labour-power (involved in communication, co-operation, and the production and reproduction of affects) occupies an increasingly central position in both the schema of capitalist production and the composition of the proletariat. Our point here is that all of these diverse forms of labour are in some way subject to capitalist discipline and capitalist relations of production. This fact of being within capital is what defines the proletariat as a class.

In the second place we need to look more concretely at the form of the struggles in which this new proletariat expresses its desires and needs. In the second half of the twentieth century, and in particular in the two decades that stretched from 1968 to the fall of

the Berlin Wall, the restructuring and global expansion of capitalist production have been accompanied by a transformation of proletarian struggles. As we said, the figure of an international cycle of
struggles based on the communication and translation of the common desires of labour in revolt seems no longer to exist. The fact
that the cycle as the specific form of the assemblage of struggles
has vanished, however, does not simply open up to an abyss. On the
contrary, we can recognise powerful events on the world scene that
reveal the trace of the multitude's refusal of exploitation and that
signal a new kind of proletarian solidarity and militancy.

Consider the most radical and powerful struggles of the final years
of the twentieth century: the Tiananmen Square events in 1989, the
Intifada against Israeli State authority, the May 1992 revolt in Los
Angeles, the uprising in Chiapas that began in 1994, the series of
strikes that paralysed France in December 1995 and those that crip-
pled South Korea in 1996. Each of these struggles was specific and
based on immediate regional concerns in such a way that they could
in no way be linked together as a globally expanding chain of revolt.
None of these events inspired a cycle of struggles because the desires
and needs they expressed could not be translated into different contexts. In other words, (potential) revolutionaries in other parts of the
world did not hear of the events in Beijing, Nablus, Los Angeles,
Chiapas, Paris or Seoul and immediately recognise them as their
own struggles. Furthermore, these struggles not only fail to communicate to other contexts, but they lack even a local communication
and thus often have a very brief duration where they are born, burning out in a flash. This is certainly one of the central and most urgent
political paradoxes of our time: In our much celebrated age of communication, *struggles have become all but incommunicable.*

This paradox of incommunicability makes it extremely difficult to
grasp and express the new power posed by the struggles that have
emerged. We ought to be able to recognise that what the struggles
have lost in extension, duration and communicability they have
gained in intensity. We ought to be able to recognize that although
all of these struggles focused on their own local and immediate circumstances, they all nonetheless posed problems of supranational
relevance, problems that are proper to the new figure of imperial
capitalist regulation. In Los Angeles, for example, the riots were
fuelled by local racial antagonisms and patterns of social and economic exclusion that are in many respects particular to that (post)
urban territory, but the events were also immediately catapulted to a
general level insofar as they expressed a refusal of the post-Fordist
regime of social control. Like the Intifada in certain respects, the
Los Angeles riots demonstrated how the decline of Fordist bargaining regimes and mechanisms of social mediation has made the man-

agement of racially and socially diverse metropolitan territories and populations so precarious. The looting of commodities and burning of property were not just metaphors but the real global condition of the mobility and volatility of post-Fordist social mediations. In Chiapas, too, the insurrection focused primarily on local concerns: problems of exclusion and lack of representation specific to Mexican society and the Mexican State, which have also to a limited degree long been common to the racial hierarchies throughout much of Latin America. The Zapatista rebellion, however, was also immediately a struggle against the social regime imposed by NAFTA and more generally the systematic exclusion and subordination in the regional construction of the world market. Finally, like those in Seoul, the massive strikes in Paris and throughout France in later 1995 were aimed at specific local and national labour issue (such as pensions, wages and unemployment), but the struggle was also immediately recognized as a clear contestation of the new social and economic construction of Europe. The French strikes called above all for a new notion of the public, a new construction of public space against the neo-liberal mechanisms of privatization that accompany more or less everywhere the project of capitalist globalisation. Perhaps precisely because all these struggles are incommunicable and thus blocked from travelling horizontally in the form of a cycle, they are forced rather to leap vertically and touch immediately on the global level.

We ought to be able to recognise that this is not the appearance of a new cycle of internationalist struggles, but rather the emergence of a new quality of social movements. We ought to be able to recognise, in other words, the fundamentally new characteristics these struggles all present, despite their radical diversity. First, each struggle, although firmly rooted in local conditions, leaps immediately to the global level and attacks the imperial constitution in its generality. Second, all the struggles destroy the traditional distinction between economic and political struggles. The struggles are at once economic, political and cultural—and hence they are biopolitical struggles, struggles over the form of life. They are constituent struggles, creating [new] public spaces and new forms of community.

We ought to be able to recognize all this, but it is not all that easy. We must admit, in fact, that even when trying to individuate the real novelty of these situations we are hampered by the nagging impression that these struggles are always already old, outdated and anachronistic. The struggles at Tiananmen Square spoke a language of democracy that seemed long out of fashion; the guitars, headbands, tents and slogans all looked like a weak echo of Berkeley in the 60s. The Los Angeles riots, too, seemed like an aftershock of the earthquake of racial conflicts that shook the United States in the 1960s.

The strikes in Paris and Seoul seemed to take us back to the era of the mass factory worker, as if they were the last gasp of a dying working class. All these struggles, which pose really new elements, appear from the beginning to be already old and outdated—precisely because they cannot communicate, because their languages cannot be translated. The struggles do not communicate despite their being hypermediatised, on television, the Internet and every other imaginable forum. Once again we are confronted by the paradox of incommunicability.

We can certainly recognise real obstacles that block the communication of struggles. One such obstacle is the absence of a recognition of a common enemy against which the struggles are directed. Beijing, Los Angeles, Nablus, Chiapas, Paris, Seoul: the situations seem all utterly particular, but in fact they all directly attack the global order of Empire and seek a real alternative. Clarifying the nature of the common enemy is thus an essential political task. A second obstacle, which is really corollary to the first, is that there is no common language of struggles that could "translate" the particular language of each into a cosmopolitan language. Struggles in other parts of the world and even our own struggles seem to be written in an incomprehensible foreign language. This too points toward an important political task: to construct a new common language that facilitates communication, like the languages of anti-imperialism and proletarian internationalism did for the struggles of a previous era. Perhaps this needs to be a new type of communication that functions not on the basis of resemblances but on the basis of differences: a communication of singularities.

Recognising a common enemy and inventing a common language of struggles [are] certainly important political tasks and we will advance them as far as we can in the course of the book, but our intuition tells us that this line of analysis fails to grasp the real potential presented by the new struggles. Our intuition tells us, in other words, that the model of the horizontal articulation of struggles in a cycle is no longer adequate to recognize the way in which contemporary struggles achieve global significance. Such a model in fact blinds us to their real new potential.

Marx tried to understand the continuity of the cycle of proletarian struggles that were emerging in nineteenth-century Europe in terms of a mole and its subterranean tunnels. Marx's mole would surface in times of open class conflict and then retreat underground again—not to hibernate passively, but to burrow its tunnels, moving along with the times, pushing forward with history so that when the time was right (1830, 1848, 1870) it would spring to the surface again. "Well grubbed old mole!"[2] Well, we suspect that Marx's old mole has

2. Karl Marx (New York; International Publishers, 1963).

finally died. It seems to us, in fact, that in the contemporary passage to Empire the structured tunnels of the mole have been replaced by the infinite undulations of the snake. This is the image that Deleuze gives in his analysis of the passage from disciplinary societies to societies of control. (Deleuze claims that contemporary society had gone beyond the disciplinary forms that Foucault analysed. Today the disciplinary institutions, the school, the family, the prison, the factory, are all in crisis. This doesn't mean that disciplinary logics are breaking down; what is breaking down rather are the institutional boundaries that once defined and limited their application to one social space. The disciplinary logics spread out across society, they are generalized and in some respects intensified. The generalised disciplinarity is what defines the society of control.) "The old mole," Deleuze writes, "is the animal of closed environments, but the snake is the animal of the societies of control. We have passed from one animal to another, from the mole to the snake, in the regime we live under, but also in our way of living and our relations with others." The depths of the modern world and its subterranean passageways have in postmodernity all become superficial. Today's struggles slither silently across the superficial, imperial landscapes. Perhaps the incommunicability of struggles, the lack of well-structured, communicating tunnels, is in fact a strength rather than a weakness—a strength because all of the movements are immediately subversive in themselves and do not wait on any sort of external aid or extension to guarantee their effectiveness. Perhaps the more capital extends its global network of production and control, the more powerful any singular point of revolt can be simply by focusing their own powers, concentrating their energies in a tense and compact coil, these serpentine struggles striking directly at the highest articulations of imperial order. Empire presents a superficial world, the virtual centre of which can be accessed immediately from any point across the surface. If these points were to constitute something like a new cycle of struggles, it would be a cycle defined not by the communicative extension of the struggles but rather by their singular emergence, by the intensity that characterizes them one by one. In short, this new phase is defined by the fact that these struggles do not link horizontally but each leaps vertically, directly to the virtual centre of Empire.[3] From the point of view of the revolutionary tradition, one might object that the tactical successes of revolutionary actions in the nineteenth and twentieth centuries were all characterized precisely by the capacity to blast open the *weakest link* of the imperialist chain, that this is the ABC of revolutionary dialectics, and thus it would seem today that the situation is not very promising. It is certainly

3. See Gilles Deleuze, "Postscript on Control Societies in Negotiations," trans. Martin Joughin (New York: Columbia University Press 1995), pp. 177–82.

true that the serpentine struggles we are witnessing today do not provide any clear revolutionary tactics, or maybe they are completely incomprehensible from the point of view of tactics. Faced as we are with a series of intense subversive social movements that attack the highest levels of imperial organisation, however, it may be no longer useful to insist on the old distinction between strategy and tactics. In the constitution of Empire there is no longer an "outside" to power and thus no longer weak links—if by weak link we mean an external point where the articulations of global power are vulnerable. To achieve significance, every struggle must attack at the heart of the Empire, at its strength. That fact, however, does not give priority to any geographical regions, as if only social movements in Washington, Geneva or Tokyo could attack the heart of Empire. On the contrary, the construction of Empire and the globalisation of economic and cultural relationships means that the critical centre of Empire can be attacked from any angle. The tactical preoccupations of the old revolutionary school are thus completely irretrievable; the only strategy available to the struggles is that of a constituent counter-power that emerges from within Empire.

Those who have difficulty accepting the novelty and revolutionary potential of this situation from the perspective of the struggles themselves might recognize it more easily from the perspective of imperial power, which is constrained to react to the struggles. Even when these struggles become sites effectively closed to communication, they are at the same time the maniacal focus of the critical attention of Empire. They are educational lessons in the classroom of administration and the chambers of government—lessons that demand repressive instruments. The primary lesson is that such events cannot be repeated if the processes of capitalist globalisation are to continue. These struggles, however, have their own weight, their own specific intensity, and moreover they are immanent to the procedures and developments of imperial power. They invest and sustain the processes of globalisation themselves. Imperial power whispers the names of the struggles in order to charm them into passivity to construct a mystified image of them, but most important to discover which processes of globalisation are possible and which are not. In this contradictory and paradoxical way, the imperial processes of globalisation assume these events, recognising them as both limits and opportunities to recalibrate Empire's own instruments. The processes of globalisation would not exist or would come to a halt if they were not continually both frustrated and driven by these explosions of the multitude that touch immediately on the highest levels of imperial power.

Methodology Again

Returning to the methodological or axiomatic point we spoke of at the beginning, one can see how this argument about international cycles of struggles and capitalist globalisation is based on the fundamental axiom: that resistance comes before power (in Deleuze/Foucault terms) or that proletarian struggles precede and prefigure the successive forms of capitalist society and rule (in Marxist/ *operaismo* terms).

Now, it is perfectly reasonable to ask if it is in fact true that resistance comes before power and that social struggles precede and prefigure capitalist restructuration. We have not offered an argument for it, really—precisely, we have treated it as an axiom. Our book tries to demonstrate that it is plausible to read the history from below, but that is really not a proof. What is more interesting, though, is the *political effect* of this axiom, that it highlights the power of resistance and the power of social struggles.

Today, when facing the forces of capitalist globalisation and our new world order, it is all too easy and all too common to feel ourselves and our social movements powerless. This method can work as a kind of antidote to that cynicism and sense of powerlessness. It is not a matter of pretending that we are powerful when we are not, but rather recognizing the power we really have; the power that created the contemporary world and can create another.

SLAVOJ ŽIŽEK

Have Michael Hardt and Antonio Negri Rewritten the *Communist Manifesto* for the Twenty-First Century?[†]

Capitalism is not just a historical epoch among others. In a way, the once fashionable and now half-forgotten Francis Fukuyama was right: global capital is "the end of history." A certain excess which was, as it were, kept under check in previous history, perceived as a localizable perversion, as an excess, a deviation, is in capitalism elevated into the very principle of social life, in the speculative movement of money begetting more money, of a system which can survive only by constantly revolutionizing its own conditions—that is to say, in which the thing can survive only as its own excess, constantly exceeding its own "normal" constraints. And, perhaps it is only

† From *Rethinking Marxism* 13, 3/4 (2001). Reprinted by permission of Taylor & Francis. Posted at http://egs.edu/faculty/zizek/zizek-have-michael-hardt-antonio-negri

today, in global capitalism in its "postindustrial," digitalized form, that, to put it in Hegelian terms, really existing capitalism is reaching the level of its notion: perhaps, one should follow again Marx's old, antievolutionist motto (incidentally taken verbatim from Hegel) that the anatomy of man provides the key for the anatomy of the monkey—that is, in order to deploy the inherent, notional structure of a social formation, one must start with its most developed form.

Marx located the elementary capitalist antagonism in the opposition between use-value and exchange-value: in capitalism, the potentials of this opposition are fully realized, the domain of exchange-value acquires autonomy, is transferred into the specter of self-propelling speculative capital which needs the productive capacities and needs of actual people only as its dispensable temporal embodiment. Marx derived the very notion of economic crisis from this gap: a crisis occurs when reality catches up with the illusory, self-generating mirage of money begetting more money—this speculative madness can not go on indefinitely; it has to explode in ever stronger crises. The ultimate root of the crisis is for him, the gap between use-value and exchange-value: the logic of exchange-value follows its own path, its own mad dance, irrespective of the real needs of real people. It may appear that this analysis is more than actual today when the tension between the real universe and the real is reaching almost palpably unbearable proportions: on the one hand, we have crazy, solipsistic speculations about futures, mergers, and so on, following their own inherent logic; on the other hand, reality is catching up [in] the guise of ecological catastrophes, poverty, Third World diseases, in collapse of social life, mad cow disease.

What all this means is that the urgent task of the economic analysis today is, again, to repeat Marx's critique of political economy, without succeeding on to the temptation of the ideologies of "postindustrial" societies. It is my hypothesis that the key change concerns the status of private property: the ultimate element of power and control is no longer the last link in the chain of investments, the firm or individual who "really owns" the means of production. The ideal capitalist today functions in a wholly different way: investing borrowed money, "really owning" nothing—even indebted, but nonetheless controlling things. A corporation is owned by another corporation, who is again borrowing money from banks, who may ultimately manipulate money owned by ordinary people like ourselves. With Bill Gates, "private property in the means of production" becomes meaningless, at least in the standard meaning of the word. * * * Does today's virtual capitalist not function in a homologous way: his "net value" at zero, he directly operates just with the surplus borrowing from the future.

This, exactly, is what Michael Hardt and Antonio Negri are try-ing to do in their *Empire* (2000), a book that sets as its goal, writing the *Communist Manifesto* for the twenty-first century. Hardt and Negri describe globalization as an ambiguous "deterritorialization": victorious global capitalism pushes into every pore of our social lives, into the most intimate of spheres, and installs an ever present dynamic, which no longer is based on patriarchal or other hierarchic structures of dominance. Instead, it causes a flowing, hybrid identity. On the other hand, this fundamental corrosion of all important social connections lets the genie out of the bottle: it sets free the potentially centrifugal forces that the capitalist system is no longer able fully to control. It is exactly because [of] its global triumph that the capitalist system is more vulnerable than ever. The old formula of Marx is still valid: capitalism digs its own grave. * * * Hardt and Negri thus deserve much praise for enlightening us about the contradictory nature of today's "turbocapitalism" and attempting to identify the revolutionary potential of its dynamic. This heroic attempt sets itself against the standard view of those on the Left who are struggling to limit the destructive powers of global-ization and to rescue (what there is left to rescue) the welfare state. This standard leftist view is imbued with a profoundly conservative mistrust of the dynamics of globalization and digitalization, which is quite contrary [to] the Marxist confidence in the powers of progress.

Nevertheless, one immediately gets a sense of the boundaries to Hardt and Negri's analysis. In their social-economic analysis, the lack of concrete insight is concealed in the Deleuzian jargon of multitude, deterritorialization, and so forth. No wonder that the three "practi-cal proposals" with which the book ends appear anticlimactic. The authors propose to focus our political struggle on three global rights: the rights to global citizenship, a minimal income, and the reappro-priation of the new means of production (i.e. access to and control over education, information and communication). It is a paradox that Hardt and Negri, the poets of mobility, variety, hybridization, and so on, call for three demands formulated in the terminology of universal human rights. The problem with these demands is that they fluctuate between formal emptiness and impossible radicaliza-tion. Let us take the right to global citizenship: theoretically, this right of course should be approved. However, if this demand is meant to be taken more seriously than a celebratory formal declaration in typical United Nations Style, then it would mean the abolition of state borders; under present conditions, such a step would trigger an invasion of cheap labor from India, China and Africa into the United States and Western Europe, which would result in a populist revolt against immigrants—a result of such violent proportions that figures like Haider would seem models of multi-cultural tolerance. The same is valid with regard to the other two demands: for instance, the universal (worldwide) right to mini-mal income—of course, why not? But how should one create the necessary social-economic and ideological conditions for such a shattering transformation?

This critique is not only aimed at the secondary empirical details. The main problem with *Empire* is that the book falls short in its fundamental analysis of how (if at all) the present global, social-economic process will create the space needed for such radical measures: they fail to repeat, in today's conditions, Marx's line of argumentation that the prospect of the proletarian revolution emerges out of the inherent antagonisms of the capitalist mode of production. In this respect, *Empire* remains a pre-Marxist book. However, perhaps the solution is that it is not enough to return to Marx, to repeats Marx's analysis, but we must needs return to Lenin.

The first public reaction to such a motto is, of course, an outburst of sarcastic laughter. Marx: OK, even on Wall Street they love him today—Marx the poet of commodities, who provided perfect descriptions of capitalist dynamics; Marx of the cultural studies who portrayed the alienation and reification of our daily lives. But Lenin: no, you can't be serious! The working-class movement, revolutionary party, and similar zombie concepts? Doesn't Lenin stand precisely for the failure to put Marxism into practice, for the catastrophe that left its mark on the entire twentieth century's world politics, for the Real Socialist experiment that culminated in an economically inefficient dictatorship? In contemporary academic politics, the idea of dealing with Lenin is accompanied by two qualifications: yes, why not, we live in a liberal democracy, there is freedom of thought . . . however, one should treat Lenin in an "objective critical and scientific way," not in an attitude of nostalgic idolatry, and, furthermore, from the perspective firmly rooted in the democratic political order, within the horizon of human rights—therein resides the lessons painfully learned through the experience of twentieth-century totalitarianisms.

What are we to say to this? Again, the problem resides in the implicit qualifications which can be easily discerned by "concrete analysis of the concrete situation," as Lenin himself would have put it. "Fidelity to the democratic consensus" means acceptance of the present liberal-parliamentary consensus, which precludes any serious questioning of how this liberal-democratic order is complicitous in the phenomena it officially condemns and, of course, any serious attempt to imagine a society whose sociopolitical order would be different. In short, it means: say and write whatever you want—on condition that what you do does not effectively question or disturb the predominant political consensus. So everything is allowed, solicited even, as a critical topic: the prospects of a global ecological catastrophe, violations of human rights, sexism, homophobia, antifeminism, the growing violence not only in far-away countries but also in our megalopolises, the gap between the First and Third Worlds, between rich and poor, the shattering impact of the digitalization of our daily lives . . . there is nothing easier today than to get international, state, or corporate funds for multidisciplinary research into how to fight the new forms of ethnic, religious or sexist violence. The problem is that all this occurs against the background of a fundamental *Denkverbot*, a prohibition on thinking. Today's liberal-democratic hegemony is sustained by a kind of unwritten *Denkverbot* similar to the infamous *Berufsverbot* in Germany in the late 1960s: the moment one shows any minimal sign of engaging in political projects that aim seriously to challenge the existing order, the answer is immediately: "Benevolent as it is, this will necessarily end in a new Gulag!"

And it is exactly this same thing that the demand for "scientific objectivity" means: the moment one seriously questions the existing liberal consensus, one is accused of abandoning scientific objectivity for outdated ideological positions. * * * However, there is a point on which we cannot concede: today, actual freedom of thought means the freedom to question the predominant, liberal-democratic, "post-ideological" consensus—or it means nothing.

Although most of us probably do not agree with Jürgen Habermas, we do live in an era that could be designated by his term *neue Undurchsichtlichkeit*, the new opacity. More than ever, our daily experience is mystifying. Modernization generates new obscurantisms; the reduction of freedom is presented to us as the arrival of new freedoms. In these circumstances one should be especially careful not to confuse the ruling ideology with ideology that seems to dominate. * * *

One is therefore tempted to turn round Marx's eleventh thesis. The first task today is precisely not to succumb to the temptation to act, to directly intervene and change things (which then inevitably ends in a cul-de-sac of debilitating impossibility: "what can one do against global capital?"). Rather, the task is to question the hegemonic ideological coordinates. * * * If, today, one follows a direct call to act, this act will not be performed in an empty space; it will be an act within the hegemonic ideological coordinates. Those who "really want to do something to help people" get involved in (undoubtedly honorable) exploits like *Médecins Sans Frontières*, Greenpeace, and feminist and antiracist campaigns, which are all not only tolerated but even supported by the media; even if they seemingly enter economic territory (say, by denouncing and boycotting companies that do not respect ecological conditions or that use child labor). They are tolerated and supported so long as they do not get close to a certain limit. Let us take two predominant topics of today's radical American academia: postcolonial and queer (gay) studies. The problem of postcolonialism is undoubtedly crucial; however, "postcolonial studies" tend to translate it into the multiculturalist problematic of the colonized minorities' "right to narrate" their victimizing experience of the power mechanisms that repress "otherness" so that, at the end of the day, we learn the root of postcolonial exploitation is our intolerance toward the Other, and, furthermore, that this intolerance toward the "Stranger in Ourselves," in our inability to confront what we repressed in and of ourselves. The politico-economic struggle is thus imperceptibly transformed into a pseudo-psychoanalytic drama of the subject unable to confront its inner traumas. The true corruption of American academia is not primarily financial—it is not only that they are able to buy many European critical intellectuals (myself included, up to a point)— but conceptual: notions of "European" critical theory are imperceptibly translated into the benign universe of cultural studies chic. * * *

Lenin is for us not the nostalgic name for old, dogmatic certainty— quite the contrary. To put it in Kierkegaard's terms, the Lenin we want to retrieve is the Lenin-in-becoming, the Lenin whose fundamental experience was that of being thrown into a catastrophic new constellation in which old coordinates proved useless, and who was thus compelled to reinvent Marxism—recall his acerbic remark apropos of some new problem: "About this, Marx and Engels said not a word." The idea is not to return to Lenin but to repeat him in the Kierkegaardian sense: to retrieve the same impulse in today's constellation. The return to Lenin aims neither at nostalgically reenacting the "good old revolutionary times" nor at the opportunistic-pragmatic adjustment of the old program to "new conditions," but at repeating, in the present, the Leninist gesture of reinventing the revolutionary project in the conditions of imperialism and colonialism— more precisely, after the politico-ideological collapse of the long era of progress in the catastrophe of 1914. Eric Hobsbawn defined the concept of the twentieth century as the time between 1914, the end of the long, peaceful expansion of capitalism, and 1990, the emergence of the new form of global capitalism after the collapse of really existing socialism. What Lenin did for 1914, we should do for 1990. "Lenin" stands for the compelling freedom to suspend the stale, existing (post)ideological coordinates, the debilitating *Denkverbot* in which we live; it simply means that we are allowed to think again.

* * *

The battle to be fought is thus twofold. First—yes—anticapitalism. However, anticapitalism without problematizing capitalism's political form (liberal parliamentary democracy) is not sufficient, no matter how radical it is. Perhaps the lure today is the belief that one can undermine capitalism without effectively problematizing the liberal democratic legacy which (as some Leftists claim), although engendered by capitalism, acquired autonomy and can serve to criticize capitalism. This lure is strictly correlative to its apparent opposite, to the pseudo-Deleuzian, love-hate, fascinating/fascinated poetic depiction of capital as a rhizomatic monster/vampire that deterritorializes and swallows all—indomitable, dynamic, ever rising from the dead, each crisis making it stronger.

* * *

Today we see the signs of general unease, which is already exploding: I am, of course, referring to the events usually listed under the name of "Seattle." The long honeymoon of triumphant global capitalism is over, the long-overdue "seven-year itch" is here. Witness the panicky reactions of the big media which, from Time to the Cable News Network, all of a sudden started to warn about Marxists manipulating the crowd of "honest" protesters. The problem is now the strictly Leninist one of how to actualize the media's accusations: how to invent the organizational structure that will confer on this unrest the form of the universal political demand. Otherwise, the momentum will be lost and what will remain will be the marginal disturbance, perhaps organized as a new Greenpeace, with certain efficiency, but also strictly limited goals, marketing strategy, and so on. In other words, the key "Leninist" lesson today is: politics without the organizational form of the party is politics without politics, so the answer to those who want just the (quite adequately named) "new social movements" is the same as the answer of the Jacobins to the Girondin compromisers: "You want revolution without the revolution!" Today's blockade is that there are two ways open for the sociopolitical engagement: either play the game of the system—"engage in the long march through the institutions"—or get involved in new social movements, from feminism through ecology to antiracism. And again, the limit of these movements is that they are not political in the sense of the universal singular: they are "one-issue movements" lacking the dimension of universality—that is, they do not relate to the social totality.

Here, Lenin's reproach to liberals is crucial: they only exploit the working classes' discontent to strengthen their own positions vis-à-vis the conservatives, instead of identifying with it to the end. Is this not also the case with today's left liberals? They like to evoke racism, ecology, workers' grievances, and so forth to score points over conservatives without endangering the system. Recall how, at

Seattle, Bill Clinton himself deftly referred to the protesters on the streets outside, reminding the gathered leaders inside the guarded palaces that they should listen to the message of the demonstrators (the message which, of course, Clinton interpreted, depriving it of its subversive sting attributed to the dangerous extremists introducing chaos and violence into the majority of peaceful protesters). It's the same with all new social movements, up to the Zapatistas in Chiapas: systemic politics is always ready to "listen to their demands," depriving them of their proper political sting. The system is by definition ecumenical, open, tolerant, ready to "listen" to all. Even if one insists on one's demands, they are deprived of their universal political sting by the very form of negotiation.

To repeat Lenin is thus to accept that "Lenin is dead"—that his particular solution failed, even failed monstrously, but that there was a Utopian spark in it worth saving. To repeat Lenin means that one has to distinguish between what Lenin effectively did and the field of possibilities that he opened up, the tension in Lenin between what he effectively did and another dimension, what was "in Lenin more than Lenin himself." To repeat Lenin is to repeat not what Lenin did but what he failed to do, his missed opportunities.

TAKIS FOTOPOULOS AND ALEXANDROS GEZERLIS

Hardt and Negri's *Empire*: A New *Communist Manifesto* or a Reformist Welcome to Neoliberal Globalization?[†]

* * * Whereas an objectivist analysis at the hands of Marx & Engels led to a radical Manifesto proposing the building of a mass antisystemic movement with clear goals and means to overthrow capitalism, the hybrid of objectivism and postmodernism used by Hardt & Negri led to this pseudo-radical Manifesto, which proposes global "resistance" against a nebulous "Empire" by a multitude that does not even need clear goals and means to overthrow it. Still, this did not deter them from ending their book by extolling the "joy of being communist"—the communist militant being resembled by H&N [Hardt and Negri] to Saint Francis of Assisi (who also happens to be Mrs Thatcher's idol!).

Thus, the authors * * * end up with reformist demands and no clear vision for a future society. In this context, H&N offer three programmatic political demands of the multitude (pp. 396–407):

†   Reprinted by permission. http://democracynature.org/vol8/takis_negri

the right to global citizenship, i.e. the general right of the multitude
to control its own movement; a social wage and a guaranteed income
for all; the right to reappropriation, i.e. the multitude's right to self
control and autonomous self-production. What makes these demands
purely reformist is that, unlike the corresponding demands of the
original *Communist Manifesto*, they are not an integral part of a
comprehensive project for systemic change. Therefore, even though
such demands cannot possibly be met within the market economy
system, still, the very fact that they are not part of an antisystemic
political programme with clear long term goals about the form the
future society will take and strategies to achieve them is bound to
lead to the creation of a reformist mentality about these three
demands, which the transnational elite could easily enhance by
offering some painless (to it) reforms in connection to them. Thus,
the offer of a European Union and Nafta citizenship could be used to
undermine the demand for global citizenship. Similarly, the offer
to enhance the present safety nets in order to secure some sort of
minimum income can be used to dent the demand for a social wage
and a guaranteed income for all. Finally, the transnational elite has
already began undermining the third demand with the various projects for "participation" at the work place, the "people's capitalism"
supposedly established by the pension funds which invest in the
stock exchange etc.—the effect of all these projects simply being to
guarantee the decision-taking power of the elites and at the same
time create the illusion to the rest of society that they have some
"say" [in] its running.

H&N have thought up, however, many safety valves to guard against
a reading like our own: the general vagueness in their analysis (e.g.
they speak of "non-representational" democracy, but do not explain
either the institutions on which it will be based, or how the new society can be created step-by-step inside the old—the avoidance of the
concept of revolution *should* have led them to such a "gradual" strategy) can be considered as such a valve. If no one understands what it
is that H&N project, then almost no one will object to it. Even so, the
fact that they offer no concrete vision is no less an invitation for criticism, especially today when, after the collapse of "actually existing
socialism," a new vision is indeed quite necessary. On the contrary,
H&N openly state (p. 206) (in accordance with their postmodern
credentials) that today one cannot offer an elaboration of a political
alternative to Empire.

In closing, we urge the reader to admire the perfect agreement
between Bernstein's motto "the goal is nothing, the movement everything," and H&N's summary of their political aspirations (p. 207):

> Our pilgrimage on earth, however, in contrast to Augustine's,
> has no transcendent telos beyond; it is and remains absolutely

immanent. Its continuous movement, gathering aliens in community, making this world its home, is both means and end, or rather a means without end.

Overall, *Empire* could cause a lot of damage to the antisystemic currents within the antiglobalisation movement by disorienting them as regards the true nature of globalization and indirectly inducing them to adopt it as an "objective basis" for an alternative globalization, if not to join the reformist currents, like those dominating antiglobalization activity today through the World Social Forum and its affiliates, which are celebrated by the authors and are heavily promoted by the "progressive" mass media.[1]

JOE BENDER

What Can the @CommunistManifesto Tell Us about #Revolution in #2011?[†]

Class, Identity, and the Revolutionary Potential of the Global Working Class

The *Manifesto of the Communist Party* places the question of class struggle squarely at the center of the historical scene. All of history can (and must) be interpreted as a history of class struggle, and the capitalist epoch is defined by the struggle between the bourgeoisie and the proletariat. Yet the organization of historical process according to the bourgeois/proletarian class struggle is the defining feature of a particular period within the larger scope of history, and its identification in the *Manifesto* responds to a certain configuration of forces in the organic development of capital in 1848. In that context, the *Manifesto*, as a manifesto, is an explicitly functional document, a call to arms intended to catalyze the formation of the proletariat as a class and the political generalization of its struggle in a worldwide workers' revolution.

Reading the *Manifesto* today, its approach to mobilization seems foreclosed in certain respects. The prospect of a proletarian revolution seems to have vanished from view, eclipsed behind the Twitter feeds and advertising/news cycles, the glittering screens and empty politics, the info-war and the war on terror of the early 21st century.

---

1. No wonder that, unlike the *Communist Manifesto*, H&N's book has been published by the most prestigious university directly controlled by the transnational elite and has also been heavily promoted by the establishment media (which are controlled by the same elite), elevating it into a best seller! [see for example: *The Observer* (15 July 2001), *The Sunday Times* (15 July 2001) and *The New York Times* (7 July 2001)].
† Written for this Norton Critical Edition.

The world in which we live little resembles the mid-19th century, and the titanic struggle of bourgeoisie and proletariat no longer seems to structure the socio-political and economic context of the age. Capital has, in effect, conquered the globe and reshaped it in its own image, with devastating consequences for human life and the life of the planet. If the specific class antagonism between bourgeoisie and proletariat is no longer pertinent, the struggle against capital and the forms of domination that are inseparable from it has lost none of its urgency.

The past four decades have seen a significant restructuring of the world economy, through an intensification of the mobility of capital in the opaque world of finance, the deregulation of markets, and the growth of ever more rapid communication technologies. In the transition to post-Fordist production, the centers of material production have shifted to sites of cheap labor, outflanking the organized workers' struggles of the twentieth century and vastly diminishing their power as a force of resistance. To this shift to neo-liberal, globalized capitalism corresponds a growth in the scope and importance of the information and cultural economies, characterized by some as a shift to "cognitive capitalism" or Semiocapitalism. Capital has reconstituted the industrial proletariat in the enclaves of outsourced production, while reshaping the so-called "advanced" economies around informatic, cognitive production, precarious affective labor, and the attention economy.[1] The broad diversity of workers' situations with regard to capital and the productive process calls into question the efficacy of formal class analysis, as in the *Manifesto*, to produce and foster possibilities for struggle against the capitalist political-economic system.

If the original task of the *Manifesto* was to exhort the proletariat to new forms of resistance against the domination of capital, and to catalyze its formation as an active political force, our own task of interpretation takes shape. The aim of this essay is not to give a comprehensive overview of reformulations of class in the Marxist tradition, but rather to put forward a series of considerations for rethinking class in the twenty-first century's second decade. The increasing situational diversity of individuals with respect to contemporary processes of production and

---

1. "Affective labor" here refers to the site where an affect, the creation of an emotion in a consumer, is applied to economic activity, particularly where the creation or availability of an affective state or impression represents the creation of positive value in economic exchange. In the context of the commodification of information, which we will see below is a decisive factor in the contemporary economy, "attention economy" refers to the real subsumption of perception by capital. Through advertising and the consumption of visual commodities, the application of attention (as the consumption of information) effectively becomes another form of labor in which value is produced and captured by new forms of regulated distribution.

appropriation poses certain difficulties for the constitution of the proletariat as a potential revolutionary subject. First, we must identify critical transformations in the development of contemporary capital and the challenges they pose to class analysis. Second, from the standpoint of these challenges, how can we reinvent class analysis to respond to our contemporary situation? A reformulated understanding of class today may enable us to think in new ways about what it means to be under the domination of capital and about the task of formulating new forms of struggle pertinent to the contemporary world.

Beyond the Industrial Age

A comprehensive history of the evolution of capitalism over the last 160 years is far beyond the scope of this study and has been undertaken in different forms by far more expert scholars than I. Still, in order to take stock of the possibilities for class analysis today it is necessary to identify some of the salient transformations of the capitalist mode of production as they relate to transformations in class composition and related processes. Reflecting on the centenary of the *Manifesto* in *The 1848* Communist Manifesto *and the World Today,* excerpted in this volume, Lucien Laurat describes a transition in the first decades of the twentieth century, characterized by the growth and organization of workers' movements in Europe and North America and the establishment of the regulatory welfare state. For Laurat, "At the same time that capitalism has organized itself at the interior of national frontiers, liberalism has given way to the directed economy (however badly and fragmentarily directed)."[2] In this context, the polarity between proletariat and bourgeoisie is displaced as the old middle classes are absorbed into the proletariat and a large part of the managerial classes are likewise subjected to the wage relation. Even those professions that historically maintained a certain functional independence— doctors, lawyers, and so on—are progressively incorporated into enterprise. Laurat continues: "Whereas the *antagonism* 'bourgeois-proletariat' of the last century rested on a *social polarity,* the *difference* between the current directors of the economic process and the majority of workers [today] reflects a simple *functional hierarchy,* that of the work of administration and the work of execution."[3] Bourgeoisie and proletariat as social classes cease to be the defining elements of a political situation and are subsumed by what Laurat characterizes as the "world of work," or a combination of wage-earning and salaried labor.

2. Laurat, 1948, in this volume.
3. Ibid. Emphasis in original.

Although world-historical capitalism has again transformed the socio-economic context since the mid-20th century, Laurat's concept of the world of work is worth retaining, as it identifies a phenomenon that has only increased in importance: the diversification of positions with respect to capital and modes of production. The *Manifesto* notes that "the various interests and conditions within the ranks of the proletariat are more and more equalized, in proportion as machinery obliterates all distinctions of labor, and nearly everywhere reduces wages to the same low level," and that "the collisions between individual workmen and individual bourgeois take more and more the character of collisions between two classes." The world of work, however, describes a situation in which diversifying conditions of labor, gains in wages, and the welfare state obscure the character of class conflict, while paradoxically producing new distinctions among workers. In the post-war technocratic state, the managers and bureaucrats who make up an increasing share of the working classes bear little resemblance to the industrial proletariat. The "white collar" workforce does not sell its physical labor or produce goods as material embodiments of their labor time from which they are alienated. However, the conditions of the "salariat" bear the signs of a real subsumption of immaterial labor[4] to capital: the task of the technostructure becomes the maintenance of social reproduction and the transformation of the whole of society into a vast machine for the creation and concentration of wealth. Productivism, quotas, and results-based competition in the workplace all indicate an ongoing functional reorganization of immaterial labor according to the dictates of the production and capture of surplus value.

By taking into account a broadened category of workers whose production is progressively subsumed by capital, the world of work marks a vital shift in capitalist production beyond the direct industrial production of the factory system and into the spheres of immaterial production and social reproduction. In the last four decades, however, a further turn in the development of world historical capitalism calls into question the ability of the world of work to account for the diversity of positions with regard to the capitalist mode of production.

The period since the economic crisis of the early 1970s is marked by a reconfiguration of capital and the mode(s) of production on a global scale. Again, without pretending to give a properly detailed account of these transformations, several important features can nonetheless be identified, with significant consequences for class

---

4. The notion of immaterial labor refers to any productive activity that does not result in a physically embodied product.

analysis. In search of cheaper labor unprotected by the legislative controls enacted in the European and North American economies, large-scale industrial capital has shifted its centers of production to Asia. A political shift toward deregulation and neoliberal economic policy among the wealthy nations of the global Northwest has eased restrictions on the movement of products and capital. The often-coercive spread of the neoliberal deregulation agenda in the developing world has opened markets across the globe to capitalist exploitation. The rapid development of transportation and communication infrastructure and technological developments in the informatization and automation of production have laid the technical and infrastructural groundwork for globalized production processes. They also contribute to the ever-greater share of abstract labor in production, as tasks are broken down into ever-smaller, interchangeable units of time. As industrial production has shifted to the third world, factories in Europe and North America have closed, bringing to an end the period of industrial expansion and near-full employment in the wealthy nations and installing increasingly precarious conditions and permanent high unemployment among the working classes in the old industrial centers. An overall increase in the level of qualification in the workforces of the wealthy countries, a consequence of broad access to higher education in the mid-twentieth century (via, for example, the G.I. Bill and Higher Education Act of 1965 in the United States) has contributed to the conditions for a shift to an information-based economy, where the analysis and recombination of information becomes the primary basis for the creation of surplus value. Over the last two decades, the explosion of the global Internet and World Wide Web, the proliferation of always-on communication devices, and more generally the penetration of virtually all human societies by advanced communication technologies, both reflect and contribute to a shift to cognitive capitalism. These developments also mark an ongoing process by which all aspects of social reproduction are subsumed by the production and appropriation of surplus value.

Beyond the reconfiguration marked by Laurat's move from proletariat to world of work, the contemporary situation produces a profound fragmentation between groups of workers and their relationships to the processes of production in which they are enmeshed. Concentrations of factory workers are reconstituted in conditions of ever-greater destitution in the Special Development Zones of China and the Pacific Rim. Workers in the wealthy nations of the Northwest are increasingly divided between specialized information work in the cognitive economy and affective labor in the service industries, the latter's ranks swelled by flows of migrants seeking work far from home and driving remittance economies in their home countries. Growing numbers of the chronically unemployed of the post-industrial economies are increasingly swept aside and left with meager prospects for enough work to assure even the basic demands of social reproduction, while their attention as viewers and website visitors drives the Internet advertising economy. The organization of a flexible, precarious global workforce, "in which just-in-time production is overseen by a permanently temporary labor force, is mirrored in the form of governance characteristic of democratic imperialism, sustained . . . by appeals to urgency, permanent mobilization, suspensions of norms: governance by crisis, rule by exception."[5] The expansion of capitalist economic organization is inseparable from certain political transformations, encapsulated here under the heading "democratic imperialism," and, more broadly, the imposition of an economic rationality in political decision making, whereby acts of governance are submitted to the sole criterion of profitability. Capital accumulation seems to operate in a closed loop in the world of finance, no longer controlled by a clearly constituted class of entrepreneurs, but rather launched in a dizzying cycle of self-reproduction, as capital shifts between banks and hedge funds at the speed of thought. Immaterial, affective, and cultural labor account for an ever-greater proportion of value creation. The formal constitution of the bourgeoisie/proletariat binomial falls apart in the face of this immense and growing complexity, a situation in which the economic logics of overproduction/overconsumption, profit and competition come to dominate human activity at all levels of society. Under the banner of free market ideology, "the deregulatory practices that accompany the victory of monetary neoliberalism consist in clearing away all rules, so that only the rules of the economic dominate, uncontested. The only legitimate rule is now the strictest, the most violent, the most cynical, the most irrational of all the rules: the law of economic jungle."[6]

Class under Semiocapitalism

In recent decades, a number of schools of thought have moved toward a critical understanding of the shape of capitalism today, its development and the possibilities for struggle within and against it. The debates between them are too lengthy to go into here; in this section I will concentrate on one strand of work coming out of the Italian Marxist tradition of *Operaismo* (Workerism), particularly in the recent work of Franco Berardi.[7] It is nevertheless important to

---

5. Jason Smith, "Soul on Strike," preface to Franco Berardi, *The Soul at Work: from Alienation to Autonomy*. (Los Angeles, CA: Semiotext(e), 2009), p. 11.
6. Franco Berardi, *The Soul at Work: From Alienation to Autonomy* (Los Angeles, CA: Semiotext(e), 2009), p. 186.
7. Ben Trott, "Immaterial Labour and World Order: An Evaluation of a Thesis," *Ephemera*, Vol. 7, No. 1, February 2007, pp. 204–06.

emphasize that this is but one way of seeking to understand contemporary society, and not without its shortcomings. Not the least
of these is the risk of essentializing the knowledge worker and
abstracting her from the social relations of production, producing a
distinction that applies the material conditions of a small set of
immaterial laborers to all. As I hope to show here, the analysis of
Semiocapitalism, including its development of the "immaterial
labor thesis," while only one way of describing the contemporary
situation, opens certain possibilities for class analysis that may
enable us to move beyond the foreclosure of class struggle.

Berardi responds to several of the transformations sketched in
the previous section, particularly the post-Fordist turn and the
explosion of digital communication technologies, to describe a situation in which the capitalist logics of efficiency, profit, enterprise
and competition invade and restructure the spheres of political,
economic, and social activity. From the mastery of space, markets,
and populations, and the predominant circulation of physical objects
of exchange, capital shifts its basis in part to the commodification
of information, but also to the domination of all aspects of human
life:

> This transformation [of information into property], and the
> ensuing reconfiguration of class struggle that comes with it,
> are conditioned by the inability of capitalism to maintain its
> pace and character of historic magnification. For capitalism
> to elude the spectre of the falling rate of profit and to extend
> its degree of accumulation, capital has to turn into an image,
> and information, shared lived experience, and the commons
> be transformed into commodities—commodification turns
> inward.[8]

The tendency of profits to fall over time is an intrinsic aspect of
capitalist accumulation, and a driving force behind capitalist innova-

---

8. Dafermos, George N. "5 Theses on Informational-Cognitive Capitalism." *Proceedings
of the 22nd Chaos Communication Congress*, December 2005, §5. http://opensource.gr/
hyperdrome/usr/dafermos/immaterial_labour/22c3.html (Accessed December 15,
2010.) Dafermos distances himself from certain aspects of *Operaismo* and its descen-
dants, with whom Berardi is historically associated, in rejecting the Workerist premise
of the centrality of workers' struggles to the evolution of capital, which they see to
evolve primarily in reaction to the resistance of labor. While this debate is peripheral
to the discussion at hand, it is worth noting that Berardi has recently differentiated
himself from this aspect of Workerism, particularly the apotheosis of workers' power as
a positive, creative force of resistance in Hardt and Negri's figure of the multitude.
Berardi refers to this tendency as the "empty use of the term 'multitude'" to refer to "a
boundless positive energy, a force of liberation that cannot submit to domination in
any way" (Berardi, 2009, pp. 154–5), whereas in fact, "[t]he multitude does not manifest itself as autonomy at all, but rather as dependence from the automatisms that biopower builds and activates in everyday life, in our sensibility and psyche: we become a
swarm" (Berardi, 2009, p. 194).

tion.[9] Because the profits extracted from a given activity tend to diminish over time, capital is always seeking out new ways to increase its accumulation, by technological means (mechanization and productivity gains to derive more profits for less pay) or by subsuming ever more types of activity to appropriation. The result of this process of subsumption of all human activity to the grammar of capital is what Berardi calls Semiocapitalism.

As the *Manifesto* declares, the struggle between bourgeoisie and proletariat is inseparable from the mode of production predicated on industrial activity and factory labor. If we wish to understand the implications of Berardi's work for class analysis we must delve deeper into how Semiocapitalism has restructured human society. This transformation initially appears along four main dimensions: the informatization of production, fragmentation and distribution of different modes of production across the globe, dominance of abstract labor over other forms of lived experience, and the central role of social reproduction.

INFORMATIZATION OF PRODUCTION

In Semiocapitalism, information is commodified, and its recombination increasingly becomes the point of creation of surplus value. Cognitive labor becomes, if clearly not the sole or necessarily the quantitatively dominant form of work, its *paradigmatic* form, the driving force of value production and capital accumulation.[1] Historically correlated with the development of the Internet, and particularly with the World Wide Web, "in the 1990s . . . financial flows generated by *net trading*, the advertising cycle, venture capital and retirement funds moved to the cycle of virtual production. Cognitive labor could therefore become enterprise, entering the formation circuits of the Techno-Sphere and media-scape."[2] The recombination and creation of information as data analysis, images, cultural products, etc., became a significant source of the creation and capture of surplus value. From a position of relative autonomy, this movement of cognitive labor was influential in the first generation of the Internet economy, but was gradually co-opted by the venture capital that funded Internet enterprise in the dot.com era. In a process of real subsumption, the innovative labor processes

9. Marx, *Capital, volume* 3, chapters 13–15.
1. Cognitive labor, for Berardi, is paradigmatic in the sense that it is in the process of conception, rather than that of execution, that innovation and hence value-creation take place: "Digital technologies open a completely new perspective for labor. First of all they transform the relation between conceiving and executing, and therefore the relation between the intellectual contents of labor and its manual execution. Manual labor is generally executed by automatically programmed machinery, while innovative labor, the one that effectively produces value, is mental labor." Berardi, 2009, p. 75.
2. Ibid., p. 96.

enabled in part by technological change were reformatted by capitalism's operational logic and broken down into units of commodified time, with implications for human existence beyond the sphere of labor as such. For Berardi, capital's colonization of all spheres of human activity, especially mental labor, results from the ongoing process of abstraction of labor described by Marx in the *Grundrisse* of 1857: "The abstraction of labor, that is to say the transformation of human activities into empty performances of abstract time, is progressively expanding to all possible forms of social activity. The final point of this process is the subsumption of the productive labor of mental activity itself [by] the sphere of value-production, which results in its ultimate reduction and abstraction."[3]

As the paradigmatic form of labor evolves, so too does the class composition of the societies in which it develops. In the context of nineteenth-century capitalism, factory work was the paradigmatic form of labor and the industrial proletariat was "its special and essential product."[4] Which class(es) would be the essential product of cognitive capitalism today? In other words, as the proletariat was produced out of the social and technical organization of production in the industrial age, what class structures does the new mode of informational production generate, and what problematics of this socio-economic organization do they embody?

In his "5 Theses on Informational-Cognitive Capitalism," George Dafermos draws out the mutual constitution of processes of capital accumulation and the classes that characterize them through the opposition between a "vectoralist class" and "digital proletariat":

> A new class has arisen that is rapidly amassing increasingly more power through its ability to *veto* on [sic] the vectors of information which it controls, and which both knowledge workers and the industrial capitalists need. This is the terrain of history where class struggle is being re-written. . . . Yet, it is misleading to assume that capitalism had, or has, a hard time adapting to this reconfiguration. . . . On the contrary, the capitalist system not only required the formation of this class, but also incorporated it into its very operational logic. With the rise of this new class, which McKenzie Wark terms the 'vectoralist class', and, which, it should be noted, has its roots in the hacker universe, yet has chosen to disassociate itself from the interests of the 'digital proletariat', we witness the final stage of the transformation of information into property.[5]

3. Ibid., p. 58.
4. *Communist Manifesto.*
5. George N. Dafermos, "5 Theses on Informational-Cognitive Capitalism."

The ongoing reconfiguration of capitalism transforms the class composition of society, and brings to the fore the struggle between the vectoralist class, strategically placed to control the means of transmission and reproduction of information, and both the industrial capitalists and digital proletariat (also described by Wark as the "hacker class," "producer of new abstractions" and creator of "the possibility of new things entering the world"[6]). According to Wark, from whom Dafermos draws the vectoralist/hacker class antagonism, the vectoralists "control the vectors along which information is abstracted, just as capitalists control the material means with which goods are produced, and pastoralists the land with which food is produced."[7] As advanced digital technology tends to reduce the reproduction cost of information, and thus the real cost of immaterial production, "vectoralists try to break capital's monopoly on the production process, and subordinate the production of goods to the circulation of information." Wark continues:

> The leading corporations divest themselves of their productive capacity, as this is no longer a source of power. Their power lies in monopolising intellectual property—patents and brands— and the means of reproducing their value—the vectors of communication. The privatisation of information becomes the dominant, rather than a subsidiary, aspect of commodified life.[8]

The hacker class, on the other hand, "produces the possibility of production, the possibility of making something of and with the world—and of living off the surplus produced by the application of abstraction to nature—to any nature."[9] Because its activity is essentially one of recombination, based on existing information, the hacker class has a vested interest in the free circulation of information as its raw material, yet it equally depends on the representation of information as value, "as something from which a source of income may be derived that gives the hacker some independence from the ruling classes."[1] The reliance of the hacker class on the flow of information brings it into conflict with the vectoralist class, which seeks to privatize and control information in all its forms. At the same time the hacker class relies on the constituted value of the information it produces—predicated on a degree of control over its reproduction and dissemination—for its material survival. In other

6. McKenzie Wark, *A Hacker Manifesto [Version 4.0]*. §2. http://subsol.c3.hu/subsol_2/contributors0/warktext.html (Accessed 12/15/2010.)
7. Wark: §14.
8. Ibid., §15.
9. Ibid., §34. In Wark's usage, the "application of abstraction to nature" represents the realization of potentials of physical matter through the application of information. Cf. §4–7.
1. Ibid., §37.

words, the hacker class requires information to be both free, in order to be able to produce, and commodified, in order to make a living from its (re)production.

This apparent contradiction poses a problem for the conceptualization of the hacker class as a possible revolutionary subject. On the one hand, the digital proletariat appears as the broad spectrum of people engaged in the productive manipulation of information, but not necessarily united by a common set of relations to the mode(s) of production. In this sense, they are what Berardi refers to as a "virtual class," where "the notion of virtual class stresses the socially undefined, elusive character of the work flows produced by Semiocapital. The virtual class is the class of those who do not identify with any class, since they are not socially or materially structured: their definition depends on the removal of their own social corporeality."[2] This perspective represents both total involvement in the network—the crossover of interaction to digitally-mediated means—and withdrawal from the physical proximity at the center of traditional workers' organizations, factory councils, and the like. On the other hand, because even cognitive workers have to pay the rent, the notion of the virtual class as an aspect of cognitive labor calls for a complementary concept to express the necessarily embodied nature of human labor. For Berardi, this concept is the "cognitariat," combination of cognitive labor and the proletariat.

> The cognitariat is the semiotic labor flow, socially spread and fragmented, as seen from the standpoint of its social corporeality. The virtual class has no needs, but the cognitariat does. The virtual class is not affected by the psychic stress determined by the constant exploitation of attention. The cognitariat is affected. The virtual class cannot produce any conscious collective process except as collective Intellect. The cognitariat can identify itself as a conscious community.[3]

The virtual class then is the social labor of the intellect as recombination, intervening in and perpetuating the circulation of information, while the cognitariat is that virtual class in its embodied aspect. In this sense, "Cognitariat is the social corporeality of cognitive labor."[4]

2. Berardi, 2009, p. 104.
3. Ibid., p. 105.
4. Ibid., p. 105.

UNEVEN DISTRIBUTION

The cognitariat, then, as a reformulation of the hacker class that takes into account its material, social existence, appears as a possible site of association and political mobilization, and an essential product of Semiocapitalism. It is important, however, not to overlook the persistence and ongoing development of other groups and positions in relation to capital. As the circulation and commodification of information grow in importance, Semiocapital also produces an uneven distribution of different modes of production over the surface of the globe. Distributed logistical networks and just-in-time production bridge the distances separating industrial enclaves from centers of consumption. Factory workers in the industrial zones of outsourced industry resemble the constituted proletariat of the nineteenth century, while new high-tech centers like Hyderabad and Bangalore are home to increasing concentrations of information workers implicated in exceedingly diverse production chains. Such redistribution simultaneously produces parallelism in workers' relations to capital and their modes of production, as in the 24-hour software development operation or distributed call-center shifts, and increases perceived competition between workers across different regions.

This uneven distribution of the modes of production also operates on another dimension, within the social division of labor, which may or may not cut across geographical lines. Moreover, even within the particular case of immaterial labor we must distinguish between different positions in the relative abstraction and autonomy of production. As Rodrigo Nunes points out, "We are speaking of a category that encompasses the different realities of the software programmer and the production engineer, the call centre worker and the nurse, the loan manager and the waitress, the shop assistant and the 'IT guy', the teacher and the filmmaker, even (pushing the boundaries between production and reproduction) the student and the parent."[5] The material conditions of the software engineer or freelance designer, who "creates the form and content of the commodity she produces,"[6] differ significantly from those of the waitress, shopworker, or receptionist, whose smile represents the creation of a positive affect as surplus value for the enterprise. Their different positions with respect to the cost of reproduction of their raw materials and the commodities they produce—tending to the base cost of social reproduction and the proliferation of information for the

5. Rodrigo Nunes, "'Forward How? Forward Where?' I: (Post-)Operaismo Beyond the Immaterial Labour Thesis." *Ephemera*. Vol. 7, No. 1: "Immaterial and Affective Labour: Explored" (Feb 2007), p. 186.
6. Ibid., p. 188.

information worker, tied to the corporeal presence and subjective availability of a given affect for the call center worker or parent, etc.—are part of their concrete work conditions and must be taken into account in any analysis of their potential and/or actual associations and potential for action.

DOMINATION OF LIVED EXPERIENCE BY WORK

The paradigmatic association of wealth and consumption in the 20th century, in which wealth and success become inseparable from the ever-greater and more ostentatious consumption and display of material objects, contributes to a situation in which individuals devote ever-greater proportions of their time to work. The society of consumption responds on one hand to the principle of overproduction. "Overproduction is an immanent character of capitalistic production, since the production of goods never corresponds to the logic of human beings' concrete needs, but to the abstract logic of the production of value."[7] Markets and consumers must be created for the goods produced, aided by the explosion of advertising. The growing proportion of labor in the time of lived experience is driven in part by the manufactured desire produced by the advertising industry, and in part by the increasingly central role of ostentatious consumption in the production of social identity. Through the assimilation of social status and identity to consumption, capital produces conditions of intensified competition. This competition in turn becomes more severe as the conditions of labor shift away from long-term, relatively stable employment. As opposed to a situation where capital must buy the whole of the worker's labor time, "when we move into the sphere of info-labor, Capital no longer recruits people, it buys packets of time, separated from their interchangeable and contingent bearers."[8]

Labor in Semiocapitalism is fundamentally precarious, because the whole productive labor of the individual, to be compensated by a wage corresponding to the cost of social reproduction, is no longer the basis of value production. From this standpoint:

> Precariousness becomes the general form of social existence. Capital can buy fractals of human time, recombining them through the digital network. Digitalized info-labor can be recombined in a different location, far from the one that produces it. From the standpoint of capital's valorization, the flow is continuous, finding its unity in the produced object. Yet from the cognitive workers' perspective the work done has a fragmentary character: it consists in fractions of cellular time

7. Berardi, 2009, p. 178.
8. Ibid., p. 192.

available for productive recombination. Intermittent work cells turn on and off within the large control frame of global production. The distribution of time can thus be separated from the physical and juridical person of the worker.[9]

For Berardi, this fragmentation and recomposition of labor time has two main consequences. The worker is always available, wherever she may find herself, as when the enterprise gives its employees Blackberry devices, ensuring their permanent availability. On the other hand, since the whole labor time of the worker is no longer required by capital, more and more workers find themselves in positions of partial employment, where one or more part-time or project-based jobs supplant full-time employment and the social benefits associated with it. This phenomenon Berardi terms the "precariat": "The word 'precariat' generally stands for the area of work which is no longer definable by fixed rules relative to the labour relation, to salary and to the length of the working day."[1] Flexibility and mobility are the watchwords of this precarious workforce, whose capacity for organization is called into question by its fragile mobility. It "moves from one task to the next and never stays long in a business," and "can no longer even consolidate itself as a force, being outside the center of the production process and employed to plug the holes of what has not yet been mechanized."[2] Moreover, as competition and precariousness drive people to devote more and more of their time to work, relational modes outside the workplace atrophy and decay. Community, interpersonal relationships, and democracy all require time and effort to elaborate, elements in short supply in conditions of the fragmentation of labor and the domination of lived experience by work.

THE SOCIAL FACTORY

In Semiocapital, social reproduction takes on a central role in value creation, as precariousness and competition drive a total orientation of the individual toward present and future work. Social existence increasingly takes on the character of mobilization, where "to be mobilized is to relate to work not as an activity but as a *possibility*."[3] Each worker is called to create herself as "human resource" and the process of subjectivation—the self-fashioning of the individual in and through a given social context—becomes part of the

9. Ibid., p. 191.
1. Franco Berardi, "Info-Labour and Precarisation," trans. Erik Empson. www.generation-online.org. www.generation-online.org/t/tinfolabour.htm (Accessed 12/14/2010.)
2. The Invisible Committee, *The Coming Insurrection* (Paris: La fabrique editions, 2007), p. 31. English text available online at http://tarnac9.wordpress.com/texts/the-coming-insurrection/ (Accessed 12/15/2010.)
3. Ibid., p. 32.

creation and capture of surplus value. This process is integrated by capital on two levels: 1/ the individual's whole social identity becomes part of their qualification for work and is exploited in the workplace as an aspect of value production by the enterprise, and 2/ the process of self-fashioning of the individual is itself commodified. The Invisible Committee (*Comité Invisible*) describes the first of these tendencies in its 2007 manifesto *The Coming Insurrection*, citing a director of human resources at Daimler-Benz:

> Business associates . . . are an important part of the business's capital. . . . Their motivation, their know-how, their capacity to innovate and their attention to clients' desires constitute the raw material of innovative services. . . . Their behavior, their social and emotional competence, are a growing factor in the evaluation of their work. . . . This will no longer be evaluated in terms of number of hours on the job, but on the basis of objectives attained and quality of results. They are entrepreneurs.[4]

As behavior is valorized by capital, the sphere of human activity outside the workplace and the individual's identity itself become part of the labor process. The inward turn of capitalism "transforms labor-power into what managerial theories call human *capital*, harnessing and putting to work not an abstract, general force of labor, but the particularity, the unique combination of psychic, cognitive, and affective powers I bring to the labor process."[5] Rather than the manual act of the worker, her entire social and psychic being is mobilized as labor. The whole of lived experience is harnessed to the production of the self as human capital and to augment the individual's productivity:

> All these young people smiling for their job interviews, who have their teeth whitened to give them an edge, who go to nightclubs to boost the company spirit, who learn English to advance their careers, who get divorced or married to move up the ladder, who take courses in leadership or practice "self-improvement" in order to better "manage conflicts"—"the most intimate 'self-improvement'," says one guru, "will lead to increased emotional stability, to smoother and more open relationships, to sharper intellectual focus, and therefore to a better economic performance."[6]

Mobilized subjectivation often takes the form of explicit self-cultivation, as workers produce themselves in and for capital through the development of skills, networking, professional persona and

4. Ibid., pp. 30–31.
5. Smith, 2009, pp. 13–14.
6. Invisible Committee, 2007, p. 32.

portfolio. Individuals are motivated to creative expression in social networks, blogs, Twitter feeds, and the like, in order to fashion and project a marketable, highly performing identity. To again cite the Invisible Committee, "Producing oneself is becoming the dominant occupation of a society where production no longer has an object: like a carpenter who's been evicted from his shop and in desperation sets about hammering and sawing himself."[7]

In the context of capitalist socialization, "It now becomes possible to sell oneself rather than one's labor power, to be remunerated not for what one does but for what one is, for our exquisite mastery of social codes, for our relational talents, for our smile and our way of presenting ourselves."[8] This is the new cultural capital, where "we participate in our own exploitation, and all participation is exploited. Ideally, you are yourself a little business, your own boss, your own product."[9] Yet in the second facet of the process described above, the labor of producing oneself is subsumed by capital. The activity of subjectivation becomes commodified in what Dafermos terms "a process of generalized social abstraction," where "the commodity-form implodes to encompass and invest all of shared lived experience."[1]

> The commodity-form has gone well beyond the romantic stage of fetishism: while there is no doubt that both the use- and exchange-value of a product now largely stem from intangible characteristics, such as perceived sex-appeal, 'coolness', and ephemeral trendiness . . . commodification does not stop at the twilight of shopfronts and commodity shelves, that is, the sphere of materiality, but it extends beyond them to encompass all of the immaterial. . . . In the age of universality of the spectacle, the ultimate commodity is the time of our own lives, that is, the relationships and experiences that give meaning to its space.[2]

The commodification of processes of subjectivation includes the intimate link between consumption and display in what Dafermos refers to as the "sphere of materiality." More insidious yet is the capture and commodification of lived time and human relationships, as communication and expression, explicitly motivated by personal qualification or not, are subsumed by capital in the crowdsourced Web advertising economy. Sites like YouTube, Facebook, and location-aware applications on mobile devices monetize the activity of the

7. Ibid.
8. Ibid.
9. Ibid.
1. Dafermos, 2005, §1.
2. Ibid.

mass of their users through eye-time, data gathering and aggregation, and targeted advertising. Even more so than television sta-
tions, these websites don't produce content for an audience, having
outsourced their content production to the audience itself, but
rather sell eyeballs to advertisers through online ad agencies like
AdMob/AdSense/DoubleClick (Google), iAd/Quattro (Apple), Mobi-
clix, Traffic Marketplace (Epic Media Group), and others. The real
value for crowdsourced Web services, however, is less in selling the
space of a single ad than in the aggregation and sale of user activity
and relationships as data. The personal information we all constantly create whenever we use digital technologies is aggregated,
packaged, sold—ostensibly depersonalized but often still linked to
an IP address or mobile device's Unique Device Identifier—and
used in branding and targeted advertising.[3] Thus, as users create
their social identities through the production and recombination of
information, they provide the material basis for capital appropriation, while at the same time creating themselves as sites for targeted marketing.

Again the varied forms of labor in Semiocapital complicate class
analysis and the possibilities of organization. Where the diverse positions of workers in respect to their production processes created a
fragmentation in today's expanded world of work, yet still remained
visible as labor, many people are not even aware of the ways in
which their personal activity is commodified and appropriated as
surplus value. Apparatuses for the capture of value permeate and
intimately structure lived experience on the smallest of scales, disseminated into the everyday gestures of contemporary social activity, largely below the level of perception. With respect to the task of
organization against exploitation by capital, this omnipresence of
the logics of capital in lived experience often seems to foreclose possibilities of resistance. In the *Manifesto*, one task in catalyzing the
development of the proletariat as a class is to "point out and bring to
the front the common interests of the entire proletariat," yet how is
this possible if the very communality of those interests and the parallelism of individuals' relationships to production and appropriation are veiled?

Organization beyond Formal Class Antagonism

In the *Manifesto* the role of the Communist party is to catalyze the
formation of the proletariat into a class, an effective agent of

3. Scott Thurm and Yukari Iwatani Kane. "Your Apps Are Watching You: A WSJ Investigation finds that iPhone and Android apps are breaching the privacy of smartphone
users." *The Wall Street Journal* December 17, 2010. http://online.wsj.com/article/SB10
0014240527487046940045760200883703574602.html (Accessed January 4, 2011.)

change.[4] This process expresses "actual relations springing from an existing class struggle, from a historical movement going on under our very eyes," yet the formation of the proletariat as a class implies the expansion from a perception of the material reality of these relations into a movement. The fragmentation of workers' relationships to the modes of production in which they find themselves today poses a significant challenge to class analysis. Likewise, the infiltration of subjectivation, social reproduction and perception by appropriation calls into question the possibility of class organization, despite the broad commonality of certain relations to capital. Indeed, this shift from a macro- to a micrologic of exploitation in the contemporary situation corresponds to the decline of the working class as an identifiable social and political position in the last four decades.

> The political extinction of the working class was not and is not a consequence of any struggle between political forces, or the effect of a social elimination. Workers continue to exist, but their social action is no longer effective in relation to the dominant processes that are actually producing general social effects. What has irreversibly changed on the scene of Semiocapital is the relationship between the human factor (the workers) and sites of control and decision. Control is no longer exerted on a macrosocial or anatomic level, as bodily constriction. Control is exerted at an invisible, irreversible level, a level that cannot be ruled, since it happens through the creation of linguistic and operative automatisms structuring the way the technosphere functions.[5]

In this formulation, the dissemination of a capitalist logic into the constitutive elements of lived experience amounts to an infiltration of all human life by capital's mechanisms of control, largely through the technological apparatuses that structure our (individual and collective) existence. The micro-logic of control short-circuits the possibility for social action to produce "general social effects." For Berardi, these transformations amount to a political extinction, as the social action of the working class can only act on the macro- and not the micro-level, and therefore cannot directly impact the sites of control and decision central to Semiocapital.

Is class then off the table as a tool for organization and change? The binomial bourgeoisie/proletariat clearly no longer exhausts or is sufficient to the organic development of capital. "Paleomarxist" frameworks, particularly in a Leninist vein, derive a purely formal

---

4. "The immediate aim of the Communists is the same as that of all the other proletarian parties: formation of the proletariat into a class."
5. Berardi, 2009, p. 200.

notion of class from a structural understanding of capital, where capital is at its most fundamental a relation of exploitation in which labor is appropriated by the owners of the means of production. The proletariat then encompasses all those individuals who are (necessarily) oppressed as a result of their non-ownership of the means of production. This framework takes capital to be solely "a formal relation of exploitation: the surplus labour-time is appropriated by private hands or by the state" whereas, on the other hand, "the actual material process of exploitation/work is neglected. This formal notion of capital leads to a formal notion of working-class: a mass of exploited individuals who have to sell their labour-power due to their 'non-possession' of the means of production."[6] Moreover, Leninism and other "left-communist" movements (e.g. Council Communism) focus on the concentration of the forces of production in the wrong hands, rather than taking into account the ways in which real subsumption by capital structures all aspects of society. They "ignore the contradiction that the material form of technology (assembly line), of science (Taylorism) and socialization ('globalisation') itself is the foundation of capitalist command over the workers. The dissolution of this contradiction can only take place in a class movement that both changes the material conditions of production *and 'socializes' the forces of production along with the struggle.*[7] The restructuring of both labor processes and social activity by Semiocapitalism clearly shows the limitations of a formal notion of class in the contemporary context. However, to say that the subsumption of lived experience by capital precludes organization and resistance is to ignore the possibility of struggles to re-socialize the forces of production along different lines. Ongoing revolutionary activity in Tunisia, Egypt and elsewhere, as well as struggles of the anti-globalization movement, left political action in Latin America, organization around environmental justice, etc., indicate the persistent need for and presence of ongoing activity toward this goal.

As we have seen, the operative automatisms of the technosphere structure lived experience as a field of labor and represent the infiltration of capital into subjectivation and social reproduction in general. However, the same technologies can also enable the development of communities, raise consciousness of parallelisms in the relations of individuals to capital, and be made to serve collective struggle. On a tactical level, internet-connected cell phones and social media can become powerful means of publicizing struggles and organizing resistance, particularly in protest action. Indeed, the

6. Kolinko, "Class Composition," April 2001, §2. www.nadir.org/nadir/initiativ/kolinko/engl/e_klazu.htm (Accessed January 5, 2011.) Author's emphasis.
7. Ibid., §5f.

extensive use of social media, Internet communications, and mobile technologies are a hallmark of contemporary organization. Student protests in the United Kingdom in the last quarter of 2010 against cuts to education funding and rising tuition fees are exemplary in this regard. Protesters used Facebook messages to contest the claim by police that crowds of detained students were being treated fairly during the Whitehall march of November 24. A group of students occupying University College London on several occasions called flashmobs through their website, and on December 9 created a live Google map of police activity in real time during the Parliament Square protest.[8] Internet communications and social networking have been put to effective use by other organizations like UK Uncut and False Economy, raising the perspective of a broadly-based grassroots movement.[9] Indeed, as this is written, the overthrow of President Zine El Abidine Ben Ali in Tunisia and President Hosni Mubarak in Egypt clearly illustrate the enormous importance of communication technologies in organizing popular action. As computer security specialist Ahmad Gharbeia writes about the Tunisian revolution: "The role of the Internet was critical at the beginning," particularly in spreading the news of local struggles in Sidi Bouzid and of police violence against protesters. Gharbeia continues: "On the 25th [of January], the movements of the protesting groups were arranged in real time through Twitter. Everyone knew where everyone else was walking and we could advise on the locations of blockades and skirmishes with police. It was real time navigation through the city, and that's why it was shut down."[1] The importance of the Internet and text messaging in these popular revolts is further underlined by the Mubarak government's decision to cut off four of five Egyptian Internet service providers and to disable text messaging on January 27th.[2] Despite these efforts, a large amount of

---

8. See UCL Occupation blog at blog.ucloccupation.com for ongoing discussion of activism against education cuts in the U.K. The Live Protest Map of the December 9, 2010 protest is available on line at http://maps.google.co.uk/maps/ms? ie=UTF8&oe=UTF8 &msa=0&msid=210122421581924639063.000496f96fd6739e0982d&z=15 (Accessed January 6, 2011.)

9. Aaron Peters, "2011: The year political activism and progressive politics goes open source," *Left Foot Forward*, December 20, 2010. www.leftfootforward.org/2010/12/ 2011-open-source-political-activism-progressive-politics/ (Accessed January 3, 2011.) Guy Aitchison, "What next for the student movement?" *UCL Occupation*, December 23, 2010. http://blog.ucloccupation.com/2010/12/23/what-next-for-the-student-movement/ #more-968 (Accessed January 6, 2011.) For further information on the UK student protests see Clifford Singer, "Reflections on student protests and UK Uncut: 12 essential posts," *False Economy*, December 30, 2010. http://falseeconomy.org.uk/blog/reflections -on-student-protests-and-uk-uncut-12-essential-posts (Accessed January 6, 2011.)

1. Mike Elkin, "Cairo's Band of Geeks Survives Tahrir Square Assault," *Wired*, February 2, 2011. www.wired.com/dangerroom/2011/02/cairos-band-of-geeks-survives-tahrir-square -assault/ (Accessed February 3, 2011.)

2. Matthew Weaver, Haroon Siddique, Richard Adams and Tim Hill, "Protests in Egypt—as they happened," *Guardian.co.uk*, January 28, 2010. www.guardian.co.uk/ news/blog/2011/jan/28/egypt-protests-live-updates (Accessed February 3, 2011.)

information escaped the blockade, with effects for the protest movement in Egypt and across the region. No one technology or service can be credited with enabling the growth of these movements; rather, a general mobilization of the communication apparatus at hand enabled protesters to circumvent attempts to suppress communication and contributed greatly to the generalization of these ongoing struggles. In particular, communication technologies rendered visible a common relation between individuals and repressive state apparatuses, creating the conditions for an upwelling of solidarity in the face of state violence.

Left Foot Forward contributor Alan Peters's article "2011: The year political activism and progressive politics goes open source," evokes open source software as a model. His reference to open source operates on two levels, recalling the possibility of crowdsourced media and networks to provide both a technical basis and a model for organization. Each individual is able both to take physical action—participating in protests, occupations, and other actions—and to become an active participant in conversations that spread possibilities for struggle across social groups and across space: "In the new 'crowdsourced' paradigm the distinction between producers and consumers of dissent is dissolved—there is no organising or membership structure in place, with instead all individuals being potential 'participants' within a movement."[3] Peters's formulation recalls Rosa Luxemburg's conception of the Social Democratic party in *Leninism or Marxism?*, where she called for a workers' organization characterized, not by an hierarchically centralized party, but rather by many loosely coordinated, autonomous groups working toward a common set of goals. Simultaneously producing, mobilizing, and facilitating dissent, each member (or potential member) of such a movement draws on and innovates within a technological framework that, as it is activated and elaborated to actualize new possibilities for organization and community, is effectively re-socialized, breaking the short-circuit of consumption and identity production and enabling the innovation of new forms of collective organization.

In opening on to new forms of organization, the notion of open source politics equally evokes the vital dimension of political generalization, the necessity for organizational activity to spread from local acts of resistance to become a broader movement, in order to act effectively against existing configurations of power. To further affect the restructuring of social activity by Semiocapitalism, however, organization must link back to the relations of production in which individuals are enmeshed. It will be of great importance, for example, whether or not the Tunisian revolution goes beyond a

3. Peters, 2010.

reshuffling of government that leaves the structures of economic domination intact. As Berardi frames the issue of generalization in a discussion of the anti-globalization movement of the 2000s, "The global movement against corporate capitalism is absolutely right when it goes to the streets, organizing blockades like in Seattle, Prague, Bologna, and Quebec City, and Genoa. But this is the symbolic action that fuels the real movement of sabotage and of reshaping, which has to be organized in every lab, in all the places where cognitarians are producing and creating the technical interfaces of the social fabric."[4] Political change is necessary, but must be accompanied by a revolution in the relations of production and social reproduction that undergird the political sphere.

The open source movement is an important example of an attempt at such a revolution in the relations of production. For the logics of private property and wage labor, the open source movement substitutes the gift, contribution without explicit return other than the ability to use a common stock of tools held in common. By the same token, to the principle of personal identity produced through economic compensation and consumption, open source substitutes the autonomy of the contributor. To return to Wark's terminology, in the gift, the hacker produces herself as the producer of that gift, as contributor:

> The hacker struggles to produce a subjectivity that is qualitative and singular, in part through the act of the hack itself. The gift, as a qualitative exchange between singular parties allows each party to be recognised as a singular producer, as a subject of production, rather than as a commodified and quantified object. The gift expresses in a social and collective way the subjectivity of the production of production, whereas commodified property represents the producer as an object, a quantifiable commodity like any other, of relative value only.[5]

The gift actively constitutes a community, and in this sense is fundamentally different from capitalist exchange. Contribution is a qualitative exchange rather than a quantitative one, irreducible to monetary value, in which each party is recognized as a subject of production, and production takes on the character of collective enterprise. In this way labor, in and through an organization in which identity takes on meaning, is removed from the field of antagonism and competition that dominates the relationships between producers in capitalist production. In choosing to participate, I am no

---

4. Franco, Berardi "Bifo." "Info-Labour and Precarisation." Trans. Erik Empson. www .generation-online.org, ND. www.generation-online.org/t/tinfolabour.htm (Accessed December 14. 2010.)
5. Wark, §21.

longer competing with others for a larger share of wages in an artificial zero-sum game, but rather affirming myself as a producer in a community of producers, in which each is defined by his or her singular contribution.[6]

In the development of open source software, individuals participate freely in a project without direct remuneration, contributing their labor and knowledge to a common stock of tools from which all can draw. In this sense the full implications of the open source model for organization become clear, as its removal of labor from mechanisms of abstraction and appropriation presents a possible alternative to the wage form in immaterial production. Nevertheless, there is a risk in taking the open source movement as a model. Many of the tools produced by the open source movement are reappropriated by capitalist enterprise and put to use for profit, as in the case of the LAMP server software stack (the Linux operating system, Apache Web server, MySQL database, and PHP/Perl/Python scripting languages) that powers a large portion of Web servers and applications globally. Moreover, in this particular sector of immaterial production, the widespread adoption of digital technologies drives down the reproduction cost of information, where "the gift of information need not give rise to conflict over information as property, for information need not suffer the artifice of scarcity once freed from commodification."[7]

However, if the products of software programming and other sectors of cognitive production are immaterial, the workers who produce them are anything but immaterial. In his timely and insightful *Telekommunist Manifesto*, Dmitri Kleiner underscores the important point that, while the distribution of digitized information is immaterial, the equipment used to produce it and the social reproduction of the workers are not. In order to envision the possibility of another form of production based on contribution and a common stock of tools, we must first account for the material inputs that underlie it and, at the very least, for the subsistence costs of the workers. Taken in isolation, "immaterial, non-reciprocal production cannot do so, since to produce free software, free culture or free soup, producers must draw their subsistence from some other source."[8] We must return again to the material productive relationships in which workers are enmeshed, where the worker's mode of production and position within production as social process give rise to the forms of struggle.

6. See Marx passage cited on p. 25 of this volume.
7. Wark, §21.
8. Dmitri, Kleiner. *The Telekommunist Manifesto* (Network Notebooks 03, Institute of Network Cultures, Amsterdam, 2010), p. 22.

For Kleiner, the central aspect of class conflict today is the immense power conferred to capitalist interests by their financial control of political processes. This political control relies on the continual ability to capture the value of labor through venture capitalism. Peer production, by capturing a greater portion of the value produced by labor, could, in principle, tip this balance, concentrating wealth in the hands of workers and allowing them to transform societies from within. On this level, peer production demonstrates a distributed organization of "independent producers employing a common stock of productive assets," a form of organization *a priori* not limited to the production of immaterial goods and able to take into account material inputs to the labor process. Because of its potential generalization to material production, peer production holds the potential to restructure the material productive relationships of society and become a threat to capitalism from the inside. In order for this to become possible, however, "an alternative to venture capitalism needs to provide a means of acquiring and efficiently allocating the collectively owned material wealth required to build free networks and free societies."[9] The alternative organizational form that Kleiner proposes, Venture Communism, is essentially a model of association in which a portion of the resources that independent producers currently return to the capitalist system as appropriated labor is diverted to the venture commune, a distributed network of peer producers organized toward developing a common stock of the tools necessary for labor and social reproduction.

Kleiner's venture commune (VC) is a collective organization, taking the form of a firm in which each member holds an equal share. The VC "holds ownership of all productive assets that make up the common stock employed by a diverse and geographically distributed network of collective and independent peer producers."[1] Each member agrees to forego private ownership of tools that would otherwise be purchased individually and instead to acquire them through the VC; conversely, "The function of the venture commune is to acquire material assets that members need for living and working, such as equipment and tools, and to allocate them to its members."[2] If a member requires a piece of equipment, the VC acquires it through the sale of bonds to its members issued against a rental agreement. The member requiring the equipment then rents it from the VC, with the rents distributed equally to the bondholders until the bonds are redeemed. If the member no longer requires the use of the equipment or no longer wishes to pay the rent, the equipment reverts to the commune, where another member may rent it or

9. Ibid., p. 8.
1. Ibid., p. 23.
2. Ibid., p. 24.

where it may be liquidated if necessary to redeem outstanding bonds. Once the bonds are redeemed, it becomes fully owned by the commune, and any further rents are distributed equally to all members. This process allows the VC to progressively build a stock of productive assets. Thus, "Venture communism is taking control of our own productive process, retaining the entire product of our labor, forming our own capital, and expanding until we have collectively accumulated enough wealth to achieve a greater social influence than those that defend exploitation."[3]

Although it merits a far more detailed analysis than can be undertaken here, Kleiner's venture communism is both a remarkable model in its own right and more generally an incitement to cooperation in order for workers to build a common stock of productive assets and gradually retain a greater share of the value they produce. Beyond tipping the balance of economic power, innovative forms of organization around labor and social reproduction have the potential to re-socialize the automatisms that underlie both production and everyday life, while contributing to the availability of the infrastructure to support innovative forms of struggle. Moreover, they have important implications for the productive use of networks in other important aspects of organization. In order to preserve and enrich the possibility for collective action as a point from which the consciousness of political struggles can be generalized, access of workers to means of communication and organization must be preserved and strengthened. The struggle to re-socialize production and forge new forms of organization, by activating what Berardi called the operative autonomisms of the technosphere toward other ends, can also be seen as another facet of the struggle against the organization of lived experience according to a capitalist grammar.

By way of conclusion then, we may say that the task of organization is marked by a double imperative: to re-socialize production in a way that both enables workers to retain a larger portion of the value they create and to shift the automatisms that structure lived experience toward a practice of identity beyond financial wealth and ostentatious consumption. Innovative forms of organization around labor and social reproduction have the potential to re-socialize the automatisms that underlie both production and everyday life, while contributing to the availability of the infrastructure to support innovative forms of struggle. As needs for transformation are felt differently in different places and under different material conditions of production, they may tend to create more direct forms of action in some places than in others. Writing in the winter of 2011, the ongoing popular uprisings in Tunisia, Egypt, Libya, and

3. For a full discussion of the venture commune, see Kleiner, 2010, pp. 23–25.

across the Middle East and North Africa stand out as an extraordinary moment of socio-political transformation, of a scale similar to the Eastern European reconfigurations of the late 1980s and early 1990s. These movements underline in the strongest possible terms both the urgent necessity to work toward political justice and the access of all to truly democratic processes, and the power of the people to assert their demands for political legitimacy in the face of organized state violence. However, these struggles to do away with repressive political regimes in bed with international economic and political actors are not necessarily a case of Hardt and Negri's multitude rising up against Empire, since those struggles so far maintain a national or regional character and attack particular structures of power within the nation-state. As successive waves of protest in Tunisia demonstrate, the importance of the popular movement goes beyond the removal of one president to the constitution of new collective responses to integrated world capitalism. In Kolinko's terms, "The main question will be from which points of uneven development struggles can socialize/globalise themselves as a new 'force of production.' Which struggles will be able to express the possibility and hope for a better form of production due to the material conditions (state of technology, science, division of labour etc.) they arise from?"[4] In addition to the tangible effects of these movements on social and political systems, their symbolic importance should not be underestimated. Who knows what new movements the popular revolts of the Arab Spring, anti-austerity protests in London and Athens, or the occupation of the Puerta del Sol might inspire? Whether emerging from North Africa, China, Western Europe or elsewhere, such struggles demonstrate, as Marx's *Manifesto* foretold, that we still have a world to win.

4. Kolinko, 2001, §5f.

Selected Bibliography

This is intended as a select bibliography for undergraduate students and is limited to those works in English that bear directly on the *Communist Manifesto*'s central themes. Advanced students will find further bibliographic guides in the footnotes to the text and to the critical articles included in this volume. Works excerpted or reprinted herein are not included here.

ON THE *COMMUNIST MANIFESTO*

Cowling, Mark, ed. *The Communist Manifesto: New Interpretations*. New York: NYU Press, 1998.

Davidson, Rondel V. "Reform versus Revolution: Victor Considérant and the *Communist Manifesto*." *Social Science Quarterly* 58.1 (June 1977): 74–85. [Excerpted in the Norton Critical Edition of the *Communist Manifesto*, 1st ed., 93–104.]

Finocchiaro, Maurice A. "Judgment and Argument in the *Communist Manifesto*." *The Philosophical Forum* 14.2 (winter 1982–83): 135–56.

Kautsky, Karl. "The *Communist Manifesto* after Six Decades." From "Vorwort" to the 1906 edition of the *Communist Manifesto*. Berlin: Buchhandlung Vorwärts, 1908. [Excerpted in the Norton Critical Edition of the *Communist Manifesto*, 1st ed., 127–31.]

Laski, Harold J. *The Communist Manifesto of Marx and Engels*. New York: Seabury Press, 1967.

Prawer, S. S. "[Literary Traces in the *Communist Manifesto*]." From *Karl Marx and World Literature*. Oxford: Oxford UP, 1976, 138–40. [Excerpted in the Norton Critical Edition of the *Communist Manifesto*, 1st ed., 105–6.]

Riazanov, David. *The Communist Manifesto of Karl Marx and Friedrich Engels*. London: Martin Lawrence, 1930.

Schumpeter, Joseph A. "The *Communist Manifesto* in Sociology and Economics." *Journal of Political Economy* 57 (1949): 199–212. [Excerpted in the Norton Critical Edition of the *Communist Manifesto*, 1st ed., 178–89.]

Struik, Dirk. The Birth of the *Communist Manifesto*. New York: International Publishers, 1971.

RELATED WORKS OF MARX AND ENGELS

Bender, F. L., ed. *Karl Marx: The Essential Writings*. Boulder: Westview, 1986.

Easton, Loyd D., and Kurt L. Guddat. *Writings of the Young Marx on Philosophy and Society*. Garden City: Doubleday, 1967.

Engels, Friedrich. "On the History of the Communist League." *Marx and Engels: Selected Works in Two Volumes*. New York: International Publishers, n.d. Vol. 2.

Marx, Karl, and Friedrich Engels. *Collected Works.* 25 vols. to date. New York: International Publishers, 1975–. Especially vols. 3–10.
McLellan, David. *Karl Marx: Selected Writings.* Oxford: Oxford UP, 1977.
Tucker, Robert C. *The Marx-Engels Reader.* New York: Norton, 1978.

HISTORICAL BACKGROUND

Hamen, Oscar J. *The Red '48ers.* New York: Scribner's, 1969.
Hamerow, Theodore S. *Restoration, Revolution, Reaction: Economics and Politics in Germany, 1815–1871.* Princeton: Princeton UP, 1966.
Harrison, J. F. C. *Quest for the New Moral World.* New York: Scribner's, 1969.
Lehning, Arthur. *From Buonarroti to Bakunin: Studies in International Socialism.* Leiden: Brill, 1970.
Lichtheim, George. *Marxism: An Historical and Critical Study.* New York: Praeger, 1965.
Lindemann, Albert S. *A History of European Socialism.* New Haven: Yale UP, 1983.
Manuel, Frank E., and Fritzie P. Manuel. *Utopian Thought in the Western World.* Cambridge: Harvard UP, 1979.
McLellan, David. *Karl Marx: His Life and Thought.* New York: Harper & Row, 1973.
Robertson, Priscilla. *Revolutions of 1848: A Social History.* Princeton: Princeton UP, 1952.

STUDIES OF MARX'S THOUGHT

Avineri, Shlomo. *The Social and Political Thought of Karl Marx.* Cambridge: Cambridge UP, 1969.
Cohen, G. A. *Karl Marx's Theory of History: A Defense.* Princeton: Princeton UP, 1978.
Eagleton, Terry. *Why Marx Was Right.* New Haven: Yale UP, 2011.
Elster, Jon. *Making Sense of Marx (Studies in Marxism and Social Theory).* Cambridge: Cambridge UP, 1985.
Gouldner, Alvin W. *The Two Marxisms.* Oxford: Oxford UP, 1980.
Heller, Agnes. *The Theory of Need in Marx.* London: Allison & Busby, 1976.
Kolakowski, Leszek. *Main Currents of Marxism.* Oxford: Clarendon, 1978.
Korsch, Karl. *Marxism and Philosophy.* Trans. Fred Halliday. New York: Monthly Review, 1970.
Lukács, Georg. *History and Class Consciousness: Studies in Marxist Dialectics.* Trans. Rodney Livingstone. Cambridge: M.I.T. Press, 1972.
Mandel, Ernest. *An Introduction to Marxist Economic Theory.* New York: Pathfinder, 1974.
Ollman, Bertell. *Alienation: Marx's Conception of Man in Capitalist Society.* Cambridge, Cambridge UP, 1971.
Rader, Melvin. *Marx's Interpretation of History.* New York: Oxford UP, 1979.
Rotenstreich, Nathan. *Basic Problems of Marx's Philosophy.* Indianapolis: Bobbs-Merrill, 1965.
Sweezy, Paul M. *The Theory of Capitalist Development: Principles of Marxian Political Economy.* New York: Monthly Review, 1942.
Waters, Mary-Alice. *Feminism and the Marxist Movement.* New York: Pathfinder, 1994.
Wessell, Leonard P. *Prometheus Bound: The Mythic Structure of Karl Marx's Scientific Thinking.* Baton Rouge: Louisiana State UP, 1984.

Class Struggles in France
      (Marx), 109, 113, 118,
      125, 193
classes
   in cognitive capitalism,
      241–44
   concept of, 192–93
   conservative, 71
   dominant ideology and,
      32–33
   global working class and,
      234–36
   hacker, 243–45
   in historical materialism,
      29–30
   in precapitalist societies,
      29–30
   revolutionary, 35–36, 71
   Ricardo on, 7–8
Clerical Socialism, 85
Clinton, Bill, 232
Cobbett, William, 174–75, 180
cognitariat, 244–45
cognitive capitalism, 238–39,
      241–44
Cologne Communist trial
      (1852), 51, 55
colonial countries, 139–40
Coming Insurrection, The
      (The Invisible Committee),
      248
commodification
   of information, 241–44
   of labor, 21, 67–68
   of self, 249–50
   of women, 195–99
commodity(-ies)
   defined, 21
   domination of, 22–23
   price of, 67–68
common enemy, 222
communes
   agricultural, 5
   venture, 257–58
communication technology

cognitive capitalism and,
      238–39
   in revolutions of 2011,
      252–54
Communism
   accumulated labor under, 177
   as acknowledged power, 60
   Adler on, 130–33
   bourgeois life juxtaposed
      with, 178–79
   buying and selling abolished
      under, 76
   as classless society, 24–25
   democratization and, 155
   economic goal of, 41
   egoistic values and, 26
   free association in, 25
   general goal of, 193–94
   as historical movement, 27
   ideology and, 80–81
   initial steps in, 82–83
   nationality and, 80
   private property under, 40,
      74, 75
   religion and, 80–81
   socialism vs., 53
   state apparatus in, 26, 82–83
   utopianism and, 132–33
   women and, 79–80
   work under, 41
Communist Correspondence
      Committees, xi, 1, 13, 104
Communist Internationals, see
      First International; Second
      International; Third
      International
Communist League, vii,
      10–19
   anti-Marxist minority in, 109
   Blanquists and, 6, 109,
      118–19
   Chartists and, 8
   Correspondence Committees
      merged with, 1, 13–14, 104
   dissolution of, xiii, 51